Globalisation
and
Tertiary Education
in the Asia-Pacific
The Changing Nature of a Dynamic Market

Globalisation
and
Tertiary Education
in the Asia-Pacific

The Changing Nature of a Dynamic Market

Editors

Christopher Findlay
University of Adelaide, Australia

William G Tierney
University of Southern California, USA

Published by

World Scientific Publishing Co. Pte. Ltd.

5 Toh Tuck Link, Singapore 596224

USA office: 27 Warren Street, Suite 401-402, Hackensack, NJ 07601

UK office: 57 Shelton Street, Covent Garden, London WC2H 9HE

British Library Cataloguing-in-Publication Data
A catalogue record for this book is available from the British Library.

GLOBALISATION AND TERTIARY EDUCATION IN THE ASIA-PACIFIC
The Changing Nature of a Dynamic Market

ISBN-13 978-981-4299-03-9
ISBN-10 981-4299-03-0

Typeset by Stallion Press
Email: enquiries@stallionpress.com

Printed in Singapore.

Foreword

The Association of Pacific Rim Universities (APRU) aims to promote scientific, educational, and cultural collaboration among Pacific Rim economies. In both its objectives and guiding principles, APRU embodies a commitment to global academic and research standards. Formed in 1997, APRU is a consortium of 42 leading research universities in the Pacific Rim.

The Pacific Economic Cooperation Council (PECC) is an independent, multi-stakeholder organisation committed to the promotion of cooperation and dialogue in the Asia–Pacific. Founded in 1980, PECC is a network of member committees composed of individuals and institutions dedicated to this mission. The Council is one of the three official observers of the APEC process.

This book is the outcome of a two-year research project undertaken by a task force composed of experts from APRU and PECC: Young-Chul Kim, Korean Educational Development Institute; Philippa Dee, the Australian National University; Jane Knight, Fulbright New Century Scholar Program; Lesleyanne Hawthorne, University of Melbourne and OECD; Federico Macaranas, Asian Institute of Management, the Philippines; Morshidi Sirat, National Higher Education Research Institute, Malaysia; Rui Yang, the

University of Hong Kong; David Ang and Jayantee Mukherjee Saha, Singapore Human Resources Institute; and Christopher Pokarier, Waseda University, Japan. In addition to the lead authors of the papers, we would like to acknowledge the input and work of the many people who supported these papers.

The editors of the volume are Professor Christopher Findlay, Head of the School of Economics, University Adelaide; and Professor William Tierney, Wilbur-Kieffer Professor of Higher Education and Director of the Center for Higher Education Policy Analysis, University of Southern California.

This project would not have been possible without the support of the APRU Steering Committee and the PECC Standing Committee as well as their respective members. We thank the APRU and PECC Secretariats for their support for the project, especially Dr Kenneth McGillivray and Mr Eduardo Pedrosa. We thank all of those involved in organising the initial brainstorming session for the authors, especially Jim Short, formerly of the Australian National University.

This project has benefited greatly from the wisdom and advice of a panel of advisors selected for their expertise and experience in the way tertiary education in our region is changing. We thank Dr David Strangway, Dr Edilberto de Jesus, and Mr Vincent Quah for taking time to share with us their knowledge and experience in the field of education. Thanks also to Claire Hollweg for research assistance.

While acknowledging comments and input from our panel of advisors and the project team, any omissions and errors in the report are solely our responsibility.

William G. Tierney
APRU

Christopher C. Findlay
PECC

Contents

Contributors

David Ang
Executive Director
Singapore Human Resources Institute (SHRI)
Secretary General and Treasurer
World Federation of Personnel Management Associations (WFPMA)
Singapore

Philippa Dee
Crawford School of Economics and Government
Australian National University
Canberra, Australia

Yang Farina
School of Chemical Sciences
Faculty of Science and Technology
Universiti Kebangsaan Malaysia
Selangor, Malaysia

Christopher Findlay
Head
School of Economics
University of Adelaide
Adelaide, Australia

Lesleyanne Hawthorne
Associate Dean International (Director, Faculty International Unit)
Faculty of Medicine, Dentistry and Health Sciences
University of Melbourne
Melbourne, Australia

Dato' Dr Ibrahim Komoo
Director
Southeast Asia Disaster Prevention Research Institute (SEADPRI)
Principal Fellow
Institute for Environment and Development (LESTARI)
Universiti Kebangsaan Malaysia
Selangor, Malaysia

Young-Chul Kim
President
Korea Educational Policy Research Institute
Seoul, Korea

Jane Knight
Comparative, International and Development Education Center
Ontario Institute for Studies in Education
University of Toronto
Toronto, Canada

Koo Yew Lie
School of Language Studies and Linguistics
Faculty of Social Science and Humanities
Universiti Kebangsaan Malaysia
Selangor, Malaysia

Federico M. Macaranas
W. SyCip Graduate School of Business
Asian Institute of Management
Manila, the Philippines

N.S. Nik Meriam
Director
Institute for Research Management and Consultancy
University of Malaya
Kuala Lumpur, Malaysia

S. Morshidi
Director
National Higher Education Research Institute (IPPTN)
    and Dean of Research
Platform for Social Transformation Research
Universiti Sains Malaysia
Penang, Malaysia

Ahmad Farhan Sadullah
Director-General
Malaysian Institute of Road Safety Research (MIROS)
Kuala Lumpur, Malaysia

Jayantee Mukherjee Saha
Senior Manager (Projects and Research)
Research Centre of Singapore Human Resources Institute (SHRI)
Singapore

Norzaini Azman
Department of Educational Foundation
Faculty of Education
Universiti Kebangsaan Malaysia
Selangor, Malaysia

Christopher Pokarier
School of International Liberal Studies
Nishi-Waseda Campus
Waseda University
Tokyo, Japan

William G. Tierney
Wilbur-Kieffer Professor of Higher Education
Director, Center for Higher Education Policy Analysis
University of Southern California
Los Angeles, USA

Rui Yang
Faculty of Education
University of Hong Kong
Hong Kong

Walter C. K. Wong
Deputy Pro Vice-Chancellor
Monash University Sunway Campus
Bandar Sunway, Malaysia

Introduction and Overview

Christopher Findlay and William Tierney

The rapid development and adoption of technology, along with more open economies, has created an integrated global economy. The globalisation process has brought with it significant changes in all areas of life, including tertiary education.

Tertiary education remains at the centre of economic well-being. It is necessary for growth, through its direct contribution to skills and workforce quality, but also in the ways in which it adds what APEC Education Ministers have referred to as the 'key competencies of the 21st century [that are] critical thinking, creativity, teamwork and self-learning ...'[1] These contribute to entrepreneurship, mobility, and the capacity to process information and new ideas. The waves of globalisation affect the ways in which the sector makes these contributions.

Governments and institutions must act quickly to adapt to a new wave of globalisation in this sector and to capture its advantages. Regional cooperation can add value by reaching a deeper understanding

---

[1] http://www.apec.org/apec/ministerial_statements/sectoral_ministerial/education/2008_education.html

of the forces for change, sharing experiences to build confidence in the ability to adjust and to capture the benefits on offer, and removing impediments to integration.

The scope and issues associated with the new wave of globalisation of education were the topics of a research project whose results are reported in this volume. Drawing on the work of the contributors, in this chapter we draw out five more-specific trends in the education sector that are associated with this new wave, and then identify the challenges for institutions and for governments. We conclude with comments on the scope for regional cooperation to help build the confidence to capitalize on emerging opportunities.

THE NEW WAVE OF GLOBALISATION

The first wave of the globalisation of tertiary education primarily meant the movement of students across borders. The new wave of globalisation includes the movement of teachers and whole institutions into overseas markets, joint-degree programs offered by institutions in different economies, and distance learning programs, to mention just a few of its characteristics. It has a higher level of commercial motivation: Knight stresses in Chapter 4 not only the shift from student mobility to program and provider mobility, but also the shift in orientation in the relationships between universities from development cooperation to what she calls 'competitive commerce'. She also provides a framework for classifying international education (adapted from Knight, 2005) and examples of the forms in which international cooperation occurs. We later discuss in more detail some of the issues involved in the choice between these modes of supply.

The new wave offers access to skills in delivery, experience in curriculum design, teaching resources, quality assurance systems and research capacity, and an international perspective, all of which can add value for local partners. But it also brings competition and pressure for adjustment.

In the following section we outline five key trends associated with the new wave of globalisation in education.

FIVE TRENDS IN THE TERTIARY EDUCATION SECTOR

In the early years of the 21st century, five trends have been prevalent throughout the Asia–Pacific with regard to tertiary education:

1. *International student mobility continues to increase significantly*

In Chapter 2, Kim reports forecasts that the number of international students will increase from 1.8 million in 2000 to 7.6 million in 2025, which implies an annual growth of about 6 per cent a year over this period, compared to about 4 per cent in the last two decades of the last century. Asia expects to account for 70 per cent of global demand by 2025. Healey (2008) stresses in his review of the various forecasts that the outlook for mobility depends on changes in the capacities of students' home institutions.

Mobility is a consequence of the combination of the impact of economic growth and structural change on the demand for education and the differences in demographic patterns among the region's economies. Important on the supply side are the established capacities in the developed but ageing economies. Commenting on the drivers of internationalisation, Healey (2008) highlights the response of institutions to incentives created by government policy, including research-intensive institutions. His list includes the response to the declining public subsidies for domestic students and the deregulation of tuition fees for foreign students.

The US and Europe remain important destinations for students moving out of Asia in these forecasts. Of the OECD members, Australia has the highest proportion of international students (19.3 per cent of all students at Australian universities in 2005). However, new competitors are emerging for these traditional host countries, including some of the important sending countries, such as China and Singapore.

Furthermore, now linked to student mobility is the trend towards two-step migration by international students into their host economies, which we discuss further below.

2.   Providers and programs are increasingly mobile

The Asia–Pacific accounts for the bulk of the world's program and institutional mobility. A number of projects that illustrate the new wave of globalisation are reported by Kim in Chapter 2. He finds that many schools and universities in the Asia–Pacific region have recently begun developing joint programs with foreign educational institutions and e-learning programs, as well as selling or franchising courses to foreign educational institutions. These operations could be in cooperation with local partners (in forms of franchising) or as stand-alone operations. They offer varying combinations of teaching and research cooperation. While some new providers are working on partnerships with traditional institutions, others are developing new ways and are offering vocational and specialised services that challenge traditional academic teaching programs that operate jointly with research.

China, which is the subject of extensive study by Yang in Chapter 11, reported a nine-fold increase between 1995 and 2003 in joint programs between Chinese and foreign institutions. In early 2003 there were 712 such programs, 37 per cent at a post-secondary or higher education level. By June 2007, this number had risen to 745, of which 169 were qualified to offer overseas awards. Over 50,000 students are enrolled in these sorts of partnerships. Yang reviews the issues associated with this rapid growth, including matters of quality assurance, legal status of the joint ventures and the cultural appropriateness of the curricula, as well as the tensions between the commercial motivations for the partnerships and their contributions to institutional development. He points out that the changes in the structure of the sector also raise challenges for its governance. These issues are not peculiar to China.

The Singapore experience is also important (Olds, 2007). Mukherjee and Ang review aspects of the Singapore approach in Chapter 9. Some proposals for new projects in Singapore have not been completed in their proposed format, including the establishment of a division of Johns Hopkins University in Singapore and of the University of New South Wales Asia. The experience highlights a number of issues for both host countries and foreign institutions in setting up offshore. Drawing on the experiences of both these cases, Sidhu (2008) concludes that, while the forces for internationalisation are powerful and the expectations are high, there is a danger of overstating the ease of implementation in a set of activities that involve direct interaction between people with different experiences and communication styles.

3. *The importance of public provision is diminishing*

Tertiary education was once largely the domain of public provision in Asia, but it is currently undergoing dramatic privatisation. The forms of privatisation are manifold, such that institutions are no longer 'only' public or 'only' private. In Chapter 7, Tierney reviews the forms of tertiary education in Malaysia. The rise in the share of private institutions and the fall in the number of students studying overseas and in public institutions is striking. The entry of new and private providers shifts the relative importance of the government's role from that of a provider to one of a regulator that oversees quality assurance.

4. *The extent of public funding is also shifting*

The weight on private contributions is increasing. The provision of public funding that remains is also likely to shift to consumers rather than providers. For example, in Australian institutions, the significance of Australian government grants has declined from 58 per cent of university revenue in 1995 to 41 per cent in 2006, while the share from overseas fee-paying students has nearly tripled and that from domestic students has risen from 17 per cent to nearly 30 per cent.[2] Again, this experience is not specific to Australia. As the sources of funding diversify, public institutions are becoming more corporate and autonomous, leading to the application of more business-oriented

---

[2] http://www.rba.gov.au/PublicationsAndResearch/Bulletin/bu_jun08/aus_exports_education_services.html

decision-making criteria. In Chapter 10, Pokarier points out that Japan already has a relatively high level of private contributions and a greater role of private universities.

5. *The interest in international research cooperation is widening and deepening*

The research community is being asked to respond to issues that apply across borders, for example, climate change. Cooperation is valuable as institutions respond to these sorts of issues. Cooperation and cross-border projects have a number of advantages (discussed by Brody, 2007). They include:

- building research capacity and drawing together the required research expertise,
- studying problems *in situ*,
- providing research students with an international experience,
- combining research beneficiaries and helping to avoid problems of free-riding and therefore underfunding,
- helping to capture economies of scale,
- avoiding costly duplication,
- capturing the benefits arising from differences in relative costs in research inputs,
- gathering the insights from comparative studies,
- adding to the impact of research results,
- reducing technology transfer costs.

There are real drivers for international cooperation, which is not merely reputation setting for newcomer or mid-ranked institutions. These include the growth of cooperative research activity; in the region, China, Korea and especially Singapore show high growth rates in research cooperation in the private sector (von Zedtwitz, 2004, 2006). Macaranas provides a number of examples, including a reference to Yale's operations in China, in Chapter 6. Taking a supply chain perspective, he identifies the relative contributions of the partners to the research process, including technology development (Yale) and procurement for research (the local partners). As noted above, the extent to which research cooperation is tied to the delivery of offshore teaching is not clear, but a range of business models have attempted to elucidate this.

CHALLENGES AHEAD

The adjustment to the five trends discussed above is significant. The entry of new providers and the development of competition can undermine institutional and regulatory structures and lead to significant and painful adjustments for mature private and public institutions or systems of tertiary education that have been slow to anticipate these developments. Entrenched interests and government practices can inhibit adaptation.

Questions remain about strategic planning within institutions in the context of such market-driven developments. There are questions about the design of policy at the domestic level, and about the opportunities for cooperation within the region.

Challenges at the institutional level include meeting the demand for a highly skilled body of academic staff for both teaching and research. Teaching is about to undergo a sea change in the manner of conducting a class, but there is almost no infrastructure for upgrading the skills of faculty in some Asia–Pacific education systems. Developing economies focus on hiring academic staff with advanced degrees and research capacity. Access to capacity for research training for their staff is a priority. Many countries will need to build capacity to attract and keep academic staff.

Many institutions will have to adapt to competition from new and possibly foreign competitors that undermine their traditional funding models. They must adapt to the separation of funding for teaching and research while meeting community expectations of their contribution to growth and development and participation in international collaborations. They will need to capture a larger share of research benefits as their funding sources diversify. They will also need to develop more partnerships with the private sector for research cooperation, including across borders.

The previous model for the internationalisation of higher education was based on student mobility, alongside faculty exchange, research collaboration, internationalisation of curricula to include foreign languages and international perspectives, and networks of institutions. Added now to this set is program and provider mobility. Using the latter options with respect to higher education in general is akin to a 'buy', rather than a 'make', decision by local institutions in economies with higher demands for education. Issues involved in that choice are discussed in detail by Macaranas. They include quality assurance by the foreign provider and 'hold-up' problems once a commitment is made, plus uncertainties associated with policy change in source and host economies. Macaranas argues that the choice of model will vary between stages of development. Institutions based in emerging economies may prefer the 'buy' option, while others prefer intermediate options. A further implication is that partner institutions in more mature economies have to think about how their associations and linkages add value to their objectives and how the activities are divided between the partners for greatest overall gain. However, as experience in the region has already shown, all models confront significant costs in doing business internationally.

Many economies in the region face substantial policy reform challenges in order to capture the benefits of globalisation in this sector. These challenges vary according to the stage of development.

Pokarier's study of Japan highlights the challenges associated with demographic change. It signals the difficulties facing economies at high levels of development. Japan's university system has met the expectation of universal education. Pokarier reviews the contributors to that success, including the role of private institutions and private contributions to the cost of education. But he points out how the rapid growth of the education system has brought problems of quality and longer-term problems of structural adjustment, especially now with the decline in the student population. Not surprisingly, Japan has set goals for rapid growth in the number of international students in its institutions. Japan, too, may join the 'war for skills'. In June 2008, a group of Liberal Democratic Party policymakers proposed to the Prime Minister to raise the foreign share of the Japanese population from less than 2 per cent to 10 per cent over the next 50 years.

Other economies at earlier stages of development continue to work towards providing higher levels of access to tertiary education. The nature and pace of adjustment in all economies depends on the extent of integration of education markets.

In Chapter 3, Dee lists examples of the various policy impediments that might apply in these modes. She finds that countries tend to have relatively higher restrictions on commercial presence than on study abroad. The effect of these restrictions is not to stop international transactions in either mode, but to reduce their volume to levels below what they might be otherwise. In principle, both are important. However, in econometric work Dee finds that the indicators of restrictions on the movement of students offshore are not significantly related to student flows: the apparently high levels of restrictiveness in China, Vietnam, Indonesia or Korea, for example, are therefore not affecting student outflows. Dee nevertheless finds that the policies affecting commercial presence have significant effects on student movement. Barriers in the source economy to importing education services via the inward movement of foreign campuses boosts the number of students from the source economy seeking overseas enrolment. Dee finds that 'the magnitudes suggest that if an economy with sample average barriers to FDI imports were to liberalise completely, it would send about 60 per cent fewer students overseas' (at the average level of restrictions on sending students abroad).

Dee also points out that these barriers to imports are not the only ones that matter for adjustment in markets for international education. These impediments are important. She finds a significant statistical relationship between these scores and the movement of students and reports econometric results that if 'an economy with sample average barriers to the inward movement of students were to liberalise completely, it would attract about 250 per cent more students — more than twice as many'.

This result is significant for the institutions involved in providing education exports. As Dee points out, restrictions on exports may allow the providers to earn larger incomes than otherwise from the provision of services to international students, since prices in the market for their services will be higher. Some part of this income may be dissipated in the management of systems required within institutions in such highly regulated markets. But some other part of that income can be used to support other activities of the institutions that are not income-generating, such as basic research. The split of income for these purposes is not clear and is a topic for further work. This concern is related to the earlier point regarding the challenges of funding research in more open markets.

More specific challenges at the economy level include the following:

1. *Institutional type and the definition of quality*

International rankings are often reported, leading institutions and ministries to target higher rankings. There is a risk involved in this. Rankings create a 'one size fits all' mindset and privilege research institutions. Although certain institutions in certain countries will be research-focused, the majority of institutions in all countries will be more focused on providing a quality education to an increasing number of students. The comparative ranking of universities in 'league tables' has the potential to diminish the credibility of these universities and to distract them from addressing the legitimate knowledge demands of their own people.

2. *Institutional diversity and competition*

Will the tertiary system produce graduates and re-graduates with the skills required? How will internationalisation and the capacity to operate in the global economy be handled, how will programs for re-training those already in the workforce be designed, and will curricula be able to capture local as well as international cultures in more open markets for education? The proliferation of programs and players and the redirection of funding flows through the hands of households means these questions are more likely to be, and can efficiently be, resolved in markets. The growth of diversity can help meet the expectations of industry for workforce skills, such as for specific skills on top of general capabilities, and for the interest in and capacity for lifelong learning.

In Chapter 9, Mukherjee and Ang stress the growing market in many economies for continuing or 'in-employment' education. This area attracts particular specialist providers, not necessarily those providing a full package of research and teaching. Pokarier also discusses some interesting cases of corporate universities in Japan. Traditional universities might operate in this market, but there are other models of provision emerging.

3. *Quality assurance*

Much is at risk if low-quality or fraudulent qualifications become closely linked with international transactions in education, as Knight explains. Those concerns might include lack of recognition of awards by local employers. Providers, too, find challenges in quality control in their more distant operations, yet they too have strong incentives to avoid reputational risk.

As governments around the region shift from funding public providers to funding consumers, the Ministry of Higher Education plays a greater role in the design or certification of quality assurance systems, which involves the recognition and establishment of the status of foreign providers. It should also apply to providers operating in new modes of supply (e.g., distance). Knight refers to examples of assurance systems in China, Malaysia and Hong Kong. Setting up these systems may have high opportunity costs in some economies; they may thus adopt less elaborate mechanisms. At least a considered decision on quality assurance will be required: the principle will be to adopt arrangements that are not unduly burdensome given the nature of domestic regulatory capacity.

The solution is not only in the hands of the government. More players are now involved in accreditation, including professional bodies and other non-government organisations, such as associations of particular disciplinary groups or schools. A significant aspect of quality assurance in higher education will be the active engagement of the staff themselves in international academic networks. In addition, international communities of good practice in higher education management and services increasingly play a role.

4. *Funding research*

The funding of research will cease to be a complement to or packaged with the funding of teaching. Separate funding systems will be required as private, specialist teaching providers compete for students, at least at earlier levels of tertiary education, and diminish the surpluses earned by the traditional providers. The funding challenges also apply to graduate and PhD programs. Private participation in funding of research alongside government funding will matter more in the future, but not all countries have the institutional structures in place to organise those contributions or to provide evaluations of the returns to public funding that will become more transparent and open to scrutiny.

International cooperation in the design and delivery of research, integrated with research training, will become more valuable. Drawing on a case study of Malaysian experience, in Chapter 8 Morshidi *et al.* observe a number of different methods, and various points of entry, for institutions of different types. They stress the importance of understanding the links between teaching and research and the ability to use the expanding market for education as a 'driving force' for research. Given the variety of types of institutions in the region and the cultural variations, they also discuss the value of working on an 'Asia–Pacific framework for research and innovation'. Participation in various professional networks is seen as one of the building blocks.

5. *Design of migration policies in host economies and the 'war for skills'*

The pool of international students in some economies has become an important source of skilled migration. In Chapter 5, Hawthorne documents the extent to which many APEC and OECD economies are using this 'two-step' approach to migration. Competition for international students for this purpose through changes in immigration regulations will become more intense. Hawthorne argues that the level of future competition of this form will be 'unprecedented'. However, instability in student flows may follow. There is, in addition, the scope for migration-driven flows to rapidly distort international student movements by sector and discipline. Private-sector respondents to the opportunities created by migration-driven student flows add to the problems of quality assurance.

The critical parameters influencing the link between student flow and migration policy include the demographic trends in both source and host economies and the sensitivities of student flows to the particularities of migration policies. Hawthorne suggests continuing surveillance and monitoring of export education and migration policies, checking that student flows leading to migration are driven by workforce demands. In addition, she proposes establishing expectations about long-term trends in demography in the region and its impact on likely student flows. She also recommends work to find out which economies might shift from sending students to providing education.

REGIONAL COOPERATION

What should be done to build a regional community that is credible in terms of its strategy for the education sector? We conclude with some responses to this question.

A simple first step is to develop new data collection systems that will support institution and policy decision-making. More importantly, there are five areas where further cooperation is valuable.

1. *Research cooperation*

The proliferation of modes of supply of international education makes possible more linkages in research. Research cooperation will be required at the regional level to resolve pressing issues, many of which also require a range of disciplinary inputs. Options for consideration include the joint funding of PhD programs, involving the sending economy's scholarship organisations and institutions/employers, and foreign research and training providers. The returning students with research training provide the basis for extending research networks across the region. Laboratories working jointly at different stages of the same research project are already being established according to comparative advantage. There are different models of how to build research and innovation systems, and there may be no single answer on how to get those right, other than stating that integration pays. The trends identified here facilitate the experimentation with and development of those systems across borders and disciplines.

2.   *Human resource development*

Domestic and regional associations can work together to increase the teaching and research capacity of the academic staff in the region. Staff mobility might be one mechanism. Commitment to openness in that mode of supply will be important. This mobility also supports the evaluation of innovation systems across borders. Another possibility is greater collaboration between business and industry and tertiary institutions.

3.   *Removing border measures and complementing the role of the GATS*

Student-sending economies would send 60 per cent fewer students on average if the barriers to foreign campus establishment were liberalised completely. As discussed, if an economy with average barriers to inward student movements were liberalised totally, it would attract more than twice as many students. Restrictive policies waste opportunities for gains from international exchange. The ability of the GATS to deal with these issues is limited. Some impediments are of a form that GATS does not specify as being required to be listed. Nor is it clear where impediments applying to foreign consumers (i.e., to exports of services) would be scheduled. Further, the GATS approach tends to be mode by mode whereas most education providers work with packages of modes. A sector-wide convention or model is valuable and could be designed at a regional level.

4. *Codes of practice on quality assurance*

Codes of conduct are being developed for international delivery, including those by UNESCO[3] and the OECD. Some of the voluntary codes are based on global networks. The relevance of these for APEC members can be examined. A review of options and some evaluation of those already available and of the possible complementary role of regional academic networks and other private actors will help accelerate progress towards good quality assurance systems.

While there is value in sharing experiences in the design of solutions and the contribution of these complementary mechanisms, a single regional or international body is less likely to be successful in the Asia–Pacific given the diversity in the region. As Knight points out, there is no 'one way' to quality assurance.

5. *The brain drain*

In open markets and with the aggressive migration policies of developed economies, developing economies will continue to be concerned about the risks they face from the loss of talent. Their concerns are heightened when their own public funds are used to pay for the education of the internationalised students. Analysis of the actual movement of students after graduation, the rate and timing of their return, the distribution of the costs of higher degree education between the home and host economies in the context of research cooperation, the implications for home and host labour markets, and the students' contribution to the regional community through diaspora effects are all topics for conversation at a regional level to understand the significance of the issue.

---

[3] See http://www2.unescobkk.org/elib/publications/087/APQN_Toolkit.pdf.

REFERENCES

Brody W (2007). College goes global. *Foreign Aff*, 86(2), 122–133.

Healey NM (2008). Is higher education *really* 'internationalising'? *Higher Education*, forthcoming.

Knight J (2005). Cross-border education: An analytical framework for program and provider mobility. In *Higher Education: Handbook of Theory and Practice*, J Smart and W Tierney (eds.). Springer, Dordrecht.

Olds K (2007). Global assemblage: Singapore, foreign universities, and the construction of a 'Global Education Hub'. *World Devel*, 35(6), 959–975.

Sidhu R (2008). The 'brand name' research university goes global. *Higher Education*. doi: 10.1007/s10734-008-9136-2.

von Zedtwitz M (2004). Managing foreign R&D laboratories in China. *R&D Manage*, 34(4), 439–452. http://ssrn.com/abstract=591620.

von Zedtwitz M (2006). Internationalization of R&D — perspectives from outside and inside of China. Presentation, 20 October 2006. http://www.oecd.org/dataoecd/29/49/37738049.pdf.

The Asia–Pacific Education Market and Modes of Supply

Young-Chul Kim

1 INTRODUCTION

Globalisation has compressed the world in both time and space, enabling easy cross-border mobility. Political, economic and social forces have also boosted the cross-border mobility of students, teachers, programs and institutions. With the expansion of the international mobility of human resources, increased competition to recruit such resources is anticipated, both among countries and among educational institutions.

With the advance of the ubiquitous 'information age' as a result of the rapid development of information and communication technologies (ICT), the delivery systems of educational services have become diversified. As a result, cross-border education is feasible in cyberspace through the internet, without the actual movement of people, programs or institutions. Hence, the development of ICT has accelerated international mobility in education.

The boundaries of education are now expanding from the traditional education limited by national borders to international education. Hence, more and more students are going abroad to study or enrolling in foreign educational programs and institutions in their home countries. Furthermore, many advanced countries are recruiting foreign students and establishing branch campuses in foreign countries, adopting a revenue-generating approach.

The Asia–Pacific is the largest education market in the world.[1] This market has grown very rapidly during the last decade and will continue to expand even more rapidly in the future because of the infinite growth potential of human resources and the great enthusiasm for international education. In recent years many Asian countries have adopted open education market policies to raise their national competitiveness and to actualise personal achievement. Hence, more Asian students are going abroad to study compared to non-Asian students. In this regard, it is relevant to study the Asia–Pacific education market in terms of modes of supply.

This paper provides an overview of the Asia–Pacific education market, identifies the modes of supply of educational services, reviews recent trends in modes of supply and provides an outlook for this market and, finally, describes the links between demand for education and developments in trade and foreign investment.

---

[1] In this paper the Asia–Pacific refers to countries on the Pacific Rim. In this regard, PECC member countries are the major target group, including India. The PECC member countries are Australia, Brunei, Canada, Chile, China, Chinese Taipei, Colombia, Ecuador, Hong Kong, Indonesia, Japan, Korea, Malaysia, Mexico, New Zealand, Peru, the Philippines, Singapore, Thailand, the United States and Vietnam, and associate members are France and Mongolia. The OECD classifies the Asia–Pacific region as: East Asia (China, Hong Kong, Japan, Korea and Taiwan), Southeast Asia (Cambodia, Indonesia, Laos, Malaysia, Myanmar, the Philippines, Singapore, Thailand and Vietnam), South Asia (Afghanistan, Bangladesh, Bhutan, India, Maldives, Nepal, Pakistan and Sri Lanka), and Pacific (Australia, the Cook Islands, Fiji, Kiribati, the Marshall Islands, Micronesia, Nauru, New Zealand, Papua New Guinea, Samoa, the Solomon Islands, Tonga, Tuvalu and Vanuatu).

2 AN OVERVIEW OF THE ASIA–PACIFIC EDUCATION MARKET

More than two-thirds of the world's population live in the Asia–Pacific region that encompasses enormous political, economic and cultural variations. There are population giants such as China, India, the US and Indonesia, and economic giants such as the US and Japan.

An OECD report in 2004 described the sub-regional characteristics of the Asia–Pacific region as follows: four East Asian nations with dynamic export economies, strong national identities and some common cultural elements; eight diverse Southeast Asian nations, most with sizeable populations and a large Chinese diaspora, and some with a substantial Muslim element; two global hub cities, Singapore and Hong Kong; eight South Asian nations, including nations with very large populations; two modernised and advanced nations in Oceania; and the tiny nations of the Pacific, with larger underdeveloped nations (OECD, 2004). As well as these countries, PECC includes three OECD nations in North America and three Pacific nations in South America on the boundary of the Asia–Pacific region.

Because of the enormous variation in socio-economic development in the Asia–Pacific region, there is a wide range of educational participation and resources among different nations. This wide range of conditions facilitates mobility of education in the region, such as cross-border education. It is the largest regional source of international students and contains the largest education export countries, mainly the United States, Australia and Canada, as well as the largest education import countries, such as China, India, Japan and Korea (see Table 1).

More precisely, the OECD (2004) classified the Asia–Pacific region into five groups of educational typology of cross-border education: developed exporter nations with strong domestic capacity and a minor role as importers of education (the US, Australia, Canada and New Zealand); developed nations with strong domestic capacity but active as importers (Japan and Korea); developed or intermediate nations with inadequate domestic capacity, active as both importers and exporters (Singapore and Hong Kong); intermediate nations

Table 1. **Number of students enrolled in all levels of education and tertiary education in the Asia–Pacific region**

Country	Year	Number of students in all levels of education	Number of students in tertiary education
Australia	2005	6,021,137	1,024,589
Canada	2004	6,486,632	1,254,833
Chile	2005	4,549,989	663,694
China	2003	259,915,907	15,186,219
India	2004	260,556,785	11,852,936
Indonesia	2003	50,210,781	3,441,429
Japan	2005	22,288,745	4,038,302
Korea	2005	11,580,617	3,210,184
Malaysia	2003	6,870,927	632,309
Mexico	2005	31,747,673	2,384,858
New Zealand	2005	1,259,422	239,983
Peru	2003	8,991,847	830,345
Philippines	2003	22,675,367	2,427,211
Thailand	2003	16,504,375	2,251,453
United States	2005	73,959,016	17,272,044

Source: OECD Online Education Database.
Note: OECD Online Education Database supplies student enrolment data of individual countries. However, it does not cover all PECC member countries. Hence, only the student enrolment of the above 15 countries out of the 21 PECC member countries will be reviewed.

with inadequate domestic capacity, active as importers while relatively underdeveloped as exporters (China, Vietnam, Indonesia, etc.); and relatively undeveloped nations, characterised by both low domestic participation and work demand for cross-border education (Laos, Cambodia, etc.).

3 MODES OF SUPPLY OF EDUCATION SERVICES

Internationalisation in higher education has two dimensions: purely domestic education and cross-border education (OECD, 2004). Domestic education refers to the international and intercultural dimensions of the curriculum, the teaching–learning process, research and extra-curricular activities. In fact, many such activities help students to develop international understanding and intercultural skills without ever leaving their countries. This can be referred to as 'internationalisation at home'.

Meanwhile, cross-border education refers to situations when students, teachers, researchers, programs, an institution/provider or course materials cross national jurisdictional borders. Depending on who or what crosses the border, cross-border education can take three different forms, as shown in Table 2: people mobility, when students and teachers go abroad for educational purposes; program mobility, when educational programs go abroad; and institution mobility, when institutions or providers go or invest abroad for educational purposes (OECD, 2004).

Popular methods of cross-border program mobility are franchising, twinning, double or joint degree, articulation, validation, and e-learning or distance learning (Knight, 2007). Major forms of cross-border provider mobility include a branch campus, an independent institution, an acquisition/merger, a study centre or teaching site, and affiliation/networks (Knight, 2007). In addition to these three kinds of mobility, Knight added project mobility, such as joint curriculum development, research, bench-marking, technical assistance, e-learning platforms, professional development and other capacity-building initiatives especially in the information technology area. All forms of cross-border education are currently delivered under a variety of contractual arrangements through development aid, not-for-profit partnerships and, increasingly, trade (OECD, 2004).

The issue of trade liberalisation in educational services has been included in the current negotiations under the General Agreement on Trade in Services (GATS) in the World Trade Organization (WTO). The GATS is a multilateral, legally enforceable agreement governing international trade in services, which was negotiated by members of the WTO and entered into force in 1995. The GATS distinguishes between four modes of supply through which services can be traded (OECD, 2004).

Cross-border supply (mode 1) means that the educational services cross borders. This does not require the physical movement of

Table 2.   Types of cross-border education activities

Type	Main forms	Examples	Size
1. People			
Students/ trainees	Student mobility	– Full study abroad for a foreign degree or qualification – Part of academic partnership for home degree or joint degree – Exchange programs	Probably the largest share of cross-border education
Teachers/ trainers	Academic/ trainer mobility	– For professional development – Part of academic partnership – Employment in a foreign university – Teaching in a branch institution abroad	An old tradition in the education sector, which should grow given the general emphasis on the mobility of professionals and internationalisation of education
2. Programs			
Educational programs	Academic partnerships	– Joint course or program with a foreign institution	Academic partnerships represent the largest share of these activities
	E-learning	– E-learning programs – Selling/franchising a course to a foreign institution	E-learning and franchising are small but rapidly growing activities
3. Institution/ providers	Foreign campuses Foreign investment	– Opening of a foreign campus – Buying (part of) a foreign educational institution – Creating an educational provider abroad	A trend increasing very quickly from a modest starting point

Source: OECD (2004). *Internationalisation and Trade in Higher Education: Opportunities and Challenges.*

the consumers or the providers. Consumption abroad (mode 2) is the movement of educational consumers to the country of the supplier. Commercial presence (mode 3) is the establishment of facilities by educational service providers in another country to provide the service. The presence of natural persons (mode 4) refers to temporary travel of educators to another country to provide educational services (see Table 3).

Modes of supply are closely related to types of cross-border education activities (OECD, 2004). Cross-border education via people mobility includes student and academic mobility: student mobility corresponds to mode 2 (consumption abroad), academic mobility to mode 4 (presence of natural persons). Cross-border education through institution mobility corresponds to mode 3 (commercial presence). Cross-border education through program mobility corresponds to mode 1 (cross-border supply) when it takes the form of distance education or e-learning.

Table 3. Characteristics of the main modes of international supply of educational services

Mode	Education examples	Types of cross-border education
1. Cross-border supply	Distance education Online education Commercial franchising of a course	Program mobility
2. Consumption abroad	Students who go to another country to study	People (student) mobility
3. Commercial presence	Local university or satellite campuses Branch campus, including joint venture with local institutions	Institution mobility
4. Presence of natural persons	Professors, teachers, researchers working temporarily abroad	People (academic) mobility

Source: OECD (2004). *Internationalisation and Trade in Higher Education: Opportunities and Challenges.*

4 RECENT TRENDS IN THE MODES OF SUPPLY AND OUTLOOK FOR THE ASIA–PACIFIC EDUCATION MARKET

As the largest education market in the world, the Asia–Pacific region has very competitive educational institutions on the supply side. Hence, the major five education export countries (the US, Australia, Canada, Japan and New Zealand) in the region receive 40 per cent of all foreign students studying abroad in the world. On the demand side, the region also has affluent human resources: more than two-thirds of the world's population live in the region, and more than 50 per cent of foreign students studying abroad are Asian. Most of them are studying in Asia–Pacific countries because the advanced countries in the region, in general, offer reputable and quality education.

4.1 International Student Mobility in a Global Context

International student mobility represents one form of cross-border education and probably has the largest market share of cross-border education. Each year the OECD conducts a survey on student mobility and foreign students in higher education, and publishes the results in *Education at a Glance: OECD Indicators*. The information on student mobility in this section has been taken mainly from *Education at a Glance: OECD Indicators 2007* and the OECD Online Education Database.

Study-abroad students make up the major form of cross-border higher education. In 2005, 2.7 million foreign students in higher education were enrolled outside their country of citizenship, of which 2.3 million (or 85%) studied in OECD countries (see Table 4). It means that most countries where students go abroad to study are advanced countries, including the OECD countries. The total number of foreign students has grown dramatically from 0.6 million worldwide in 1975 to 2.7 million in 2005 — more than a four-fold increase. This accelerated growth in the internationalisation of higher education during the past 10 years mirrors the growing globalisation of economies and societies.

Table 4. Trends in the number of foreign students in tertiary education outside their country of origin

Year	2000	2001	2002	2003	2004	2005
Worldwide	1,818,759 (100)	1,896,265 (104)	2,188,544 (120)	2,425,915 (133)	2,598,660 (143)	2,725,996 (150)
OECD countries	1,545,534 (100)	1,604,565 (104)	1,856,600 (120)	2,040,574 (132)	2,195,550 (142)	2,296,016 (149)

Source: OECD (2007). Education at a Glance: OECD Indicators 2007.

Although there is some unspecified data regarding the geographic regions of the students' origin, 46.9 per cent of foreign students come from the Asia region. If the data are adjusted, more than half of total foreign students may be Asians (see Table 5).

According to the statistics in 2005, at least 5 out of 10 foreign students were attracted to a relatively limited number of destinations. Only four countries hosted the majority of foreign students enrolled outside their country of citizenship. The United States received the most foreign students (in absolute terms) with 21.6 per cent of all foreign students worldwide, followed by the United Kingdom (11.7%), Germany (9.5%) and France (8.7%). Altogether, these four major destinations account for 51.5 per cent of all higher education students pursuing their studies abroad. Other than these four major destinations, significant numbers of foreign students are enrolled in Australia (6.5%), Japan (4.6%), the Russian Federation (3.3%), Canada (2.8%) and New Zealand (2.5%).

Related to the international education market share, Lasanowski and Verbik (2007) classified major countries in the international student market into the major players (the US, the UK and Australia), the middle powers (Germany and France), the evolving destinations (Japan, Canada and New Zealand) and the emerging contenders (Malaysia, Singapore and China). The common characteristics of the major players are that all of these countries are English-speaking, receive extremely high numbers of students from China and India,

Table 5.   Foreign students in tertiary education by geographic regions of origin (2005)

Geographic regions	Africa	Asia	Europe	North America	Oceania	South America	Not specified	Total
Number	326,519	1,277,690	679,797	81,797	17,371	166,919	175,903	2,725,996
Share (%)	12.0	46.9	24.9	3.0	0.6	6.1	6.5	100.0
Adjusted	12.8	50.1	26.7	3.2	0.7	6.5	—	100.0

Source: OECD (2007). *Education at a Glance: OECD Indicators 2007.*

Note: Sum of geographic regions does not equal the total because of 'not specified' data.

Table 6. Changes in number of foreign students in major countries of destination

Country	2000	2005
United States	475,159 (26.1)	590,167 (21.6)
United Kingdom	222,936 (12.3)	318,399 (11.7)
Germany	187,033 (10.3)	259,797 (9.5)
France	137,085 (7.5)	236,518 (8.7)
Australia	105,764 (5.8)	177,034 (6.5)
Japan	66,607 (3.7)	125,917 (4.6)
Russia	41,210 (2.3)	90,450 (3.3)
Canada	40,443 (2.2)	75,249 (2.8)
Italy	24,929 (1.4)	44,921 (1.6)
New Zealand	8,210 (0.5)	69,390 (2.5)
Korea	3,373 (0.2)	15,497 (0.6)
Worldwide	1,818,759 (100.0)	2,725,996 (100.0)

Source: OECD (2007). *Education at a Glance: OECD Indicators 2007.*

and have education organisations that have developed impressive marketing strategies.

As shown in Table 6, the United States saw a significant drop as a preferred destination for foreign students, from 26.1 per cent of the global intake in 2000 to 21.6 per cent in 2005, although the total number of foreign students has increased. The United Kingdom and Germany also saw a slight decline in their market share over the same five-year period (2000–2005). In contrast, the market shares of Australia, Japan, Canada, New Zealand and Korea expanded continually. The growth in market position was most impressive for New Zealand, with a five-fold increase from 0.5 per cent in 2000 to 2.5 per cent in 2005, followed by Korea, with a trebling from 0.2 per cent to 0.6 per cent.

These trends reflect different emphases of internationalisation policies, ranging from proactive marketing policies in the Asia–Pacific region to a more passive approach in the traditionally dominant countries such as the United States, whose foreign student intake was also affected by the tightened entry regulations in the aftermath of the September 11 attacks.

Table 7.   International higher education market shares of major countries (2005)

Countries	Foreign students received (out-bound)		Students going abroad (in-bound)		Ratio of out-bound to in-bound
	Number	Shares (%)	Number	Shares (%)	
United States	590,167	21.6	38,672	1.4	15.3:1
United Kingdom	318,399	11.7	21,847	0.8	14.5:1
Germany	259,797	9.5	66,811	2.5	3.9:1
France	236,518	8.7	53,868	2.0	4.4:1
Australia	177,034	6.5	9,151	0.3	19.3:1
Canada	75,249	2.8	42,373	1.6	1.8:1
Japan	125,917	4.6	62,853	2.3	2.0:1
Russia	90,450	3.3	42,959	1.6	2.1:1
New Zealand	69,390	2.5	3,734	0.1	18.6:1
Korea	15,497	0.6	96,423	3.5	1:6.2
India	7,738 (2004)	0.3	139,223	5.1	1:18.0
China	—	—	404,664	14.8	—
OECD countries	2,296,016	84.2	776,483	28.5	3.0:1

Source: OECD (2007). *Education at a Glance: OECD Indicators 2007.*

Table 7 presents the major education service-exporting countries and major education service-importing countries. Major advanced countries including the US, the UK, Germany, France, Australia, Canada and Japan are typical education-exporting countries. An excessive export surplus can be seen especially in the US, the UK, Australia and New Zealand, with a ratio of out-bound to in-bound of more than 10. It is no coincidence that all these countries are English-speaking. Meanwhile, China, India and Korea are typical education-importing countries. Contrary to education-exporting countries, the ratio of in-bound to out-bound students in these countries is very high.

By the regions of origin of foreign students, Asian countries, which sent 1.2 million students abroad in 2004, are the largest sending countries followed by the European ones (0.7 million). These two regions of origin account for 70 per cent of all foreign students.

The statistics on the regions of origin and countries of destination for foreign students show that the US, the UK, Australia, Canada and Japan receive most of their foreign students from Asian countries. Meanwhile, Germany receives a majority of its foreign students from European countries, especially Eastern European ones, and France receives the greatest number of foreign students from African countries, especially Northern African countries (see Table 8).

The demand for international higher education has grown dramatically since 2000. The average annual growth rate of international students was 4.1 per cent in the 1980s and 4.2 per cent in the 1990s, respectively. However, the growth rate in the 2000s (2000–2005) rapidly increased to 8.4 per cent. Assuming the same growth rate in the five years from 2000, the number of international students will increase from 2.7 million in 2005 to 4.1 million in 2010, and to 9.1 million in 2020.

The Global Student Mobility 2025 report (Böhm, 2003) foresees that the demand for international higher education will increase from 1.8 million international students in 2000 to 7.6 million in 2025. Asia was thought to have by far the greatest growth potential and was expected to account for 70 per cent of global demand in 2025. Within Asia, China and India were identified as the main growth markets and estimated to account for 50 per cent of the global demand for international higher education in 2025. Similarly, the British Council projected that overall demand for international higher education would increase from 2.1 million places in 2003 to approximately 5.8 million by 2020 (Böhm *et al.*, 2004). Demand for student places in the five main English-speaking destination countries (Australia, Canada, New Zealand, the UK and the US) alone was predicted to rise from 1 million to 2.6 million in 2020, with students from Asia again accounting for the majority of this demand. Language of instruction is one of the major underlying factors students consider when choosing a country of study. The dominance of English-speaking destinations may be largely attributed to the fact that students intending to study abroad are most likely to have learnt English in their home country and/or wish to improve their English language skills through immersion and study abroad programs (OECD, 2004).

Table 8.   Foreign students by region of origin and destination (2005)

Classifications	Destination countries							
	US	UK	Germany	France	Australia	Canada	Japan	Worldwide
Regions of origin								
Africa	37,705	29,429	23,255	109,701	5,740	14,662	904	326,519
	(6.4)	(9.2)	(9.0)	(46.4)	(3.2)	(11.0)	(0.7)	(12.0)
Asia	373,254	147,384	94,722	39,974	138,982	53,657	118,661	1,277,690
	(63.2)	(46.3)	(36.5)	(16.9)	(78.5)	(40.3)	(94.2)	(46.9)
Europe	73,747	104,522	127,760	48,433	10,171	21,605	2,801	679,797
	(12.5)	(32.8)	(49.2)	(20.5)	(5.7)	(16.2)	(2.2)	(24.9)
North America	29,907	18,765	3,935	3,639	6,681	8,359	1,824	81,797
	(5.1)	(5.9)	(1.5)	(1.5)	(3.8)	(6.3)	(1.4)	(3.0)
Oceania	4,680	2,291	399	299	3,764	861	543	17,371
	(0.8)	(0.7)	(0.2)	(0.1)	(2.1)	(0.6)	(0.4)	(0.6)
South America	70,834	8,488	7,931	9,648	1,937	8,687	1,189	166,919
	(12.0)	(2.7)	(3.1)	(4.1)	(1.1)	(6.5)	(0.9)	(6.1)
Total	590,167	318,399	259,797	236,518	177,034	132,982	125,917	2,725,996
	(21.6)	(11.7)	(9.5)	(8.7)	(6.5)	(4.9)	(4.6)	(100.0)

Source: OECD (2007). *Education at a Glance: OECD Indicators 2007.*
Note: Countries of destination are selected from countries receiving the greatest number of foreign students. The number for Canada is based on 2004 data.

4.2 Program and Institution Mobility

The bulk of cross-border post-secondary education through program and institution mobility occurs in the Asia–Pacific region (Vincent-Lancrin, 2007). Singapore, Malaysia and Hong Kong are probably the main importers of cross-border education through institution and program mobility. This type of activity is also increasingly being developed in mainland China.

Many schools and universities in the Asia–Pacific region have recently begun developing joint programs with foreign educational institutions and e-learning programs, as well as selling or franchising courses to foreign educational institutions. Academic partnerships represent the largest share of these activities. E-learning and franchising are small but rapidly growing activities (OECD, 2004). For example, in Korea, 14 universities were operating dual-degree programs, and four universities were operating joint-degree programs as of 2006. (MOEHRD and KEDI, 2006). Another example of a joint program is the establishment of the Logistics Institute — Asia–Pacific by the National University of Singapore and Georgia Institute of Technology to conduct research and provide education. The Massachusetts Institute of Technology (MIT), the National University of Singapore and Nanyang Technology University have jointly implemented the Singapore–MIT Alliance Program to operate graduate programs.

In recent years many branch campuses of foreign universities have been established in the Asia–Pacific region, and this trend will continue. Many Asian countries are trying to attract branch campuses of foreign universities, with Singapore being the most successful. Many world-class universities, including the Chicago School of Business, INSEAD, MIT, Johns Hopkins, Georgia Institute of Technology, Stanford University and the University of New South Wales, are operating branch campuses or joint programs in Singapore. Similarly, the University of Nottingham, Monash University, Curtin University of Technology and FTMS–De Montfort University are operating branch campuses in Malaysia. China and Korea are also trying to play host to foreign university campuses. Ningbo, China has invited the University of Nottingham campus, and the Shipping and Transport

College of Rotterdam is establishing a branch campus in Kwangyang, Korea. At its peak, Japan housed 36 foreign university campuses, but most of these branch campuses closed in the mid-1990s because they failed to meet the minimum requirements for university recognition. The few that remain include Temple University Japan, Southern Illinois University Carbondale in Niigata, Kyoto International University and Roosevelt University.

Since 1996, the Malaysian government has encouraged foreign universities to establish branch campuses, and five branch campuses of foreign universities and over 600 private colleges now offer both local and foreign qualifications. In Hong Kong, approximately 165 foreign educational institutions and professional bodies offered a total of 856 courses in June 2003, alone or with local partners (Garrett and Verbik, 2003). Finally, China reported a nine-fold increase between 1995 and 2003 in foreign programs (Garrett and Verbik, 2003). In early 2003, there were 712 such programs, 37 per cent of them at a post-secondary or higher education level.

5 LINKS BETWEEN DEMAND FOR EDUCATION AND DEVELOPMENTS IN TRADE AND FOREIGN INVESTMENT

Overall demand for education in the Asia–Pacific region has increased rapidly during the last several decades. The demand has changed from primary and secondary education to higher education, and some demand has moved away from domestic education to international education. Many Asia–Pacific students have gone abroad to receive reputable and quality education in the advanced countries in the region. This trend has been accelerated and facilitated by an increase in personal income levels and open market policies of the governments.

According to the recent United States international student statistics (2006/07), Asia is the largest sending region and accounts for 59 per cent of total US international enrolment. The top five countries of origin are all Asian countries (India, China, Korea, Japan and Taiwan). Similarly, among the international student enrolments in

Table 9.   Relative number of students going abroad to study

Country	Population	Students going abroad to study	Students going abroad per 10,000 people
China	1,319,315,450	404,664	3.07
India	1,169,016,000	139,223	1.19
Korea	48,224,000	96,423	19.99
Japan	127,750,000	62,853	4.92

Sources: UN estimates and Government Statistics Bureau.

Australia, 9 of the top 10 source countries are Asian countries. China, India and Korea are the major sources of international students in both the US and Australia. The percentage of students from China and India enrolling in higher education is low as their income levels are low (see Table 9). As a result, even though the absolute number of students going abroad in both countries is very high, the relative number of students going abroad (the number of students going abroad per 10,000 people) is relatively low. This means that their potentiality in the future education market will be enormous as their income levels increase.

Foreign students themselves have become a major income source for universities in some countries (the US, Australia and Canada).[2] In 2006–7, international students in the US contributed approximately 14.5 billion dollars to the US economy through their expenditure on tuition and living expenses (Institute of International Education, 2007). In 2001, the UK earned 11.1 billion dollars from foreign students, Australia earned 2.1 billion dollars, Canada earned 0.7 billion dollars and New Zealand earned 0.4 billion dollars. In the same year,

---

[2] In recent years, the focus of government and institutional policies on international education seems to have shifted from educational and cultural aspects to financial motives. In this regard, an increasing number of countries including Australia, New Zealand and the United Kingdom have adopted the so-called revenue-generating approach to the internationalisation of higher education. These countries utilise foreign students as resources to bring economic benefits to institutions as well as to the national economy as a whole by restricting or preventing the provision of subsidised educational services to overseas students.

Table 10. Export earnings from foreign students and import payments by national students studying abroad (2001)

Country	Export earnings (billion US dollars)	Import payment (billion US dollars)
United States	14.5	2.4
United Kingdom	11.1	—
Australia	2.1	0.4
Canada	0.7	0.5
New Zealand	0.4	—

Source: OECD (2004). *Internationalisation and Trade in Higher Education: Opportunities and Challenges.*

American students abroad spent 2.4 billion dollars, Canadians spent 0.5 billion dollars and Australians spent 0.4 billion dollars (see Table 10). Larsen *et al.* (2002) estimated that the international market for student mobility alone amounted to around 30 billion dollars in exports or 3 per cent of global service exports in 1998. However, the world market for post-secondary education is not confined to student mobility in tertiary education, and the figure would be much higher if data were available for all forms of cross-border education, such as program mobility and institution mobility (OECD, 2004).

Major education export countries in the Asia–Pacific region have common characteristics. They are all English-speaking nations, and they demand high tuition fees, adopting a higher fee system for international students than for domestic students.[3]

Meanwhile, countries that send too many students to foreign countries are suffering from an imbalance of trade in educational services. For instance, the number of Korean students studying at higher education institutions abroad was slightly over 13,000 in

[3] Tuition fee policies vary from country to country (OECD, 2004). English-speaking countries, such as the US, Canada and Australia, have adopted higher tuition fees for international students than for domestic students. Meanwhile, other countries, such as Japan and Korea, have the same tuition fees for international and domestic students. Moreover, the Nordic countries, the Czech Republic and Iceland charge tuition fees for neither international nor domestic students.

1980; after 25 years, the number has skyrocketed to 190,000, a 14-fold increase. The growing number of students studying abroad has resulted in a severe imbalance of trade in educational services. According to the Bank of Korea, the amount of money related to the import of educational services soared from 958 million dollars in 2000 to approximately 4.5 billion dollars in 2006, while the export of educational services remained at 28 million dollars in 2006 (The Bank of Korea, 2007). To alleviate this matter, the Korean government established 'The Educational Service Export Plan' in 2007. It includes inducing foreign students to study in Korea, facilitating the establishment of overseas branch campuses of domestic universities and expanding overseas development aids in education and manpower training.

The Asia–Pacific region has the largest education service-exporting countries as well as the largest education service-importing countries. Both have developed their own strategies based on their position. Education-exporting countries have developed aggressive strategies by building branch campuses and expanding their internet-based systems. Governments in some countries support international exchange programs and remove regulatory obstacles for international education. These countries will develop a more aggressive education-exporting strategy, based on the revenue-generating approach.

Education-importing countries have developed diverse cross-border education strategies. Generally, countries with advanced school systems maintain an open market policy under free trade principles, whereas governments in many countries with less developed school systems intervene in cross-border education. Intervention takes two forms: positive and negative. Some countries maintain selected regulatory policies, restraining studying abroad in early childhood, prohibiting the establishment of schools by for-profit organisations or regulating the remittance of school operation proceeds to home countries.

6 CONCLUSIONS

Education has become increasingly international. Options for students are no longer constrained by national borders. As a result, more and more students choose to study abroad, enrol in foreign educational programs and institutions in their home country or simply use the internet to take courses at colleges and universities in other countries. Internationalisation of education will be accelerated by free trade systems such as the FTA as this will catalyse commercialisation, privatisation, marketisation and liberalisation of service sectors, including education, between various countries.

International higher education now plays a significant role in the economy. Foreign students have become a major source of income for universities in some countries and are actively recruited by, for example, the US, the UK, Australia and Canada. International students contribute to the national economy through their expenditure on tuition and living expenses. Hence, higher education is described as a major service sector export. However, the world market for higher education is not confined to student mobility, and the figure would be much higher if data were available for all forms of cross-border education. Some universities and other institutions offer English as a Second Language (ESL) programs, which are a source of considerable income. Universities in the advanced nations (the US, the UK and Australia) have opened branch campuses abroad as a means of earning income as well as internationalising themselves. Such market forces are driving the academic world towards greater internationalism.

The largest education service-exporting countries (the US, Australia and Canada) and importing countries (China, India, Japan and Korea) in the Asia–Pacific region have developed their own strategies to meet the demands fuelled by the international education fever. Education-exporting countries have developed aggressive strategies by building branch campuses and expanding distance education programs according to the revenue-generating approach. Comparatively, education-importing countries have developed diverse cross-border education strategies to meet the demand of their people. As the world becomes more global and the need for internationalisation increases, the number of people demanding international education services will continue to grow. Countries facing either the export or import aspect of this matter will be required to modify and diversify their programs and regulations to meet the needs of these globalising citizens.

REFERENCES

Altbach PG (1998). *Comparative Higher Education: Knowledge, the University, and Development*. Ablex Publishing Corporation, London.

Australian Education International (2007). http://aei.dest.gov.au.

Bank of Korea (2007). *Economic Statistical Yearbook*. Seoul.

Böhm A (2003). *Global Student Mobility 2025: Analysis of Global Competition and Market Share*. IDP Education Australia, Sydney.

Böhm A et al. (2004). *Vision 2020: Forecasting International Student Mobility: A UK Perspective*. British Council, London.

FKI (Federation of Korean Industry) (2007). *Inducement of Foreign Universities in Major Countries and its Implications* (in Korean). Seoul.

Ihm C-S (2006). A strategy for internationalization in higher education: Korea. Paper presented at the 1st International Symposium on A Strategy for Internationalization in Higher Education, Seoul, 15 December, 61–74.

IMD (2007). *World Competitiveness Yearbook 2007*. IPP Books.

Institute of International Education (2007). http://www.opendoors.iienetwork.org.

Kim G-J (2006). Internationalization of Higher Education in Republic of Korea: Groping Around for Establishing the New Initiatives. Paper presented at the 1st International Symposium on A Strategy for Internationalization in Higher Education, Seoul, 15 December, 3–14.

Kim Y-C (2007). Internationalization and Global Competitiveness of Higher Education in Korea. Paper presented at the Joint Annual Conference of ICKS-KAUPA on Impending Changes on the Korean Peninsula and the Future of US–Korean Relations, Honolulu, 28–29 June.

Knight J (2003). *GATS, Trade and Higher Education: Perspective 2003 — Where Are We?* The Observatory on Borderless Higher Education, UK.

Knight J (2007). Cross-border tertiary education: An introduction. In *Cross-border Tertiary Education: A Way Towards Capacity Development*, OECD and World Bank (eds.). OECD, Paris.

Larsen K, Martin J and Morris R (2002). Trade in educational services: Trends and issues. *World Econ*, 25(6), 849–868.

Lasanowski V and Verbik L (2007). *International Student Mobility: Patterns and Trends*. The Observatory on Borderless Higher Education, UK.

Lee S-H et al. (2006). *Gains and Losses of Youngsters' Studying Abroad from the Human Developmental Viewpoint* (in Korean). Korean Educational Development Institute. Seoul.

MOEHRD and KEDI (Ministry of Education & Human Resources Development and Korean Educational Development Institute) (2006). *White Paper on Education* (in Korean). Seoul.

OECD (2004). *Internationalisation and Trade in Higher Education: Opportunities and Challenges.* OECD, Paris.

OECD (2006). *Education Policy Analysis: Focus on Higher Education 2005–2006.* OECD, Paris.

OECD (2007). *Education at a Glance: OECD Indicators 2007.* OECD, Paris.

Rhee B-S *et al.* (2004). *Policy Study on Internationalization and Upgrading of University Education* (in Korean). Korean Educational Development Institute, Seoul.

Samsung Economic Research Institute (2006). *University Innovation and Competitiveness* (in Korean). Seoul.

Shin H-S (2005). *Higher Education Reform Policies* (in Korean). Hakjisa, Seoul.

Yoo H-S *et al.* (2004). *Policy Study on the Education Service Sector in FTA: Singapore and Japan* (in Korean). Korean Educational Development Institute, Seoul.

Vincent-Lancrin S (2007). Developing capacity through cross-border tertiary education. In *Cross-border Tertiary Education: A Way Towards Capacity Development*, OECD and World Bank (eds.). OECD, Paris.

International Student Movements and the Effects of Barriers to Trade in Higher Education Services

Philippa Dee

1 INTRODUCTION

As with many other activities, higher education is undergoing rapid globalisation. A recent OECD report documents the following trends (OECD, 2007). The first is a shift from student mobility to program and provider mobility. The number of students seeking education in foreign countries is still increasing, and is by far the most important method by which higher education services are traded. But increasing emphasis is being placed on delivering foreign academic courses, programs and projects to students in their home country. The second trend is a move from development cooperation to competitive commerce, or from 'aid to trade'.

The same OECD report notes that the number of foreign students in OECD countries more than tripled in 25 years to a total of 2.3 million by 2004. This represented about 85 per cent of the world's foreign students in that year. Conversely, about 66 per cent of the foreign students studying in OECD countries in 2004 were from outside the OECD area. Asia accounted for about half of those (48%), followed by Europe (27%), Africa (12%), South America (7%), North America (4%) and Oceania (1%). Student mobility, therefore, appears to be truly universal.

The OECD report also notes that the bulk of cross-border post-secondary education delivered through program and institution mobility occurs in the Asia–Pacific region. Singapore, Malaysia and Hong Kong are probably the main importers of cross-border education through institution and program mobility. This type of activity is also increasingly being developed in mainland China, which reported a nine-fold increase between 1995 and 2003 in such programs, all offered in cooperation with local institutions (as required by Chinese legislation). Just over a third of these were at the post-secondary level. Lasanowski and Verbik (2007) report how, by importing institutions and programs, these countries are becoming emerging contenders to export higher education services via the inward movement of foreign students.

Despite the size of, and growth in, international student movements, some commentators argue that there is significant unmet demand:

'Since Yr 2000 there has in reality been very little cross-border trade in higher education, despite the hype that exists in the press and in the many OECD countries that compete in similar markets and have become more reliant on the income they earn from foreign students than was the case in past decades. Today barely 2.5 per cent of global tertiary enrolments are students that enrol in foreign universities — and although this number continues to grow, it is very small when one considers the unmet supply and demand that exists in the global higher education sector' (Perkinson, 2006, p. 16).

But the growth of program and institution mobility raises the question of whether this is not a more efficient method of trade than via international student movements. It also raises the question of whether the various, and numerous, regulatory barriers to trade in higher education services are skewing service delivery away from more efficient methods. If this is the case, then international negotiations on barriers to trade in higher education services, such as those occurring under the General Agreement on Trade in Services (GATS) as part of the Doha Round, provide a way of redressing the problem.

However, little is known empirically about what drives trade in higher education services, and even less is known empirically about the role of barriers to that trade. Without such empirical insights, trade negotiators have little basis for prioritising their negotiating efforts. This paper offers contributions on both fronts. It develops and tests a model of international student movements, recognising that higher education in many countries is price-controlled and entry is typically subject to non-price rationing. It investigates the role of trade barriers, and finds significant effects of barriers in both the sending and receiving countries, which in turn distort the methods of service delivery. It explores the policy implications, finding that barriers in the receiving country appear not to be covered by the GATS. It also explores areas for further research.

The next section summarises the empirical work on barriers to services trade to date, and discusses why trade in higher education services is different. The third section develops a model of international student movements, and compares it to other models found in the literature. The fourth section tests the model empirically and investigates the role of trade barriers, while the concluding section draws out policy implications and areas for further study.

2 SERVICES TRADE AND BARRIERS TO THAT TRADE

Services are often delivered face-to-face. This means that trade in services often takes place via the movement of people (consumers or individual producers) or capital (service-producing firms).

First, the consumer may move to the producer's economy. This happens with services such as education and health, when the student or patient moves to another economy for education or treatment.

In the language of the GATS under the WTO, this mode of services trade is called 'consumption abroad', or mode 2.

Alternatively, the producer may move temporarily to the consumer's economy. This also happens in education, where teachers move to another economy to teach short courses. It is also very common for professionals to travel temporarily to the economy into which they are delivering professional services. In the language of the GATS, this mode of service delivery is called the 'movement of natural persons' (to distinguish it from the movement of corporate or other legal entities), or mode 4.

Many other services are delivered to other economies via 'commercial presence'. In banking and telecommunications, for example, it is common for companies to set up a permanent corporate presence in another economy and to make their sales from their foreign affiliate. Universities may also establish offshore campuses. The GATS also recognises commercial presence, or mode 3, as a mode of services delivery.

Finally, services may be traded 'cross-border', at arm's length rather than face-to-face. Services are typically intangible, so the internet is an important vehicle for such cross-border trade. Distance education and program mobility are examples, as is internet banking. This is GATS mode 1.

With services traded via the movement of people or capital, the transaction typically occurs behind the border. Even when cross-border trade takes place via the internet, it is not easily observed by customs officials. Thus, services transactions are not amenable to tariff protection. Instead, services trade barriers are typically behind-the-border, non-price regulatory measures.

Since services trade barriers typically operate behind the border, measurement has generally been on some behind-the-border assessment of economic performance. Papers that have quantified the effects of regulatory barriers to services trade include Barth, Caprio and Levine (2004); Boylaud and Nicoletti (2000); Claessens, Demirgüç-Kunt and Huizinga (2001); Clark, Dollar and Micco (2004); Doove et al. (2001); Fink, Mattoo and Neagu (2001); Fink, Mattoo and Rathindran (2002); Gonenc and Nicoletti (2000);

Kalirajan (2000); Kalirajan *et al.* (2000); Kang (2000); Nguyen-Hong (2000); Steiner (2000) and Warren (2000). The literature is summarised and some of the methodological issues canvassed in Dee (2005).

For most of the services trade barriers studied, the predominant mode of service delivery has been via the movement of *producers*:

- through foreign direct investment (banking, distribution, electricity generation, professions, telecommunications); or
- through the temporary movement of individual producers (professions).

Accordingly, most measurement work has concentrated on supply-side effects, behind the border, within the importing country.

In that context, a key issue has been whether the trade barriers create rents (raise markups), or raise real resource costs. The welfare costs of the latter can exceed that of the former by a considerable margin, even if the 'height' of the trade barriers is the same — compare the shaded areas in Figs. 1(a) and 1(b).

Theory can provide some guidance on whether barriers are rent-creating or cost-escalating. Rents are likely to be created by quantitative and other barriers that limit entry (or exit, though this is far less common). Some red-tape measures may add to resource costs. There are also many ways in which rents can be dissipated or

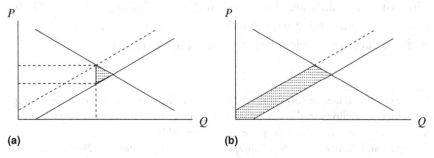

(a)   (b)

Figure 1. (a) **Welfare cost of rent-creating non-tariff barriers; (b) Welfare cost of cost-escalating non-tariff barriers**

capitalised. So non-tariff barriers that may once have been rent-creating for the initial incumbent become cost-escalating for subsequent incumbents.[1]

The limited empirical evidence tends to accord with this intuition.[2] In banking and telecommunications, where explicit barriers to entry are rife, barriers appear to create rents. In distribution services, where indirect trade restrictions also apply, barriers appear to increase costs. In air passenger transport and the professions, barriers appear to have both effects. Theoretical arguments suggest that barriers in maritime and electricity generation primarily affect costs.[3]

2.1 Higher Education is Different

Higher education is different in at least three respects:

- the main way in which higher education services are traded is via the movement of *consumers* (international students), although as noted in the introduction, delivery via the movement of capital (off-shore campuses) or individual producers (teachers) is gaining ground rapidly, as is cross-border trade (through program mobility, if not distance education);
- some barriers to trade in higher education restrict the movement of consumers, not producers; and
- some barriers to trade in higher education services affect exports, not imports.

The last two points are illustrated in detail in Tables 1 and 2. These tables give illustrative examples of the types of barriers to trade in higher education services that are found in various countries.

---

[1] For example, Kalirajan (2000) provides indirect evidence that some of the zoning and other restrictions in the wholesale and retail sector have created rents that are subsequently capitalised into the price of commercial land.

[2] Gregan and Johnson (1999); Kalirajan *et al.* (2000); Kalirajan (2000); Nguyen-Hong (2000); OECD (2005); Copenhagen Economics (2005).

[3] Steiner (2000); Clark, Dollar and Micco (2004).

Table 1. **Examples of barriers to imports of education services**

Mode	Limitations on market access	Derogations from national treatment
MODE 1: Cross-border trade, e.g., downloading courses from the internet	Restrictions on downloading educational material from the internet, be it from a domestic or foreign supplier	Restrictions on downloading educational material from foreign internet sites
	Requiring foreign suppliers of internet education courses to be in a partnership or joint venture with a local institution	Restrictions on which courses foreign suppliers of distance education can provide
	An economic needs test attached to registration, authorisation or licensing of all education providers, including those supplying via distance education	Restrictions on the import and distribution of educational materials or software from foreign institutions providing distance education
	Restrictions on the recognition of qualifications obtained from any distance education supplier	Restrictions on the local accreditation of foreign distance education suppliers, or on the recognition of qualifications obtained from a foreign distance education supplier
		Restrictions on cross-border payment or credit card transactions
MODE 2: Consumption abroad, e.g., home students moving overseas to study	Since the home country has no jurisdiction over the foreign service supplier, it can mostly limit foreign supply only *indirectly* by restricting the local consumer. Such restrictions on consumers are unlikely to also affect local suppliers. Hence it is unlikely that there would be limitations on market access for *imports* of education services delivered via this mode.	Restrictions on foreign education institutions advertising locally or recruiting local students

(Continued)

Table 1. (*Continued*)

Mode	Limitations on market access	Derogations from national treatment
		Quotas on the number of local students going overseas to study
		Foreign currency restrictions on local students studying abroad
		Restrictions on the recognition of overseas qualifications for institutional credit
		Restrictions on the recognition of overseas qualifications for professional licensing and accreditation
MODE 3: Commercial presence, e.g., foreign institutions establishing a local campus	An economic needs test attached to registration, authorisation or licensing of all education providers	An economic needs test attached to registration, authorisation or licensing of foreign education providers
	A requirement that the foreign institution incorporate locally	A restriction that prevents foreign tertiary institutions from using the term 'university' in the title of their local campus
	A requirement that the foreign institution operate in a joint venture with a local institution	Restrictions on the scope of services that the local campus of a foreign institution can provide
	Restrictions on the number of foreign teachers that local institutions can employ	Restrictions on the number of students that the local campus of a foreign institution can service
	Limits on foreign equity in local institutions	A residency requirement on the management of the local campuses of foreign institutions

(*Continued*)

Table 1.   (*Continued*)

Mode	Limitations on market access	Derogations from national treatment
		Discriminatory quality assurance requirements on the local campuses of foreign institutions
		Restrictions on the ability of the local campuses of foreign institutions to grant degrees, or restrictions on the recognition of those degrees
		Restrictions on the ability of the local campuses of foreign institutions to charge fees
		Restrictions on the ability of the local campuses of foreign institutions to gain access to producer subsidies
		Restrictions on the ability of the students of local campuses of foreign institutions to gain access to consumer subsidies
MODE 4: Movement of natural persons, e.g., foreign teachers coming to deliver short courses	An economic needs test attached to registration, authorisation or licensing of all education providers, including foreign teachers	Nationality of citizenship requirements to teach locally
	Quotas or economic needs tests on the numbers of temporary staff employed by local institutions	A prior residency requirement to teach locally
	Labour market testing for the contract employment of foreign teachers	Restrictions on the recognition of the qualifications of foreign teachers

Source: WTO (1998); WTO (2001); IDP Education Australia (2002).

Table 2.   Examples of barriers to exports of education services

Mode	Restriction
MODE 2: Consumption abroad, e.g., foreign students entering to take local courses	Numerical limits on the entry of foreign students
	Limits on what courses foreign students can enrol in
	Discriminatory enrolment criteria for foreign students
	Restrictions on local institutions recruiting foreign students
	Restrictions on foreign students gaining access to local employment while studying
	Restrictions on foreign students gaining access to tuition or other (e.g., transport) subsidies while studying
MODE 4: Movement of natural persons, e.g., local teachers moving overseas to deliver courses	Exit restrictions on domestic teachers
	Education or employment bond requiring teachers to serve a minimum term of employment locally before they can go overseas
	Restrictions on funds transfers overseas by domestic teachers

Source: WTO (1998); WTO (2001); IDP Education Australia (2002).

Table 1 lists barriers to the *import* of education services under two headings:

- limitations on market access;
- derogations from national treatment.

The key distinguishing feature is that derogations from national treatment imply that foreign service providers are discriminated against, *vis-à-vis* domestic suppliers. The discrimination may be *de facto* or *de jure* (WTO, 2001). By contrast, limitations on market access may affect both foreign and domestic suppliers (WTO, 2001).

The GATS disciplines on market access are limited to six specific types of measures (GATS Article XVI.1 and XVI.2):

- limits on the number of services suppliers;
- limits on the total value of services transactions;

- limits on the total number of services operations or total quantity of services output;
- limitations on the total number of natural persons employed;
- measures that restrict or require specific types of legal entity or joint venture; and
- limitations on the participation of foreign capital.

Thus, not all of the restrictions listed in Table 1 would necessarily appear in a country's GATS schedule. The key policy question is whether countries are required to schedule limitations on market access that limit the entry of new domestic or foreign service providers equally, but which do not take one of the above six forms. According to the Guidelines on Scheduling Specific Commitments (WTO, 2001), such measures do not have to be scheduled as limitations on market access, but they may be subject to the GATS disciplines on domestic regulation (GATS Article VI.5(a)). According to these disciplines, in those sectors where a country has made specific commitments, qualification requirements and procedures, technical standards and licensing requirements must not interfere with ('nullify or impair') a country's national treatment or market access commitments by failing to be:

- based on objective and transparent criteria, such as competence and the ability to supply the service;
- not more burdensome than necessary to ensure the quality of the service; and
- in the case of licensing procedures, not in themselves a restriction on the supply of the service.

Hence there are some weak legal sanctions on such measures, even if they do not have to be scheduled.

As noted in Table 1, a critical barrier to imports of education services is lack of recognition of the foreign qualifications so obtained. In practice, few if any countries have scheduled lack of recognition as a trade barrier (WTO, 1998).

Table 2 lists barriers to the *export* of education services. A key policy question is whether these are subject to GATS disciplines. The

GATS guidelines again provide some guidance (WTO, 2001). They note first that there is no obligation under the GATS for a member to take measures outside its territorial jurisdiction. They also note that whatever the mode of supply, obligations and commitments under the agreement relate directly to the treatment of services and services *suppliers*. They only relate to consumers so far as services or services suppliers of other members are affected. This has implications for measures affecting education exports via mode 2 (consumption abroad), whereby foreign students come to the home country to be educated. Discrimination against those foreign consumers is only relevant if it somehow implies discrimination against foreign suppliers (wherever their location).

As noted in Table 2, restrictions typically affect exports delivered via mode 2 (the inward movement of foreign students to take courses locally) and mode 4 (the outward movement of local teachers to deliver courses overseas). These restrictions could have very real effects on trade in education services. However, in most cases, they would not have to be scheduled in a country's GATS schedule, because they do not affect the viability of local service *providers* (either domestic institutions or the local campuses of foreign institutions), nor do they adversely affect offshore service providers.

Thus the GATS framework is limited in its ability to deal with barriers to the movement of international students in two important ways — it has no jurisdiction over barriers that are imposed directly on the students themselves, rather than on the service providers, and it provides only weak sanctions over non-discriminatory barriers that affect both domestic and foreign providers of higher education services, but which fall outside the six specific forms. The extent to which these and other barriers affect international student movements is examined in the next sections.

The GATS framework also appears somewhat poorly placed to deal with barriers to the growing trade in higher education delivered via the mobility of programs, providers or projects. The GATS framework encourages negotiators to negotiate mode by mode, but many of the new ways of delivering higher education services involve two or more of the GATS modes simultaneously. For example, higher education *programs* may be delivered (through twinning or franchise arrangements) via distance, face-to-face, or some combination of the two. In some cases, the program and qualification will be awarded by the foreign institution but the teaching will be done by a local institution. In other cases, the foreign institution may also be responsible for the teaching. In either case, representatives from the foreign institution are likely to travel on a regular basis to monitor progress. Therefore, delivery of a single program may involve 'cross-border' trade, 'commercial presence' and the 'temporary movement of people'.

Similarly, *provider* mobility may be temporary, permanent or some combination of the two. For example, foreign branch campuses may be established on a permanent basis, but staffed partly by individual teachers on temporary transfer from the home country. Mobility of *projects* involves the international sharing of research and curricula. Here the important barriers may be limits on the protection of intellectual property, rather than barriers under the four GATS modes of supply. The extent to which these and other barriers affect the mobility of programs, providers and projects is an area for further research.

3 A MODEL OF INTERNATIONAL STUDENT MOVEMENTS

Because some barriers to trade in higher education affect consumers as well as producers, measurement of the effects of those barriers will need to look at both sides of the higher education market.

Higher education markets differ across countries in many respects. But a key characteristic of the Canadian system identified by Finnie and Usher (2006) also applies in many other countries, particularly in Europe and Oceania. This is that tuition levels are regulated, thus the allocation of tertiary education places is subject to non-price rationing (Fig. 2). So even though some barriers to services trade affect consumers, the observed 'market' outcomes do not reflect pure demand behaviour, but rather the rationing rule — a mixture of demand and supply effects.

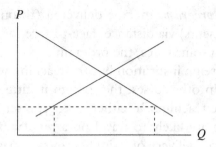

Figure 2.   The 'market' for higher education services

The hypothesis in this paper is that rationing in higher education is a mixture of:

- queuing — the number of students from a particular source country studying in a particular destination country is a function of the total length of the queue, and the proportion of places held in that queue by students from that source country; and
- screening — foreign students also have to meet the admissions criteria.

The number of foreign students from various source countries in tertiary institutions around the world will reflect these two influences.

The model is necessarily cast in cross-country terms because barriers to services trade vary on a cross-country basis, and a key aim of the paper is to measure the effects of trade barriers on the movements of foreign students. Thus, apart from the influence of trade barriers, the model of higher education needs to be robust and general enough to fit all the countries in a cross-country sample, providing little opportunity for fine-tuning.

In a cross-country context, the queuing effect means that the number of foreign students from a particular source country enrolled in a particular destination country will depend:

- positively on the population of the destination country — if foreign students were scattered randomly about the population centres of the world, this is how the length of the queues would be determined;

- positively on the population of the source country — on the basis of number of applications alone, this is how the proportion of queue places held by a particular source country would be determined;
- positively on the GDP per capita of the source country, since richer countries are more likely to be able to meet the tuition and living costs of overseas study;
- positively on the perceived quality of tertiary education in the destination country — the literature consistently suggests that this demand effect is very strong (e.g., Chapman, 1979; Murphy, 1981; Tierney, 1983; Tremblay, 2001; Shackleton, 2003; Follari, 2004; Knight, 2005; Perkinson, 2006);
- perhaps negatively on the perceived quality of tertiary education in the source country — since this may mean there is less need to go abroad to get a quality education; and
- positively on the ease with which international students can subsequently gain permanent residency or citizenship in their country of study — this demand effect is well recognised in the policy literature (e.g., Lasanowski and Verbik, 2007), but is typically ignored in empirical work.

The queuing effect will be further moderated by the operation of barriers to trade in higher education services. Accordingly, the number of foreign students from a particular source country enrolled in a particular destination country will depend:

- positively on restrictions on inward FDI (mode 3 imports) in education in the source country — assuming that inward FDI boosts the quantity and/or quality of tertiary education in the source country, so there is less need for students to go abroad (the concluding section discusses how this assumption may be tested directly);
- positively on restrictions on imports via cross-border trade (mode 1) or temporary movement of teachers (mode 4) in the source country — for similar reasons;

- negatively on restrictions on imports by the source country via the outward movement of students (mode 2 imports);
- negatively on restrictions on the inward movement of foreign students in the destination country (mode 2 exports).

The screening effect will depend on the screening criteria, which typically focus on the quality of the student applicants, and the ability of universities to monitor that quality. Accordingly, the number of foreign students from a particular source country enrolled in a particular destination country will depend:

- positively on the perceived quality of the students from the source country (or the feeder institutions from which they come), relative to the quality of the education on offer in the destination country — exporters want good students, but 'beggars can't be choosers'; and
- negatively on distance — exporters often travel extensively to source countries to assess the quality of the feeder institutions and to pre-screen the candidates, and distance affects the costs of doing so.

Thus the final model is that the number of tertiary students from a particular source country enrolled in a particular destination country will depend on (expected signs in parentheses): population at source (+), population at destination (+), distance (−), GDP per capita at source (+), quality at source (+/− but expect +, i.e., the screening effect will dominate the demand effect), quality at destination (+/− but expect +, i.e., the demand effect will dominate the screening effect), the ease of subsequent migration (+), and measures of trade restrictions at both the source and destination.

　　Kim (1998) develops a similar estimating equation to test a well-articulated model of student choice involving lifetime optimisation of earnings, but his model differs from the one above because he assumes that the market for higher education clears. This implies that the effect of quality at the destination is non-linear, because as quality goes up, tuition fees go up and eventually the price effect on demand dominates. Furthermore, in his empirical implementation he uses GDP per capita as a proxy for the quality of education, whereas in the above formulation the effects of GDP per capita and the quality of education enter separately.

Raychaudhuri and De (2007) also posit a similar empirical formulation on an ad hoc basis, and ascribe the effects of trade barriers to unobservable country-specific heterogeneity. In the above formulation, the effects of trade barriers will be tested by reference to explicit information about the regulatory policy regimes in each country.

Banks, Olsen and Pearce (2007) present a forecasting model of foreign student enrolment in which population and income are the only two behavioural determinants. They do not examine the role of trade barriers.

The qualitative literature on foreign student movements also emphasises the cultural and linguistic factors affecting student choice (e.g., Shackleton, 2003; Knight, 2005). Kim (1998) tests the possibility that a common language may boost foreign student enrolment, but finds that this factor is barely significant. Tremblay (2001) argues instead that foreign students as a proportion of total domestic enrolment tends to be low when the language of instruction is not widely used, suggesting that the influence of language is a little more indirect. Kim also tests whether a common religion boosts foreign student enrolment. Finally, Perkinson (2006) provides circumstantial evidence that tuition fees do not greatly influence student choice. He cites the study by Follari (2004) that Australia was impacted recently by a currency appreciation plus a 12 per cent annual increase in tuition fees and living costs, but continued to maintain the highest growth of foreign students of all OECD countries. He concludes that foreign students perhaps place higher value on other perceived benefits, such as program relevance, qualifications and career pathways. Furthermore, at least some international students are supported by scholarships, so do not bear the tuition costs themselves.

Some of the literature has suggested that distance (or geographic remoteness) affects the demand for higher education (e.g., Tremblay, 2001), whereas the above discussion emphasises its role in determining the cost of successfully applying screening tests. With universities increasingly marketing themselves over the internet, and also using the internet as a medium of internal communication, it is now far easier for students to obtain information about individual faculty members and about course structure and content. But admissions mistakes are costly, so universities are increasingly supplementing universal screening tests (such as the TOEFL, which tests ability in English as a second language) with their own investigations into the quality of feeder institutions and the abilities of individual student candidates. With the above formulation, it is impossible to test whether distance does now affect the supply side more than the demand side. But this indeterminacy does not matter for the current purpose, which is primarily to test the role of barriers to trade in higher education.

4 TESTING THE MODEL

The underlying model above is tested on as big a sample as possible, to test its general validity. It is then re-estimated on a smaller sample of countries for which information on trade barriers is available.

4.1 Data

In the full sample, data on numbers of foreign tertiary students are taken from the OECD Online Education Database[4] for 93 source and 35 destination country pairs for 2000. This provides a maximum of 3255 observations. Corresponding data on population and GDP per capita are taken from World Development Indicators. The GDP per capita data are measured in constant 2000 US dollars converted using market exchange rates rather than purchasing power parity exchange rates, because market exchange rates determine the purchasing power of foreign students in their destination countries. Distance is measured by the great-circle distance between capital cities.[5]

The underlying model requires data on the quality of tertiary student candidates from the source country and the quality of tertiary

---

[4] Available at http://www.oecd.org/document/54/0,3343,en_2649_33723_38082166_1_1_1_1,00.html.
[5] Available at http://gc.kls2.com.

education institutions in the destination country. It is assumed possible to use the quality of feeder institutions in the source country as a proxy for the quality of students in the source country. Arguably, institutions can be vetted more easily than individual candidates, although as noted above, exporting institutions are increasingly testing the quality of individual candidates as well. The assumption will be problematic if significant numbers of candidates have qualifications from a third country. It has not been possible to test this possibility throughout the full sample. But at the Australian National University, a major exporter of higher education services, at least 90 per cent of foreign students have prior qualifications from their home country rather than a third country.

It is also assumed here that the feeder institutions in the source countries are themselves tertiary institutions. If large numbers of foreign students are undergraduates, then their feeder institutions will be secondary schools. It is not possible to break the OECD data on student numbers down according to whether they are studying at the undergraduate or postgraduate level. About half of the foreign students at the Australian National University between 2002–2006 were enrolled at the undergraduate level. However, there is likely to be a reasonably high correlation between the quality of high schools and the quality of tertiary institutions across countries.

When it comes to quality in the destination countries, there is some debate in the literature about what drives demand behaviour more — perceived 'prestige', or genuine quality (in terms of measurable outcomes for students once they graduate). Massy (2004) argues strongly that the difference matters for welfare outcomes, because it determines whether greater competition among tertiary institutions promotes internal efficiency, or creates 'an arms race in spending without regard to educational value added' (p. 31). However, the current purpose is to capture selection processes that occur on both the demand and the supply sides of the market. Even if genuine quality is what students are concerned about, it may not be accurately observed, either by students or by those doing the screening. Thus, measures of prestige may be what both sides of the market use as proxies for quality.

The best known 'beauty pageant' rankings of universities are available only for a subset of countries. The Institute of Higher Education of the Shanghai Jiao Tong University only ranks the top 500 universities, while the Times Higher World University Rankings are only available for the top 200 universities.

This study has used data from the Webometrics ranking of world universities, which ranks 4000 universities and other research-related institutions around the world.[6] These rankings are compiled by a group from the Centro de Información y Documentación Científica (CINDOC), part of the National Research Council (CSIC), the largest public research body in Spain.

The group uses web searches to compile data on four dimensions of university web activity:

- size — the number of pages recovered from four search engines (Google, Yahoo, Live Search and Exalead);
- visibility — the total number of unique external links received (inlinks) by a university site (as obtained from Yahoo, Live Search and Exalead);
- rich files — the number of rich files on the site (.pdf, .ps, .doc and .ppt files, where these formats were evaluated as being most relevant to academic and publication activities); and
- scholar — Google Scholar provides the number of papers and citations for each academic domain.

The chosen measure of quality for this study is visibility (number of inlinks), since this best measures 'revealed' prestige. There are several reasons for preferring this measure. Some of the other measures are more about Web use than quality or prestige. The results from Google Scholar have some obvious anomalies. For example, by this measure the second-highest ranked university in the world in July 2007 (behind Harvard) was the Universidad de La Rioja. The Webometrics group themselves give visibility by far the greatest weighting in their overall index, and they note a relatively high correlation between their overall index and other ratings.

---

[6] http://www.webometrics.info

The disadvantage of the Webometrics rankings is that they have only been compiled since 2004, and the ones used here are for July 2007. This does not match the enrolment data, which are for 2000. Massy (2004) notes that measures of university prestige are stubbornly stable. Nevertheless, to test the sensitivity of the results, an alternative measure of quality is also tried. This is a standard measure of research 'impact', defined as the number of citations per publication for each country. The citation count in the numerator is the number of references made in articles published in 2003 to articles published in 1999–2001. The publication count in the denominator is the number of articles published in 1999–2001. Both are available from the National Science Board (2006), for 34 of the source countries and 30 of the destination countries in the sample.

For both source and destination countries, therefore, the chosen measure of quality is the visibility ranking of the *top* university in that country. On the demand side, the literature stresses that the top universities are the drawcards (e.g., Tremblay, 2001), although Shackleton (2003) notes that the newer universities are increasingly using systems of quality assurance to compete with the reputations of established schools.

Note that quality and quality ranking numbers have an inverse relationship to each other. Thus, while the framework of the previous section suggests that foreign student enrolment will depend positively on quality at both source and destination, the relationship with the associated quality *rankings* is expected to be negative.

For this paper, it has not been possible to collect detailed information on the ease with which international students can subsequently gain permanent entry into their chosen country of study. Instead, numbers of permanent migrants have been used as a crude indicator of the stringency of immigration policy in each destination country. This measure has several major drawbacks. First, it only measures the stringency of immigration policy generally, and does not capture whether local graduates receive any preferential treatment. Second, the stringency of immigration policy generally is highly correlated with the extent to which international students face barriers while they are studying — one of the key determinants of interest in this paper. Hence it is not possible to disentangle the separate influences of the two determinants. Nevertheless, at least some of the regressions reported in this paper use data on inflows of foreign population from the OECD's online database International Migration Data 2007.[7] This is available only for 24 destination countries, all from the OECD.

The data on trade restrictions are taken from Nguyen-Hong and Wells (2003). This paper uses raw information on regulatory barriers to trade in higher education services, of the types described in Tables 1 and 2, compiled by IDP Education Australia (2002). Because the detailed information was collected to assist Australia in its trade negotiations, it is regarded as 'sensitive' and the IDP report remains unpublished. However, Nguyen-Hong and Wells (2003) have converted the detailed qualitative information into a number of quantitative indices of barriers to trade, by mode of service delivery and also according to whether the restrictions affect higher education imports or exports. Indices of trade restrictions are available for 19 of the source countries and 12 of the destination countries in the full sample (for a maximum of 228 observations). Most of these are from the Asia–Pacific region. The IDP report was completed in 2002 and the barriers that it reports on are likely to be those applying in 2000 or 2001, closely matching the timeframe of the enrolment data.

The data on trade restrictions are shown in Table 3. They show that the countries imposing the greatest restrictions on the outward movement of international students (i.e., restrictions on importing via consumption abroad) are Vietnam and China, followed by Indonesia and Korea. The countries imposing the greatest restrictions on the inward movement of international students (i.e., restrictions on exporting via consumption abroad) are Hong Kong, Thailand, Vietnam and Chile. Some countries in the sample impose relatively high barriers on other modes of importing higher education services. Malaysia, India and China impose relatively high barriers on foreign universities establishing campuses in their countries (i.e., importing

---

[7] Available at http://www.oecd.org/document/3/0,3343,en_2649_33729_39336771_1_1_1_1,00.html).

Table 3. Indexes of restrictions on trade in higher education services

	Imports via cross-border supply (0–4)	Imports via consumption abroad (0–5)	Imports via commercial presence (0–7)	Imports via movement of people (0–3)	Exports via consumption abroad (0–6)
Argentina	0.50	0.83	0.50	0.00	2.10
Australia	0.50	0.25	1.30	0.50	2.05
Brazil	1.25	0.83	1.30	1.25	2.10
Canada	0.50	0.50	1.45	0.50	2.35
Chile	0.50	0.50	1.60	1.00	2.40
China	2.50	2.17	4.00	3.00	1.90
Hong Kong	0.75	1.33	0.60	0.50	3.00
India	1.00	1.17	4.29	1.50	2.30
Indonesia	1.50	1.83	3.76	1.00	1.90
Japan	0.50	0.50	1.40	0.50	1.60
Korea	1.25	1.83	0.80	0.50	1.30
Malaysia	0.75	0.83	4.60	2.00	1.80
Mexico	0.25	0.50	0.61	0.25	1.40
New Zealand	0.50	0.00	1.45	0.25	1.57
Singapore	1.50	1.50	2.45	1.50	2.35
Thailand	1.00	1.00	2.30	0.50	2.80
United Kingdom	0.00	0.25	0.60	1.00	1.30
United States	0.50	0.83	0.60	1.00	2.05
Vietnam	1.50	3.67	3.10	2.00	2.60

Source: Nguyen-Hong and Wells (2003).

via commercial presence). Note that these countries are important sources of international students. China also imposes relatively high barriers on cross-border importing, and on allowing the temporary entry of foreign teachers (i.e., importing via the movement of people).

4.2 Results

Theory provides no guidance on the functional form of the estimating equation outlined in the previous section. It has been estimated using a log-linear function form, because this form can provide a good first-order approximation to an arbitrary functional form.

For the full sample of 93 source and 35 destination countries, there is no data for either trade barriers or for migration levels (the proxy for the stringency of immigration policy generally). So the first results shown in Table 4 are for a smaller sample of 24 destination countries in the OECD for which there are migration data (a maximum

Table 4.   Econometric results — model without trade restrictions, with migration levels, OLS estimation

Dependent variable: Log of number of foreign students from each source country in each destination country in 2000 (1938 observations)

Dependent variable	Estimated coefficient	t score (using robust standard errors)	Significance
Ln pop_dest	0.21	4.86	***
Ln pop_source	0.56	18.33	***
Ln dist	−0.80	−22.93	***
Ln gdppc_source	0.24	4.83	***
Ln rank_dest	−0.64	−21.63	***
Ln rank_source	−0.08	−1.99	**
Ln migration_dest	0.42	10.24	***
R-squared	0.57		

* Significant at the 10 per cent level; ** Significant at the 5 per cent level; *** Significant at the 1 per cent level.

of 93 × 24 = 2232 observations).[8] The results are from estimating this model in log-linear form using OLS estimation.

The coefficients of population at source and destination and on distance are of the expected signs and highly significant. The coefficient of GDP per capita at source is also of the expected sign and significant, but its magnitude is low, given the expectation that the demand for higher education is income-elastic. One possibility is that the influence of the rationing mechanism is muting the full operation of this demand effect. In particular, GDP per capita at source and quality ranking at source are correlated with each other, so that the separate effect of each is hard to identify in the sample. Indeed, the coefficient of quality ranking at source is also of the expected sign, but is small in magnitude and not highly significant. By contrast, the coefficient of quality ranking at destination is of the expected sign, of reasonable magnitude and highly significant, confirming the strength of this demand effect. As expected, the coefficient of migration in the destination country is also highly significant. This seems to confirm the importance of permanent migration as a motivation for international student movements, although it may also reflect that countries with generous immigration policies have few barriers to international students themselves.

The *R*-squared of 0.57 indicates a reasonable goodness of fit in this purely cross-sectional context. However, diagnostic tests suggested problems of both heteroskedasticity (despite the inclusion of populations as scale variables) and problems with the functional form.

---

[8] As a sensitivity test, the model was also tested on the full sample, without migration data. In this alternative regression, notable outliers were the numbers of foreign students from Oman, Yemen and Malaysia studying in Jordan. These outliers were controlled for by using a dummy variable that took a value 1 if both countries had populations with clear Islamic majorities (as noted in the CIA World Factbook), and 0 otherwise. This is a more limited version of the common religion dummy used by Kim (1998). In the resulting regression, the coefficients of the remaining variables were similar to those in Table 4, except that the coefficient of population in the destination country was larger. This is not surprising, since population and migration in the destination country are positively correlated with each other.

The former problem has been addressed by using robust standard errors in the tests for coefficient significance.

Examination of the pattern of residuals suggests the problem of functional form may be associated with some grouping of observations at near-zero levels of enrolment. Thus, although observations with zero enrolment have been dropped from the sample (explaining why the number of observations, at 1938, is less than the maximum possible of 2232), the grouping near zero suggests that some other form of estimation may be more appropriate. The Heckman selection model is an obvious candidate.

The Heckman selection model recognises that the influence of at least some screening variables is not likely to be continuous. These screening variables set a minimum acceptable standard, and only those observations that have passed the screening test appear in the sample of data from which the model of student numbers is estimated. The screening variable whose influence may be non-continuous in this way is the rank of the institutions in the source country. When the model was estimated as a Heckman selection model with the rank at source as the relevant sample selection variable, the coefficient estimates and levels of significance were very close to those reported in Table 4. The results are not reported separately.

In a further sensitivity test, the ranking of institutions in the source and destination countries was replaced with the impact of the research done by universities in each country. The results were broadly similar to those in Table 4, given that the sample size was necessarily much smaller (699 observations). The main qualitative difference was that the impact of universities in the source countries was highly insignificant in both the OLS and Heckman formulations. This is not surprising, since destination countries are much more likely to screen incoming international students according to the quality of teaching in the feeder institutions, rather than the quality of research in those institutions. However, there is no generally acceptable measure of the quality of teaching for which data are readily available.

The econometric results from estimating the model with trade restrictions on a limited sample using OLS estimation are shown in

Table 5. Econometric results — model with trade restrictions, without migration levels, OLS estimation

Dependent variable: Log of number of foreign students from each source country in each destination country in 2000 (179 observations)

Dependent variable	Estimated coefficient	t score (using robust standard errors)	Significance
Ln pop_dest	−0.17	−1.90	*
Ln pop_source	0.46	3.98	***
Ln dist	−0.83	−4.22	***
Ln gdppc_source	0.70	4.16	***
Ln rank_dest	−1.14	−19.42	***
Ln rank_source	−0.02	−0.12	
Trade restrictiveness index			
On mode 1 imports at source	0.09	0.25	
On mode 2 imports at source	0.36	1.54	
On mode 3 imports at source	0.50	2.75	***
On mode 4 imports at source	−0.29	−0.61	
On mode 2 exports at destination	−0.61	−2.25	**
R-squared	0.68		

* Significant at the 10 per cent level; ** Significant at the 5 per cent level; *** Significant at the 1 per cent level.

Table 5. This estimation does not use a measure of migration in the destination country, because migration rates are negatively correlated with barriers to the export of higher education via consumption abroad (i.e., barriers to the inward movement of international students), and the main policy interest of this paper is in the latter.[9] The comparable Heckman selection model is shown in Table 6.

---

[9] The separate role of permanent migration as a motive for international student movements is probably better established by examining instances of 'natural experiments' — instances where countries have changed the rules regarding the eligibility of international student graduates for permanent migration, but have left unchanged other aspects of their immigration policy, as well as their treatment of international students while studying.

Table 6. Econometric results — model with trade restrictions, without migration levels, Heckman selection model

Dependent variable: Log of number of foreign students from each source country in each destination country in 2000

Dependent variable	Estimated coefficient	*t* score (using robust standard errors)	Significance
Ln pop_dest	−0.17	−1.94	*
Ln pop_source	0.47	5.11	***
Ln dist	−0.83	−4.37	***
Ln gdppc_source	0.72	4.67	***
Ln rank_dest	−1.14	−20.15	***
Trade restrictiveness index			
On mode 1 imports at source	0.08	0.24	
On mode 2 imports at source	0.35	1.52	
On mode 3 imports at source	0.48	2.92	***
On mode 4 imports at source	−0.23	−0.57	
On mode 2 exports at destination	−0.61	−2.33	**
Sample selection model			
Ln rank_source	−0.41	−17.76	***
Wald chi-squared (10)	553.42		***
Wald test of independent equations chi-squared (1)	0.04		

* Significant at the 10 per cent level; ** Significant at the 5 per cent level; *** Significant at the 1 per cent level.

In the restricted sample, coefficients of population at source and distance are similar to those in the full sample, under either method of estimation. The coefficient of GDP per capita at source is larger than in the full sample, and closer to what is expected. The coefficient of the population in the destination country is of the wrong sign and is barely significant. This could reflect the influence of countries such as Australia, which have relatively small populations but have been exporting aggressively in the Asia–Pacific region. The coefficient of quality ranking at destination is also larger than in the full sample, and still highly significant. The coefficient of rank at source is now insignificant. But when the Heckman selection model recognises that this variable may play a screening role, it becomes highly significant.

Of the various types of trade restrictions, two appear significant (under either method of estimation). Barriers in the source country to importing education services via FDI (the inward movement of foreign campuses) have the effect of boosting the number of students from the source country seeking enrolment in overseas universities. And barriers in the destination country to exporting education services via the inward movement of foreign students have the effect of reducing the numbers of such students. The magnitudes suggest that if a country with sample average barriers to FDI imports were to liberalise completely, it would send about 60 per cent fewer students overseas. If a country with sample average barriers to the inward movement of students were to liberalise completely, it would attract about 250 per cent more students — more than three times as many.

These results are consistent with barriers to education having the effects shown in Fig. 3. Barriers to mode 3 imports in the source country have the effect of artificially moving the demand curve to the right. And barriers to mode 2 exports in the destination country have the effect of artificially moving the supply curve to the left. The finding that barriers to mode 3 imports in the source country promote mode 2 imports in the source country is evidence of intermodal substitution.

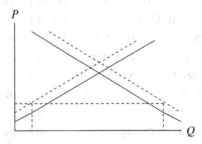

Figure 3.   The effect of barriers to services trade in higher education

5 POLICY CONCLUSIONS AND AREAS FOR FURTHER RESEARCH

The key policy issue is to explore the welfare implications of these findings. Do restrictions on mode 2 exports allow higher education providers in exporting countries to earn economic rents, along the lines of Fig. 1(a)? Or are the rents dissipated by the institutions pursuing other activities, along the lines of Fig. 1(b)? Similarly, how exactly do the restrictions on mode 3 imports in the source country affect the quality and/or quantity of higher education services in the source countries? And do the effects manifest themselves via rents or cost changes? These crucial policy questions require further research.

Theory can provide some guidance. Massy (2004) argues that a useful model of the production side of the higher education market is a model of the non-profit organisation. Universities can be seen as optimising the achievement of some non-profit objective, which could be as varied as offering a diversity of courses, offering courses to students from a variety of socioeconomic backgrounds, preserving arcane knowledge, or providing professorial employment. They do so subject to the prevailing production technology, and to the constraint that profits must always be zero. In these circumstances, they produce outputs to the point where the marginal revenue from each activity, plus its marginal contribution to the achievement of the non-profit objective, equals its marginal cost. Activities with high marginal revenue but low contribution to the non-profit objective may be exploited so as to cross-subsidise activities with a low marginal revenue but a high marginal contribution to the non-profit objective. Massy (2004) shows that such entities have an incentive to be technically efficient. But, by definition, they have an incentive to dissipate any rents on the achievement of their non-profit objective.

As in any other sphere, trade barriers may still have two types of effects. First, trade barriers may allow universities to earn rents, which they will then 'dissipate', but such dissipation is not the same as technical inefficiency. Alternatively, trade barriers may interfere directly with the production technology, causing genuine technical inefficiency. It is easy to imagine that the red tape associated with the 'managed' markets for higher education in some countries could fall into the latter category. But being able to distinguish the two cases empirically will require a productivity measurement technology that takes account of all the relevant inputs and outputs, including those outputs that are associated with the achievement of the non-profit objective. This will be the empirical challenge.

A final policy point is to reiterate that only a fraction of the significant barriers to trade in higher education services are covered by the GATS. Those imposed by exporting countries on the students themselves appear to be totally beyond the scope of the GATS. And many of the significant non-discriminatory barriers are not included if they do not fall within the narrow GATS definition of 'barriers to market access'. The results of this paper suggest that barriers to trade in higher education services have significant quality effects, and possibly significant welfare effects. But most will need to be addressed outside the current GATS framework.

REFERENCES

Banks M, Olsen A and Pearce D (2007). *Global Student Mobility: An Australian Perspective Five Years On.* IDP Education, Adelaide.

Barth J, Caprio G and Levine R (2004). Bank regulation and supervision: What works best? *J Finan Intermediation*, 13, 205–248.

Boylaud O and Nicoletti G (2000). Regulation, Market Structure and Performance in Telecommunications. Working Paper No. 237, ECO/WKP(2000)10, Economics Department, OECD, Paris, 12 April.

Chapman R (1979). Pricing policy and the college choice process. *Res High Educ*, 10(37), 57.

Claessens S, Demirgüç-Kunt A and Huizinga H (2001). How does foreign entry affect domestic banking markets? *J Bank Finance*, 25, 891–911.

Clark X, Dollar D and Micco A (2004). Port efficiency, maritime transport costs, and bilateral trade. *J Devel Econ*, 75, 417–450.

Copenhagen Economics (2005). *Economic Assessment of the Barriers to the Internal Market for Services.* Copenhagen Economics, Copenhagen.

Dee P (2005). A Compendium of Barriers to Services Trade. Prepared for the World Bank, available at http://www.crawford.anu.edu.au/pdf/Combined_report.pdf.

Doove S, Gabbitas O, Nguyen-Hong D and Owen J (2001). Price Effects of Regulation: International Air Passenger Transport, Telecommunications and

Electricity Supply. Productivity Commission Staff Research Paper, Ausinfo, Canberra.

Fink C, Mattoo A and Neagu C (2001). Trade in International Maritime Services: How Much Does Policy Matter? Working Paper No. 2522, World Bank, Washington DC.

Fink C, Mattoo A and Rathindran R (2002). Liberalising Basic Telecommunications: Evidence from Developing Countries. Paper presented at OECD–World Bank Services Experts Meeting, OECD, Paris, 4–5 March.

Finnie R and Usher A (2006). The Canadian experiment in cost-sharing and its effects on access to higher education, 1990–2002. In *Cost-sharing and Accessibility in Higher Education: A Fairer Deal?*, P Teixeira, B Johnstone, M Rosa and H Vossensteyn (eds.), pp. 159–187. Springer, Dordrecht.

Follari M (2004). *Comparative Costs of Higher Education for International Students 2004.* IDP Education, Australia.

Gonenc R and Nicoletti G (2000). Regulation, Market Structure and Performance in Air Passenger Transport. Working Paper No. 254, ECO/WKP(2000)27, Economics Department, OECD, Paris, 3 August.

Gregan T and Johnson M (1999). Impacts of Competition Enhancing Air Services Agreements: A Network Modelling Approach. Productivity Commission Staff Research Paper, Ausinfo, Canberra, July.

IDP Education Australia (2002). Identification and Analysis of Barriers to Trade and Investment in Education Services in Selected Countries. Final Report, Sydney.

Kalirajan K (2000). Restrictions on Trade in Distribution Services. Productivity Commission Staff Research Paper, Ausinfo, Canberra.

Kalirajan K, McGuire G, Nguyen-Hong D and Schuele M (2000). The price impact of restrictions on banking services. In *Impediments to Trade in Services: Measurement and Policy Implications*, C Findlay and T Warren (eds.), pp. 215–230. Routledge, London and New York.

Kang J (2000). Price impact of restrictions on maritime transport services. In *Impediments to Trade in Services: Measurement and Policy Implications*, C Findlay and T Warren (eds.), pp. 189–200. Routledge, London and New York.

Kim J (1998). Economic analysis of foreign education and students abroad. *J Devel Econ*, 56, 337–365.

Knight J (2005). Cross-border education: An analytical framework for program and provider mobility. In *Higher Education: Handbook of Theory and Research*, Vol. 21, J Smart and W Tierney (eds.), pp. 345–395. Springer, Dordrecht.

Lasanowski, V and Verbik, L (2007). *International Student Mobility: Patterns and Trends.* The Observatory on Borderless Higher Education, London.

Massy W (2004). Markets in higher education: Do they promote internal efficiency? In *Markets in Higher Education: Rhetoric or Reality?* P Teixeira, B Jongbloed, D Dill and A Amaral (eds.), pp. 13–35. Kluwer, Dordrecht.

Murphy P (1981). Consumer buying roles in college choice. *Coll Univ*, 56, 140–150.

National Science Board (2006). *Science and Engineering Indicators 2006*, Vol. 2. National Science Foundation, Arlington VA (available at www.eric.ed.gov).

Nguyen-Hong D (2000). Restrictions on Trade in Professional Services. Productivity Commission Staff Research Paper, Ausinfo, Canberra.

Nguyen-Hong D and Wells R (2003). Restrictions on Trade in Education Services. Productivity Commission Staff Working Paper, Canberra, October.

OECD (2005). Modal Estimates of Services Barriers. TD/TC/WP(2005)36, OECD, Paris.

OECD (2007). *Cross-border Tertiary Education: A Way Towards Capacity Development*. OECD and IBRD/The World Bank, Paris.

Perkinson R (2006). International Higher Education: Seizing the Opportunity for Innovation and International Responsibility. Notes for Plenary Speech presented to the 'Global 2' Education Conference, 7–8 December, Edinburgh (available at http://www.whitneyintl.com/documents/Innovation_and_International_ Responsibility.pdf).

Raychaudhuri A and De P (2007). Assessing Barriers to Trade in Education Services in Developing Asia–Pacific Countries: An Empirical Exercise. Asia–Pacific Research and Training Network on Trade Working Paper Series, No. 34, May (available at www.artnetontrade.org).

Shackleton J (2003). Opening up trade in higher education: A role for the GATS? *World Econ*, 4(4), 55–77.

Steiner F (2000). Regulation, Industry Structure and Performance in the Electricity Supply Industry. Working Paper No. 238, ECO/WKP(2000)11, Economics Department, OECD, Paris, 12 April.

Tierney M (1983). Student college choice sets: Towards an empirical characterization. *Res High Educ*, 18, 271–184.

Tremblay K (2001). Student mobility between and towards OECD countries: A comparative analysis. In *International Mobility of the Highly Skilled*, OECD (ed.), pp. 39–67. OECD, Paris.

Warren T (2000). The impact on output of impediments to trade and investment in telecommunications services. In *Impediments to Trade in Services: Measurement and Policy Implications*, C Findlay and T Warren (eds.), pp. 85–100. Routledge, London and New York.

WTO (1998). Education Services: Background Note by the Secretariat. S/C/W/49, WTO, Geneva, 23 September.

WTO (2001). Guidelines for the Scheduling of Specific Commitments under the General Agreement on Trade in Services. Adopted by the Council for Trade in Services on 23 March 2001, available at http://tsdb.wto.org/wto/ guidelines.html.

Cross-Border Higher Education: Quality Assurance and Accreditation Issues and Implications

Jane Knight*

1 INTRODUCTION

The Global Student Mobility 2025 Report (Böhm *et al.*, 2002) predicts the demand for international education will increase from 1.8 million international students in 2000 to 7.2 million international students in 2025, and that Asia will represent approximately 70 per cent of the global demand for higher education. By all accounts these are staggering figures and present enormous challenges, opportunities and potential risks. It is not known what proportion of the demand

* This an updated and adapted version of a paper prepared for the Global University Network for Innovation: Knight, J (2006). Cross-border higher education: Issues and implications for quality assurance and accreditation. Global University Network for Innovation: *Higher Education in the World 2007 — Accreditation for Quality Assurance — What is at Stake?* Palgrave, London, pp. 134–146.

will be met by student mobility, but it is clear that there will be unprecedented growth in the movement of programs and institutions/ providers across national borders.

The Asia–Pacific region is a hotbed of innovation and activity in cross-border education. Two critical challenges currently facing the growth in mobility of students, programs and providers are quality assurance of academic provision and recognition/legitimacy of the qualifications awarded. This paper focuses on the mobility of education programs and providers across national borders and addresses issues related to registration of providers, quality assurance, accreditation of programs and recognition of qualifications. Examples of new quality and accreditation initiatives for cross-border education at the national, regional and international levels are discussed. Finally, the challenge of minimising potential risks and maximising benefits is examined and the importance of collecting reliable data to inform policy development is emphasised.

2 NEW DEVELOPMENTS IN CROSS-BORDER EDUCATION

The growth and change in cross-border program and provider mobility is remarkable. There are new types of providers, new types of collaborative partnerships (foreign/domestic, public/private, profit/ non-profit), new modes of delivery, and new types of awards and qualifications granted. These realities contribute to the complexity of cross-border education and require close examination.

2.1 Diversity in Types of Providers

The increase in worldwide demand for higher education and more specifically international education has resulted in a diversity of providers delivering education at home and across borders. The providers are classified into two categories.

The 'traditional higher education institutions' are normally oriented to teaching, research and service/commitment to society and include public non-profit, private non-profit and private for-profit institutions. The majority of traditional universities are bona fide institutions that comply with domestic and foreign regulations (where they exist). However, there has been an increase in diploma mills and rogue or low-quality providers. Diploma mills are essentially web-based organisations that sell degrees or qualifications while rogue or low-quality providers are usually not recognised by bona fide accreditation/licensing bodies in either the sending or receiving countries. 'Rogue providers' are often accredited by self-accrediting groups or by agencies that sell accreditation (accreditation mills).

The 'new or alternative providers' are diverse in nature, but are typically described as companies or organisations that provide education programs and/or services for profit purposes. They are more oriented to delivering education and training programs than undertaking research and scholarly activities. Examples of commercial publicly traded companies include Raffles LaSalle, Informatics and Hartford in Singapore, Aptech and NIIT in India and SEG and Stamford College in Malaysia. Companies that sell education programs and services and are listed on a public stock exchange are growing in number and part of the Global Education Index (Garrett, 2004) but at this time there is no solid data on the actual enrolment numbers. Other new providers include corporate universities such as those run by Motorola and Toyota, and networks of universities, professional associations and organisations. These new types of cross-border providers can be brick-and-mortar institutions or virtual universities, and can complement, compete, collaborate or simply coexist with domestic higher education providers. They are raising new issues and significant challenges in terms of quality assurance and recognition of qualifications.

2.2 A Higher Education Framework for Cross-Border Education

Cross-border education refers to the movement of people, programs, providers, knowledge, ideas, projects and services across national boundaries. It is a term that is often used interchangeably with transnational, offshore and borderless education. There are subtle but important differences between these terms (Knight, 2005). In spite of the global flow of technology, goods, services and economy, borders have an increasing importance in terms of national-level regulations and context; because the term 'cross-border' recognises their existence, it is the preferred term.

Table 1 provides a framework to understand the nature of cross-border education in terms of the movement of persons, programs, providers and projects. It also illustrates two significant trends. The

Table 1.   Framework for cross-border education

	Forms of Mobility		
Category	Development Cooperation →	Educational Linkages →	Commercial Trade →
People Students Professors/scholars Researchers/ Experts/consultants	↓	Semester/year abroad Full degrees Field/research work Internships Sabbaticals Consulting	
Programs Course, program sub-degree, degree, postgraduate	↓	Twinning Franchised Articulated/validated Joint/double award Online/distance	
Providers Institutions Organisations Companies	↓	Branch campus Virtual university Merger/acquisition Independent institutions	
Projects Academic projects Services	↓	Research Curriculum Capacity building Educational services	

Adapted from Knight (2005).

first is the vertical shift downwards from student mobility to program and provider mobility. It is true that the number of students seeking education in foreign countries is still increasing; however, there is more emphasis currently being placed on delivering foreign academic courses and programs to students in their home country. The second is the shift from left to right, signifying substantial change in orientation from development cooperation to competitive commerce, or, in other words, from aid to trade.

It is important to note that this model is conceived as a higher education framework and is not based on the GATS framework for trade in services, which identifies four different modes of trade. The inclusion of education in the GATS serves as an important wake-up call as higher education has never been seen as a tradable commodity; furthermore, it is not necessary to use a trade framework to conceptualise the international mobility of education given that it has been occurring for decades — long before the advent of the GATS.

3 QUALITY-RELATED ISSUES AND IMPLICATIONS

This section focuses on the registration, quality assurance and accreditation of cross-border education programs and providers. These terms have different meanings and significances depending on the country, actor or stakeholder using the term. In fact, there is no uniformity in the way these terms are used within a region, let alone across the major regions of the world. In this discussion of cross-border education the terms are used in a generic and hierarchical way. Registration refers to the first step, which is the acknowledgement that a foreign institution/provider is present in the receiving country. Registration may only involve acknowledgement of the provider as a foreign entity or it could involve the granting of a license to operate. Registration procedures and conditions vary enormously among countries and usually differ if the provider is collaborating with a local partner or is independent. The second step focuses on the quality assurance of the incoming education program and the recognition of the qualification awarded. At this stage the process usually focuses on meeting minimum quality assurance standards and may emphasise content/curriculum more than the actual teaching/learning, admissions or evaluation processes. The criterion often used is whether the foreign program has been quality assured in the home or sending country. The next step is accreditation, which is often voluntary and refers to the recognition that the foreign program has undergone an evaluation audit and has met an explicit set of standards (frequently the same standards that are applied to domestic programs). There is no 'one way' or 'one size fits all' approach to registration, quality assurance or accreditation of cross-border education as it depends entirely on the national context and the regulations of the receiving country. Examples of the national regulations for cross-border education from three receiving countries in the Asia–Pacific region demonstrate the different approaches being used (see Section 4.4).

3.1 Registration of Cross-Border Providers in the Receiving Country

A fundamental question is whether the foreign providers that are delivering award-based programs are registered by the receiving country. The answer to this question varies. Many countries do not have the regulatory systems in place to register out-of-country providers. Several reasons account for this, including lack of capacity or political will. It is usual practice that, if an institution/provider is not registered in the receiving country, regulatory frameworks for quality assurance or accreditation do not apply. As this is the situation in many countries, foreign providers (more often 'new providers' than traditional universities) do not have to comply with the national higher education regulations of the receiving countries.

The questions and factors at play in the registration or licensing of foreign providers are many. For instance, do the criteria or conditions applicable to those providers who are part of and recognised by a national education system in their home country differ from those for providers who are not? Does it make a difference if the provider is for-profit or non-profit, private or public, an institution or a company? What conditions apply if, in fact, the provider is a company that has no home-based presence and only establishes institutions in foreign countries? How does one monitor partnerships between local domestic institutions/companies and foreign ones? Is it possible to register a completely virtual provider? Clearly, there are challenges involved in trying to establish appropriate and effective national or regional regulatory systems for the registration of cross-border providers.

Often there are bilateral cultural/academic agreements in place to facilitate and monitor the presence of foreign education providers. However, the fact that education services are now part of bilateral and multilateral trade agreements introduces new regulations and questions. A key question facing national governments, as well as international organisations, is to what extent the introduction of new national regulations to register, quality assure or accredit cross-border providers will be interpreted as barriers to trade and therefore will need to be modified to comply with new trade policies.

3.2 Quality Assurance and Accreditation of Cross-Border Education

In the last decade, increased importance has certainly been given to quality assurance and accreditation (QAA) at the institutional and national levels. New quality assurance mechanisms and national organisations have been developed in over 60 countries in this period. New regional quality networks, such as the Asia–Pacific Quality Network have also been established. The primary task of these groups has been the QAA of domestic higher education offered primarily by public and private higher education institutions (HEIs). However, the increase in cross-border education provided by both traditional institutions and new private commercial ones has introduced a new challenge (and gap) in the field of quality assurance and accreditation. Historically, with some notable exceptions such as Malaysia, Australia, Hong Kong and more recently China, national quality assurance agencies have not focused their efforts on assessing the quality of imported and exported programs. A key question now facing QAA bodies is how to deal with the increase in cross-border education provided by traditional HEIs and, more importantly, the new private commercial institutions that are not normally part of a home-based accreditation and quality assurance scheme in the sending country.

As the discussion moves forward it will be of strategic and substantive importance to recognise the roles and responsibilities of all the players involved in accreditation and quality assurance. These include individual institutions/providers, national quality assurance systems, non-government and independent accreditation bodies, professional bodies, and regional/international organisations — all of whom contribute to ensuring the quality of cross-border education. Much is at risk if low-quality providers or fraudulent qualifications become closely linked to cross-border education. It will be important to work in a collaborative and complementary fashion to build a system that ensures the quality and integrity of cross-border education and maintains the confidence of the society in international higher education and academic qualifications.

3.3 Growth in Diversity of Accrediting Bodies

The increased awareness of the need for quality assurance and/or accreditation has led to several new developments in accreditation, some of which are helping the task of domestic and international recognition of qualifications, while others are only serving to hinder and complicate matters. First, it is important to acknowledge the efforts of many countries to establish quality assurance and accreditation systems and the approval of bona fide accreditors. At the same time, it is necessary to recognise the increase in self-appointed and rather self-serving accreditors, as well as accreditation mills that simply sell 'bogus' accreditation labels.

Market forces are making the profile and reputation of an institution/provider and its courses more and more important. Major investments are being made in marketing and branding campaigns to get name recognition and to increase enrolment. The possession of some type of accreditation is part of the campaign and assures prospective students that the programs/awards are of high standing. The desire for accreditation status is leading to a commercialisation of quality assurance/accreditation as programs and providers strive to gain as many 'accreditation' stars as possible in order to increase competitiveness and perceived international legitimacy. The accreditation 'business' is growing in response to this demand and the challenge is how to distinguish between bona fide and rogue accreditors.

At the same time, there are networks of institutions and new organisations establishing their own 'self-appointed accreditation service' to provide support and accreditation status to their members. These are positive developments when seen through the lens of trying to improve the quality of the academic offer. However, there are concerns that they are not totally objective in their assessments and may be more interested in generating income from selling their accreditation services than in improving quality. While this can apply to both cross-border and domestic provision, it is particularly worrisome for cross-border provision as attention to national policy objectives and cultural orientation is often neglected.

Another disturbing development is the growth in accreditation mills. These organisations are not recognised or legitimate bodies and they more or less 'sell' accreditation status without any independent assessment. They are similar to degree mills that sell certificates and degrees with little or no coursework. Different education stakeholders, especially the students, employers and the public, need to be aware of these accreditation (and degree) mills that are often no more than a web address and are therefore usually out of the jurisdiction of national regulatory systems.

Because of this increase in self-appointed accreditors and accreditation mills, the establishment of a registry of bona fide accreditors may be a necessary next step. It is no longer enough to have recognised domestic and foreign higher education providers listed in a national database; it is now important to have a registry of approved bona fide accreditors. This is a new development being discussed at national, regional and international levels and Europe is now working on a European Registry of approved accreditors.

3.4 Role of Quality Standards from Outside the Higher Education Sector

It is probably inevitable that non-education organisations will be interested in developing international quality standards and accreditation procedures for cross-border education. ISO standards, or other industry-based mechanisms such as the Baldridge Awards, are examples of systems that might be applied or modelled for cross-border education. The education sector has mixed views on the appropriateness of quality standards being established by those outside the sector; some see merit in this idea and others see problems. At the same time, there are divergent opinions on the desirability and value of any international standards for accreditation as this might jeopardise the sovereignty of national-level systems or contribute to standardisation without necessarily improving quality standards.

3.5 Recognition of Qualifications

The credibility of higher education programs and qualifications is extremely important for students, their employers, the public at large and, of course, for the academic community itself. It is critical that the qualifications awarded by cross-border providers are legitimate and will be recognised for employment or further studies both at home and abroad. This is a major challenge facing the national and international higher education sector in light of new cross-border providers and programs.

UNESCO has long acknowledged the need for an international system to facilitate and ensure recognition of academic and professional qualifications. Regional UNESCO conventions on the recognition of qualifications were established more than 25 years ago. They are unique, legally binding instruments dealing with the mutual recognition of qualifications. But the majority of the conventions were developed when student mobility was active, not the movement of programs and providers. Thus the conventions, including the Asia–Pacific Convention, are in the slow and complex process of being updated. At the present time, there is discussion on how these

UNESCO conventions can be used as instruments to complement trade agreements and to assure students, employers and the public that there are systems in place to recognise academic and professional qualifications. Given the growth in academic mobility, the increased mobility of the labour force and the fact that the GATS is encouraging greater professional mobility, there is a clear and urgent need for national and regional education policymakers to address the issue of recognising academic and professional qualifications both at home and abroad.

4 RECENT NATIONAL, REGIONAL AND INTERNATIONAL INITIATIVES

Implicit in the discussion of the issues and challenges facing quality assurance of cross-border education is the basic assumption that the law of supply and demand in a 'market orientation' will not necessarily guarantee quality or sustainability of education programs moving between countries. Intervention, such as codes of practice, guidelines, national policy or regulations, and regional agreements are important instruments to take into consideration. This section briefly describes the different kinds of initiatives that have been taken at national, regional and international levels.

4.1 Codes of Practice

Codes of practice for cross-border/transnational education have been developed by several national university associations (e.g., Australia), quality agencies (e.g., the United Kingdom) and government departments (e.g., Mauritius). They are usually a set of principles to guide the practice of delivering programs across borders and for establishing partnerships with foreign providers. They are intended for public and private higher education institutions but have relevance for other non-traditional providers as well. The codes differ in substance and perspective but are similar in spirit and purpose, which is to assure quality in cross-border academic provision regardless of mode of delivery and partnership model, and to maintain the integrity of the academic qualification. These codes are not enforceable and are primarily awareness-raising tools.

4.2 UNESCO/OECD Guidelines for Quality Cross-Border Provision

It is timely that UNESCO and the OECD have jointly developed a set of 'Guidelines on Quality Provision in Cross-Border Education' (UNESCO/OECD, 2005). These guidelines address six stakeholder groups in higher education — governments, higher education institutions/providers, student bodies, quality assurance and accreditation entities, academic recognition bodies, and professional associations. The purpose of these guidelines is to encourage international cooperation and enhance the understanding of the importance of quality provision in cross-border higher education. They aim to protect students and other stakeholders from low-quality higher education programs, accreditation and degree mills, and other disreputable providers. The guidelines are not legally binding but countries are encouraged to use them in the manner that is most appropriate to their national context.[1]

4.3 The Asia–Pacific Quality Network

The Asia–Pacific has the greatest volume, scope and variety in cross-border higher education provision. The establishment of national regulatory frameworks for incoming and outgoing cross-border education is an important but challenging step for many countries. To this end, the Asia–Pacific Quality Network has prepared a 'Toolkit on Regulating Quality Assurance in Cross-Border Education'. The toolkit is designed to help receiving and sending countries with the issues, models, benefits and practical steps in establishing a regulatory framework for cross-border education (UNESCO/APQN, 2006). The following section briefly describes the national regulatory frameworks for incoming cross-border providers in China, Malaysia and Hong Kong. These examples have been taken from the toolkit, where more detailed information is available.

---

[1] See http://www.unesco.org/education/hed/guidelines.

4.4 Examples of National Regulations for Receiving Countries

4.4.1 *The People's Republic of China*

China is a hotbed of activity in terms of foreign entities establishing joint education ventures with Chinese partners. The demand for post-secondary education in China is enormous given the population demographics and China's desire to be a serious player in the international economic and political arena. China is one of the most interesting and desirable countries for commercial academic enterprises and, while it has opened its doors to these activities, it has done so with a national regulatory framework in place. In 2003, China established the 'Regulations on Chinese and Foreign Cooperation in Running Schools', which was supplemented the following year with additional regulations on implementation methods.[2] The law requires that all foreign institutions or companies collaborate with a local provider. Thus, only joint ventures are permitted, and these partnerships must be approved and accredited by the Chinese authorities.

If a foreign qualification is awarded it must be recognised in the home country of the awarding institution. (This raises the question of the recognition and accreditation challenges of international providers that do not have a home-based awarding institution.) If a Chinese qualification is awarded, then the Chinese institution/partner is responsible for the evaluation of the standards of the foreign institution. On top of the necessary accreditation procedures, foreign qualifications must also be recognised by the national Chinese authority, the Chinese Service Center for Scholarly Exchange.[3]

The Chinese regulations are an interesting model to study with regard to accreditation of foreign providers, given that joint ventures are mandatory. Experiences of foreign providers reveal that while the regulations are clear on paper, the implementation is still a challenge

---

[2] See http://www.moe.edu.cn/english/laws_r.htm.
[3] See http://www.cscse.edu.cn/matterpages/cscse/index_all_en.jsp.

given the size and complexity of the higher education system in China and the diversity of local/foreign, public/private, for-profit and non-profit partnerships that are being developed.

4.4.2 Malaysia

The Malaysian regulations for cross-border education provision are especially interesting as they address quality and cultural and economic requirements. All foreign providers are subject to Malaysia's national quality assurance framework but, unlike China, foreign providers are not required to cooperate with a local institution or entity.

There are three levels of assessment in the Malaysian system. The first is compulsory and provides approval to conduct programs of study. The second level sets a minimum standard that providers must meet if a qualification is to be offered. The third involves an accreditation process, and this is necessary if the qualification is to be recognised for employment purposes within the Malaysian public sector. These rules apply to both domestic and foreign providers. The Malaysian Qualifications Authority (recently formed by the merger of the National Accreditation Board and the Quality Assurance Division of the Ministry of Higher Education) is now responsible for public and private, domestic and foreign quality assurance and accreditation work.[4] Malaysia has a long history of welcoming foreign institutions and companies to offer tertiary education programs. It is a good example of a country that has developed the necessary public policy and regulations, including an accreditation process, to ensure that cross-border education: 1) helps to meet national policy objectives, 2) is of a high quality, and 3) is economically sustainable.

4.4.3 Hong Kong

Hong Kong was early to establish legislation for the regulation of higher and professional cross-border education. In 1997, it introduced

---

[4] See http://apps.emoe.gov.my/qad/main.html.

a law in order to increase access to higher education for its population by allowing more cross-border education, but at the same time to ensure consumer protection.[5] Foreign providers are free to establish an education program in their own name or to collaborate with a local institution.

According to the law, registration is mandatory for all cross-border education providers delivering face-to-face or mixed-mode programs. Every program must be formally registered but, interestingly, registration for distance education is voluntary and foreign providers who cooperate with a self-accrediting Hong Kong institution are exempted. In addition to registration, cross-border education programs and providers may choose to apply for local accreditation by the Hong Kong Council for Academic Accreditation, but thus far it has not been obligatory.

The Hong Kong regulations use comparability with the standards of home programs as the benchmark of quality for foreign institutions, companies or networks. If foreign providers choose to adapt the content of their programs to be more relevant to local Hong Kong needs and norms, they are free to do so as long as comparability with home standards is maintained. A key assumption of this benchmark is that the provider has a home institution for comparability purposes. As pointed out in the typology of cross-border providers, not all have a home base that sets standards of quality nor are they necessarily accredited by a national quality assurance system.

These are three different approaches to developing regulations to ensure that cross-border education providers are registered and, in most cases, undergo the same processes as domestic institutions in terms of quality assurance and accreditation. It is interesting to note which processes are mandatory and which are voluntary. In these examples, registration is obligatory as is some type of quality assurance but accreditation is optional depending on the level, mode of program delivery and the type of local/foreign partnership that has been established.

---

[5] See http://www.doj.gov.hk/eng/laws.

5 MINIMISING RISKS AND MAXIMISING BENEFITS

5.1 Receiving Countries

The prospect of having foreign education providers deliver academic programs, establish new institutions or collaborate with local institutions in joint ventures can bring many advantages to receiving countries. The list of potential benefits is long and varied and includes increased access to higher and continuing education, more diversity in program offerings, less brain drain of bright students to foreign institutions, and exposure to foreign teaching and education management systems. But there is also a list of potential risks, which can include an increase in low-quality or rogue providers, non-sustainable foreign provision of higher education if profit margins are low, foreign qualifications that are not recognised by domestic employers or for further study, elitism in terms of those who can afford cross-border education, or overuse of English as the language of instruction. Thus it is critical that receiving countries are clear about their objectives and expected benefits of cross-border provision, and that registration, quality assurance and accreditation processes are in place to ensure that cross-border education contributes to national policy objectives, whatever they may be.

5.2 Sending Countries

It must be emphasised that sending countries have a direct responsibility and vested interest in assuring the quality of the academic offer. The primary reasons are to ensure that students and foreign partner institutions are protected from low-quality and rogue providers, that learners have a relevant and high-quality education experience, and that the qualifications are recognised for further study and employment purposes.

There are other reasons that sending countries need to have quality assurance or accreditation systems in place for cross-border education. Sending countries cannot afford to put their domestic and international reputations at risk by delivering low-quality academic programs in another country or having academic programs close before all students have completed their studies. A tarnished international profile in an increasingly competitive environment could have negative effects on the ability to attract students, researchers, faculty and research projects at home and abroad. A sending country's investment and interest in cross-border education is also linked to the opportunity for strategic political, economic and technological alliances. This has increasing importance in the knowledge economy. Therefore, if a country's reputation is put in jeopardy because of low-quality provision overseas, it could have far-reaching political implications both domestically and internationally. Furthermore, if public institutions are the foreign providers, it is critical that a solid business plan and quality assurance plan are in effect so that public investment is protected by initiatives that are financially successful and 'sustainable.

5.3 Availability of Data on Cross-Border Education

There is a serious lack of solid data on the volume and type of cross-border program and provider mobility. Institutions and national education systems have invested much effort in gathering reliable data on student mobility, but it is only in the last five years that countries and international organisations are starting to track program and provider mobility. The paucity of information on program mobility creates an undesirable environment of speculation, confusion and often misinformation. This can have negative consequences in terms of confidence in the quality and dependability of cross-border education provision and impedes the analysis needed to underpin solid policy and regulatory frameworks, especially for accreditation. The development of a regional or global protocol for data collection on cross-border education is a project waiting to happen.

There are huge challenges in this data collection because of a lack of a common set of terms and different systems of gathering data. Australia, New Zealand and more recently the UK have gathered statistics from the recognised HEIs on the extent of their cross-border education provision. Other countries, notably in Europe, are collecting descriptive data on cross-border provision primarily focused on intra-European mobility. These efforts are primarily directed towards collecting data from traditional universities and often do not include the new and alternative providers such as companies and international networks.

6 CONCLUDING REMARKS

This paper has explored the quality assurance and accreditation issues and practices in delivering education across national borders. There is ample evidence that demand for higher education in the next 20 years will outstrip the capacity of some countries to meet their domestic need. Students will continue moving to other countries to pursue their studies and this will remain an important part of the international dimension of the higher education landscape. However, student mobility will not be able to satisfy the enormous appetite for higher education from densely populated countries in Asia that want to build national human capacity in order to fully participate in the knowledge society. Hence, the emergence and growing importance of cross-border education programs and providers merits close examination.

A review of the developments shows a diversity of new types of education providers, new delivery modes, and innovative forms of public/private and local/foreign partnerships. New courses and programs are being designed and delivered in response to local conditions and global challenges, and new qualifications/awards are being conferred. The growth in the volume, scope and dimensions of cross-border education not only has the potential to provide increased access and to promote innovation and responsiveness of higher education, but it also brings new challenges and unexpected consequences. Current realities show that unrecognised and rogue cross-border providers are active, that much of the latest cross-border education provision is being driven by commercial interests and gain, and that mechanisms to recognise qualifications and ensure the quality of academic courses/programs are still not in place in many countries. These present major challenges to the education sector. It is important to acknowledge the huge potential of cross-border education, but not at the expense of academic quality and the integrity of the qualification.

REFERENCES

AVCC (2003). *Offshore Programs of Australian Universities*. Australian Vice-Chancellors' Committee, Canberra.

Böhm A, Davis D, Meares D and Pearce D (2002). *Global Student Mobility 2025 Report: Forecasts of the Global Demand for International Education*. IDP Education, Australia.

Coleman D (2003). Quality assurance in transnational education. *J Stud Int Educ*, 7(4), 354–378.

Garrett R (2005). *Fraudulent, Sub-standard, Ambiguous — The Alternative Borderless Higher Education*. The Observatory on Borderless Higher Education, London.

Garrett R (2004). *Global Education Index 2004 Report*. The Observatory on Borderless Higher Education, London.

Hopper R (2007). Building capacity in quality assurance: The challenge of context. In *NUFFIC Cross-Border Tertiary Education: A Way Towards Capacity Development*, OECD/World Bank (eds.), pp. 109–155. OECD/World Bank, Paris.

Knight J (2006). *Higher Education Crossing Borders: A Guide to the Implications of GATS for Cross-border Education*. UNESCO and Commonwealth of Learning, Paris.

Knight J (2005). *Borderless, Offshore, Transnational and Crossborder Education — Definition and Data Dilemmas*. The Observatory on Borderless Higher Education, London.

Knight J (2005). Cross-border education: An analytical framework for program and provider mobility. In *Higher Education: Handbook of Theory and Practice*, J Smart and W Tierney (eds.), pp. 207–227. Springer, Dordrecht.

Knight J (2006). *Internationalization of Higher Education: New Directions, New Challenges. 2005 IAU Global Survey Report*. International Association of Universities, Paris.

Knight J (2006). Cross-border higher education: Issues and implications for quality assurance and accreditation. In *Higher Education in the World 2007 — Accreditation for Quality Assurance — What is at Stake?* Global University Network for Innovation (ed.), pp. 134–146. Palgrave, London.

Larsen K, Momii K and Vincent-Lancrin S (2004). *Cross-Border Higher Education: An Analysis of Current Trends, Policy Strategies and Future Scenario*. The Observatory on Borderless Higher Education, London.

Middlehurst R and Woodfield S (2003). The Role of Transnational, Private and For-Profit Provision in Meeting Global Demand for Tertiary Education: Mapping, Regulation and Impact. Report for the Commonwealth of Learning and UNESCO.

OECD (2004a). *Quality and Recognition in Higher Education: The Cross-Border Challenge*. Organization for Economic and Community Development, Paris.

OECD (2004b). *Internationalization and Trade of Higher Education — Challenges and Opportunities*. Organization for Economic and Community Development, Paris.

OECD/World Bank (2007). *Cross-Border Tertiary Education: A Way Towards Capacity Development*. OECD/World Bank, Paris.

UNESCO/APQN (2006). *Toolkit: Regulating the Quality of Cross-Border Education*. UNESCO, Bangkok.

UNESCO/OECD (2005). *Guidelines for Quality Provision in Cross-Border Higher Education*. UNESCO/OECD, Paris.

Verbik L and Jokivirta L (2005). *National Regulatory Frameworks for Transnational Higher Education: Models and Trends. Part 1 and Part 2*. The Observatory on Borderless Higher Education, London.

Demography, Migration and Demand for International Students

Lesleyanne Hawthorne

1 DEMOGRAPHIC SHIFT AND THE LOOMING 'WAR FOR SKILLS'

Striking demographic shifts are underway in developed nations, where fertility decline is fuelling interest in and competition for high-skilled migrants. According to the Chief Economist of the OECD in 2005, 'Over the next couple of decades nothing will impact on (member) economies more profoundly than demographic trends and, chief among them, ageing' (Cotis, 2005, p. 1). Within a generation, select OECD nations are at risk of contracting by a third, with severe productivity implications. The majority of members have fertility rates below replacement level (for example, Australia at 1.8, the UK at 1.8 and Canada at 1.5), with labour market impacts set to be intensified by 'baby boomer' retirements. Countries with traditionally high birth rates are contracting (Mexico to 2.2), while others are approaching free-fall (Japan, Germany, Italy, Spain, the Czech

Republic at 1.3 and the Republic of Korea at 1.1) (OECD, 2007). This 'fertility revolution' is being replicated across Asia, where overall population growth is predicted to halve from 2.1 to 1.0. The process is well underway: Indonesia's fertility reducing from 5.1 to 2.4 between 1970 and 2006, China's from 4.9 to 1.6 (0.9 in Shanghai), and Thailand's from 5.0 to 1.7 (Hugo, 2007).

Within this context, international students represent an increasingly attractive human resource to governments and employers, with the decision to study overseas often a symbolic first step towards a global career (Salt and Millar, 2007). By 2006, North America (the US and Canada), the European Union (the UK, Germany and France) and the Asia–Pacific (Australia, China, Japan and Singapore) were the major recipients of international student flows (see Table 1), with China (804,919), India (329,354), the Republic of Korea (306,963), Japan (250,641), Malaysia (173,728) and Indonesia (127,501) the dominant sources (Hugo, 2007). Host-country fertility rates seem certain to influence career choice, in particular the opportunity to engage in two-step migration. The 'war for skills' is rapidly intensifying — global employers are competing to attract the best human capital, in a context where international students are characterised by youth, host-country language ability, full credential recognition, significant acculturation and domestically relevant professional training (Hawthorne, 2005). In New Zealand, for instance, 88 per cent of skilled migrants by 2006 had first arrived as students or temporary workers, contributing to 'demographic survival' in a country where 2.3 million arrivals from 1955–2004 had translated to a net population gain of just 208,000 people (Bedford, 2006).

Migration represents a strong and longstanding motivation for international study. As early as 1994, an Australia-wide survey found 78 per cent of students recruited from China, 64 per cent from Hong Kong, 46 per cent from Fiji and 43 per cent from Malaysia and Singapore to be motivated by future migration, despite the then existence of a three-year eligibility bar (Nesdale *et al.*, 1995). Responding to the opportunity for immediate migration since 1999, demand for Australian tertiary courses has soared. Within five years, 52 per cent of

Table 1. Top international student destination countries by 2006 (share of world's higher and vocational education market)

Top 10 international student destination countries	International students enrolled in higher/vocational education	World market share (%)
US	565,000 (2006)	22
UK	330,000 (2005–06)	12
Australia	281,633 (2005–06)	11
Germany	248,000 (2006)	10
France	201,100 (2006)	10
China	141,000 (2005)	7
Japan	118,000 (2006)	5
Singapore	66,000 (2005)	2
Canada[1]	62,000 (2006)	2
Malaysia	55,000 (2006)	2
New Zealand	42,700 (2006)	3

Source: Adapted by Hawthorne from Lasanowski and Verbik (2007), *International Student Mobility: Patterns and Trends*, The Observatory on Borderless Higher Education, London; and Citizenship and Immigration Canada (2007).

Australia's main skilled category consisted of former international students, with an extraordinary 66 per cent of all Indian and 38 per cent of Chinese (PRC) students electing to stay. By 2005, China and India had become Australia's major international student source countries, from a negligible base (Birrell and Rapson, 2004). Migration-driven enrolments such as these had become essential to Australia — offsetting a sustained decline in those from Commonwealth–Asian source countries such as Malaysia, Singapore and Hong Kong, in a context where international student fees were required to compensate for severe federal government funding cuts[2] (see Table 2). By 2008, export education had become Australia's third largest industry, including 370,000 students from 190 countries onshore, and a further

---

[1] Estimates of international student numbers in Canada have declined in recent years as a result of the decision to waive visa applications for students enrolled for less than six months. A December 2007 Canadian government report suggests the total number to be far higher: around 160,000 in all.

[2] From 1993 to 2003 Australia reduced public funding per tertiary student by 30 per cent.

Table 2. International student enrolments in Australia by top 10 source countries (2005–06)

Nationality	2005 enrolments	2005 growth (%)	2006 enrolments	2006 growth (%)
China	81,730	15.8	90,287	10.5
India	27,605	33.0	39,166	41.9
South Korea	26,319	10.5	31,257	18.8
Hong Kong	21,343	-7.1	20,523	-3.8
Malaysia	19,362	-3.2	19,166	-1.0
Thailand	16,514	1.2	17,889	8.3
Japan	19,053	-4.9	17,804	-6.6
Indonesia	16,121	-11.1	15,038	-6.7
United States	12,585	-1.6	12,045	-4.3
Brazil	7,081	49.7	10,190	43.9
Other nationalities	98,366	3.3	110,453	12.3
Total	346,079	6.4	383,818	10.9

Source: Australian Education International statistics, March 2007, Canberra.

120,000 students studying by distance (Birrell, Hawthorne and Richardson, 2006; Australian Education International, 2008).

Migration options exist in a growing array of countries. Chinese students, for instance, are vigorously exploring global options: enrolments in France doubled from 8774 in 2003 to 15,963 in 2006, and rose from 35,155 to 50,755 in the UK, compared to 62,582 in the US by 2006, 63,543 in Australia and 74,292 in Japan. At the same time, it is essential to note that China has become a destination as well as a source of supply — ranked sixth in the world by 2006 with 141,000 international students. While the majority of such students were derived from Asia, growing numbers were from OECD nations, attracted by:

'[China's status as] the world's largest and fastest growing economy ... a place where leading industrial players want to be doing business ... For this reason, the international students of today understand Chinese higher education as a strategic investment in future employment. As an emerging player in the global education market ... China is in the fortunate position of being able to select from among the more successful practices of other nations ... By channelling as much as US$4 billion into a select few of its more research-intensive institutions, China is taking great strides to transform the overall quality of higher education in the country' (Lasanowski and Verbik, 2007, pp. 23–24).

Location of study influences early career choices. By 2005, 8,050,901 foreign workers were resident in Asia, most notably 2,640,000 in Malaysia, 2,300,000 in Thailand, 900,000 in Japan and 620,000 in Singapore. While many were low-skilled, growing numbers are also knowledge workers recruited to work in the expanding Shanghai, Tokyo, Singapore and other global financial and/or biotechnology hubs — many of them first arriving as international students (Beaverstock and Boardwell, 2000; Beaverstock, 2002; Appold, 2005).

According to Hugo, while much demographic change is predictable, '[a]nticipating and preparing for demographic shifts influencing the future shape of [a] population' is essential, along with 'see[ing] population policy not as a freestanding separate policy but as a facilitator in economic, social, environmental and political policy' (Hugo, 2007, slide 9). The student-migration phenomenon is the subject of current OECD research, with trends being assessed across 10 member nations (Australia, Canada, the Czech Republic, France, Germany, Japan, the Netherlands, Norway, the UK and the US).[3] Indeed, each of these countries is in the process of expanding export education, while introducing new or revised skilled migration policies. In the period ahead, this connectivity between export education and skilled migration seems certain to grow.

2 THE ATTRACTION OF INTERNATIONAL STUDENTS AS SKILLED MIGRANTS

The reasons that international students are increasingly sought as skilled migrants by governments can be demonstrated by two brief Asia–Pacific case studies. As early as 2001, Canada and Australia were

---

[3] Lesleyanne Hawthorne was engaged in this research while employed by the OECD in 2007–08, including policy fieldwork across member nations.

Table 3.   The proportion of migrant professionals in Canada and Australia by select field (2001)

Professional field	Canada overseas-born (%)	Australia overseas-born (%)
Engineering	50	48
Computing	51	48
Medicine	35	46
Science	36	37
Commerce/business	27	36
Architecture	49	36
Accountancy	35	36
Arts/humanities	24	31
Nursing	23	24
Teaching	15	20
Engineering	50	48

Source: Adapted by Hawthorne from Canadian (Statistics Canada) and Australian (Australian Bureau of Statistics) 2001 Census data.

dependent on migration for one-third to half of all professional workers, most notably in the fields of engineering, information technology (IT), medicine, accounting and architecture/building (see Table 3). By 2012, Canada estimates 100 per cent of net growth in all professions will be migration-dependent (Finley, 2008). In the recent period, to address workforce supply, both Canada and Australia have prioritised skilled migration, diversified immigrant source countries, utilised points systems designed to improve selection objectivity while maximising employment outcomes, and in particular enhanced the scope for 'two-step' migration (migrants' immediate transition from temporary to permanent resident status) (Hawthorne, 2008).

This process, however, has often failed to deliver the desired economic dividend. In Canada, for instance, the recent primary source countries for skilled migrants have been China, India, the Philippines, Pakistan and Romania — nations associated with poorly resourced education systems and often disappointing employment outcomes (*Times Higher Education Supplement*, 2007; Shanghai Jiao Tong University, 2006). In contrast to the US, UK, French and Australian workers whom Canadian employers choose, Canadian government selection to date has treated all degrees as equal, regardless of likely domestic recognition levels (Sweetman and McBride, 2004; Hiebert, 2006). Host-country language ability has not been independently screened (Ferrer, Green and Riddell, 2004). In consequence, large numbers of skilled migrants have been admitted to Canada with limited English/French fluency and non-recognised qualifications, frequently trained in fields associated with low labour market demand (Hawthorne, 2008). The consequence for many has been labour market displacement — the latest available data show economic migrants to be 'the new face of the chronically poor' in Canada, securing employment outcomes inferior to migrants under the 'Family' category and taking 28 years (if ever) to secure wage parity with comparably qualified Canadians (Picot, Feng and Coulombe, 2007) (see Table 4).

Given evidence of similar trends in Australia, since 1999 economic applicants at risk of delayed or de-skilled employment have been excluded from migration at point of entry, through mandatory pre-migration English screening, credential assessment, analysis of labour market demand, and the allocation of bonus points to former international students with Australian qualifications (Birrell and Hawthorne, 1999; Department of Immigration and Multicultural Affairs, 1999). This process has ensured their growing workforce participation (see Table 5). Australia's 2006 economic migration review (the most extensive since 1988) affirmed the effectiveness of these initiatives in delivering immediate labour market outcomes — 83 per cent of skilled migrants secured work within six months, with substantial numbers rewarded by unprecedented remuneration (Birrell, Hawthorne and Richardson, 2006). In fine-tuning the program further, new measures since September 2007 have included enhanced English language ability, plus a stronger focus on former students' Australian work experience (see Section 4 for the rationale).

3 GROWING GLOBAL COMPETITION FOR INTERNATIONAL STUDENTS

In the context of demographic change, large numbers of APEC and OECD nations are now facilitating this type of 'two-step' migration,

Table 4. Employment outcomes for degree-qualified migrants in Canada by 2001 (1996–2001 arrivals)

Arrival date	Source country	Own profession	Other prof/ management	Any work S/Total	Unemployed	Not in labor force	Number
	Canada	33.6	27.5	84.7	3.9	11.4	1,888,276
1996/2001	South Africa	39.5	30.5	86.6	5.2	8.2	1,992
	Australia/New Zealand	29.9	36.5	80.0	6.3	12.1	855
	USA	26.5	31.0	76.1	5.3	18.6	5,696
	UK/Ireland	25.8	37.3	83.2	5.5	11.3	4,219
	North West Europe	25.0	33.8	80.0	7.9	12.1	8,701
	HK/Malaysia/Singapore	19.1	22.1	65.1	11.2	23.8	6,436
	Central & South Americas	17.9	19.0	68.1	13.8	18.1	11,803
	Eastern Europe	17.7	22.6	70.5	13.8	15.7	31,622
	South Eastern Europe	16.0	20.1	67.3	16.7	16.1	6,710
	China (exc. Taiwan)	14.9	20.7	58.3	18.7	23.0	48,952
	Other Middle East/N Africa	14.3	19.1	56.6	21.2	22.2	16,059
	India	12.2	18.9	71.5	12.8	15.7	29,059
	Other South/Central Asia	11.5	16.8	60.5	16.6	23.0	35,659
	Taiwan	10.3	18.0	44.9	14.5	40.6	7,955
	Iraq	8.8	15.5	50.6	20.7	28.7	2,116
	Philippines	8.3	10.3	77.1	9.1	13.8	17,869
	Other	15.5	21.6	65.0	14.8	22.9	22,010
	Total migrants						257,714

Source: 2001 Census (Canada), reported in *Labour Market Outcomes for Migrant Professionals — Canada and Australia Compared*, Hawthorne (2007).

Table 5. Top 10 countries of citizenship for skilled migration applicants to Australia 2003/04 to 2005/06

2003–04	No.	%	2004–05 (July–June)	No.	%	2005–06 (July–Nov)	No.	%
India	7,103	19	UK	5,959	18	India	2,363	19
China	5,506	15	India	5,145	15	China	2,258	18
UK	4,698	13	China	4,338	13	UK	2,071	16
Malaysia	2,029	6	Malaysia	1,947	6	Malaysia	536	4
Indonesia	1,990	5	Indonesia	1,525	5	Philippines	431	3
Singapore	1,490	4	Hong Kong	1,439	4	Indonesia	430	3
Hong Kong	1,199	3	Singapore	1,242	4	Hong Kong	404	3
Korea	1,033	3	Sri Lanka	1,028	3	Korea	391	3
Sri Lanka	925	3	Philippines	986	3	Sri Lanka	331	3
Philippines	919	3	Korea	856	3	Singapore	291	2

Source: Birrell, Hawthorne and Richardson (2006), *Evaluation of the General Skilled Migration Categories,* Commonwealth of Australia, Canberra.

targeting students and temporary workers. In particular, governments are:

- monitoring successful competitor models;
- developing high-skilled migration policies, including categories designed to attract and retain international students;
- expanding the scale of international student flows, through enhanced global promotion, marketing structures and research functions;
- providing access to 'job search' postgraduate year(s) designed to extend student stay;
- expanding this opportunity to all locations and disciplinary fields (following preliminary focus on science and engineering); and
- constructing student pathways from temporary to permanent resident status, supported by priority processing, and/or uncapped migration categories (International Centre for Migration Policy Development, 2006; Lasanowski and Verbik, 2007).

Given developments such as these, there is now unprecedented competition for international students, including across APEC nations. By 2005, Singapore, for instance, was attracting 2 per cent of the global market (66,000 students), with 13 per cent of its tertiary sector enrolment from overseas (in particular from China (15,000), Indonesia and Malaysia). Marketing itself as 'the best of East and West ... the Global Schoolhouse', Singapore aims to attract 150,000 additional students by 2015, a process expedited by strong international academic rankings (in 2007, the National University of Singapore was ranked 33rd in the *Times Higher Education Supplement*). Malaysia had secured 55,000 international students by 2006, setting goals to achieve 100,000 by 2010. While Asia remains the dominant source region to date (China, Indonesia, Thailand, Bangladesh, Singapore), increasing flows are also being attracted from Saudi Arabia and the Gulf States, supported by the Ministry of Education investment of US$4.8 billion to boost development of the tertiary sector (Lasanowski and Verbik, 2007). Malaysian universities have also started to experiment with delivery mode, opening a private-sector campus in Botswana (Gabarone) in their first offshore initiative in mid-2007.

Global surveillance of competitor strategies is unprecedented, supported by systematic neutralisation of any perceived academic barriers or disincentives. A surprising number of providers now deliver courses in English (including in Norway, the Netherlands, Germany, China and Japan), recognising the attraction of English as the global language (Marginson and van der Wende, 2007). The Netherlands, for example, by 2007 was offering 1200+ courses taught wholly in English, including around 900 Bachelor's and Master's degrees — a process currently being promoted through seven global offices (including those in Mexico, Indonesia and Vietnam). The UK has launched two major international student recruitment initiatives in the past eight years (in 1999 and 2006) designed to challenge Australia's contention for key markets (e.g., Malaysia), while reversing past declines in the number of Asian students. The new UK migration policy (announced in February 2008, strongly influenced by the Australian model) is designed to expand international students' scope to stay, including their immediate access to work permits and (if employed) subsequent high-skilled migration. The US is in the process of launching fresh policy initiatives to stem the post-September 11 international student decline, based on an easing of visa regulations, supported by new strategic initiatives favouring flows from China, Chile and Morocco. Germany, having achieved 62 per cent international student growth since 1997, promulgated a skilled migration policy in 2005, targeting students while maintaining a policy of zero international student fees. New Zealand has abolished international PhD students' fees — an effective step in cultivating doctoral student numbers. Canada is fine-tuning a 'Canadian Experience Class' intended to facilitate students' stay, with the Minister for Immigration visiting India to canvass the scope for more effective South Asian promotion.

Within this heightened competitive environment, cost represents an important factor and this will impact many traditional providers. According to a recent US study, raised tuition fees were a primary cause of international student decline post September 11, when the US dollar was high, rather than changed security measures (Lowell, Bump and Martin, 2007). Enrolments are rising again with the dollar's slide. As demonstrated by Table 6, by 2006, US, UK and Australian fees far exceeded those charged by Canada, Germany, France, New Zealand and Japan, as well as emerging Asian competitor nations. Cost may become a decisive issue, once Europe promotes its new English-medium degrees.

4 TWO INTERNATIONAL STUDENT MIGRATION CASE STUDIES

4.1 Foreign Doctoral Students in the US

The rewards of targeted international student migration are significant. According to a recent US study, 'In the last half of the twentieth century, America was the location of choice for the best and brightest scientific minds in the world ... with 62 per cent of the world's stars as residents' — many first arriving as international students. Indeed,

Table 6.   Comparative fees by select undergraduate course, OECD/APEC nations (2007)

Destination country	Course/University	Fees in US$
Australia	**University of Sydney**	
	Business/Management	US$18,383
	Mechanical Engineering	US$20,164
	Philosophy	US$16,204
Canada	**Laval University**	
	Business/Management	US$10,634
	Mechanical Engineering	US$11,852
	Philosophy	US$11,852
China	**Shanghai Jiao Tong University**	
	One fee for all courses	US$3,300
France	**University of Paris (Sorbonne)**	
	One fee for all courses	US$235
Germany	**University of Heidelberg**	
	No fees for courses at this stage	Nil
	(policy under review)	
Japan	**University of Tokyo**	
	One fee for all courses	US$4,652
Malaysia	**University of Malaya**	
	Business/Management	US$1,704
	Mechanical Engineering	US$1,464
	Philosophy	US$1,656
New Zealand	**University of Otago**	
	Business/Management	US$12,120
	Mechanical Engineering	US$13.687
	Philosophy	US$11,050
United Kingdom	**Oxford University**	
	Business/Management	£10,360
	Engineering	£11,840
	Philosophy	£10,360
United States	**University of California**	
	General UG course per year	US$27,335

Source: Adapted by Hawthorne from Lasanowski and Verbik (2007), *International Student Mobility: Patterns and Trends*, The Observatory on Borderless Higher Education, London, with extra data sourced from Oxford University and University of California websites (accessed November 2007).

in the past two decades, the US share of global doctoral students has risen from 13.5 per cent to 28.3 per cent, with such 'stars' frequently trained by 'the research universities which produce them' (Zucker and Darby, 2007, p. 1; Marginson and der Wende, 2007).

By 2006, as we have seen, the US was the main global destination for international students, with 565,000 enrolled across 4000 accredited institutions. Seven of the top ten source countries were in Asia: India (76,503), China (62,582), South Korea (58,847), Japan (38,712), Canada (28,202), Taiwan (27,876), Mexico (13,931), Turkey (11,622), Germany (8829), Thailand (8765), followed by Indonesia (7575) (Lasanowski and Verbik, 2007). By 2007, export education had become the fifth largest industry in the US, with 46.3 per cent of students undertaking graduate courses (up 13.2% over the past year). In 2006/07, enrolments included 108,033 foreign doctoral students compared to 122,385 in Master's degree programs. The global promotion of US education is intensifying, underpinned by a message from the Secretary of State that 'America's mission in this new century must be to welcome foreign students to our nation' (Institution of International Education, 2007, p. 2).

Increases in numbers from six of the top ten US source countries have occurred in the past year, particularly from India (10% increase to 83,833), China (8% increase to 67,723) and South Korea (6% increase to 62,392) — an outcome favoured by the US currency slide. Doctoral students from these countries move seamlessly into postdoctoral work, taking positions eschewed by domestic graduates on the grounds of poor remuneration and long tenure-track requirements. Indeed, while enrolled in the US, international students 'help teach large undergraduate classes, provide research assistance to the faculty, and make up an important fraction of the benchworkers in scientific labs'. Tuition fees vanish once students have achieved part-time employment status (Borjas 2002; 2006). In 1976, international students constituted 11.3 per cent of enrolments in US graduate programs, compared to 24.4 per cent by 2000. However, much higher levels prevailed in select fields: 50.7 per cent of all doctorates awarded in engineering, compared to 36.5 per cent in the physical sciences and 25.7 per cent in the life sciences.

The presence of these foreign postdoctoral students is viewed as essential — major US employer groups are now lobbying Congress for automatic provision of Green Cards (i.e., permanent residence) to all international students completing US doctoral degrees. Recent studies estimate extended stay rates to include up to 85–95 per cent of Indian and Chinese graduates, allowing for substantial scientific contributions to be made in select fields (see, e.g., Finn, 2003; Borjas, 2006; Regets, 2001, 2007; National Science Foundation, 2008). According to the National Science Foundation (Regets, 2001, p. 17), the 'availability of foreign students may allow many graduate departments to expand or maintain graduate programs. In other cases, foreign students may allow more elite programs to maintain very high standards by choosing among the best of both foreign and native applicants' in a context where 'graduate programs are also important sources of new knowledge and research' and student participation boosts the US competitive advantage in the production of knowledge, goods and services.

The National Institutes of Health (NIH), for instance, each year hosts over 2000 foreign postdoctoral students 'to receive training and conduct biomedical research'. Such ex-students are attracted to NIH appointments by 'international prestige, its clout in financing biomedical research, and its many research opportunities'. Their presence is deemed vital:

> 'As fewer American students select biomedical careers, US training institutions are forced to increasingly rely on the admission of foreign students to maintain enrolment levels (and hence, ensure the survival of graduate academic departments) and satisfy labour market demand. [The program has become] a de facto seamless and efficient recruitment mechanism whereby American academe can, at minimal cost, indirectly evaluate, select and hire biomedical scientists from a large and constantly-renewing pool of foreign candidates that includes talented and promising young biomedical scientists from around the world' (Diaz-Briquets and Cheny, 2003, pp. 433, 438, 430).

According to the American Council on Education (2006, p. 9), foreign doctoral students are filling precisely the science and technology fields that US graduates are vacating, at a time when domestic shortages are rising. Within this context, alternative global destinations are viewed as a threat, in particular Europe's growing dominance (the destination now for close to half of all international students), with recent French and Japanese gains described as 'phenomenal'. A range of papers confirm the US government's determination to maintain its export education lead, taking all necessary steps to achieve this. A Congress-commissioned report outlines the immigration reform that was sought in 2007, one major aim being to 'ease the restrictions on foreign students in scientific and technical disciplines' (Matthews, 2007, p. 1). While in theory just 65,000 H-1B visas are available each year to temporary degree-qualified foreigners, in practice one million workers are annually resident by this means, with great latitude afforded to doctorally qualified former students.

According to a testimony to the House Subcommitttee on 21st Century Competitiveness and Education, future US 'security and quality of life' will depend on continuing to attract 'the most capable students and scholars of other countries' (Matthews, 2007, p. 18). Access to permanent residence for foreign graduates is viewed as central to this process, as outlined in the recently released *Science and Engineering Indicators 2008* report:

'Consider a hypothetical case of a bachelor's level engineer who enters the United States with a student F visa to pursue a doctorate, who spends 6 years completing the doctorate, followed by 2 years in a postdoc position, and then is hired by an employer for a permanent job on a temporary work visa. The employer applies for a permanent work visa for their new worker, who receives it 2 years after starting work. Now, 10 years after entering the United States, a 5-year waiting period begins after receiving a permanent visa, before the engineer can apply for citizenship. The engineer applies soon after becoming eligible, and after 1 year, becomes a US citizen, 16 years after entry to the United States' (National Science Foundation, 2008, pp. 3–52).

In an increasingly competitive environment, there are risks associated with uncertain and/or elongated migration processes.

4.2 Australia

Australia, in contrast to US practice, from 1999 facilitated immediate access for international students to permanent residence status. Since 2001, they have been eligible to apply for skilled migration onshore, with virtual certainty of selection (unless they fail health or character checks). In redesigning its selection criteria, the Australian government affirmed the program's original intent — to select migrants deemed able to make an immediate economic contribution. A parallel goal was to reduce skills wastage among recent arrivals, together with the level of government investment required to support migrants' labour market adjustment. The previous model of selection had proven flawed — delivering principal applicants lacking the 'knowledge economy' attributes employers seek (sophisticated English language ability, recognised credentials, and qualification in fields associated with buoyant labour market demand).

In terms of qualifications, applicants in regulated fields are now required to apply for pre-migration screening by the relevant Australian national or state licensing bodies (typically a three-month postal process) — a strategy designed to avoid years of forced labour market displacement resulting from non-recognition. Priority processing and up to 20 bonus points are awarded to people in high-demand fields, a measure associated with clearly beneficial outcomes. Recognising the importance of host-country language ability, candidates are required to achieve 'vocational' or higher level scores on the independently administered International English Language Testing System (or equivalent), provided globally and monthly by the British Council for a modest fee. The level set has not been draconian — the minimum standard for economic eligibility until September 2007 was defined as 'Has partial command of the language, coping with overall meaning in most situations, though is likely to make many mistakes. Should be able to handle basic communication in own field.'

In terms of impact, it is important to note that these policy changes from 1999 have not discouraged or distorted skilled flows to

Australia. Intakes rose to 97,500 in 2005–06 from 77,800 in 2004–05 (compared to one-third that level in the mid-1990s), with the 2007–08 target set at 102,500. Racial and ethnic diversity have been maintained — in 2006–07 the top five source countries were the UK (18%), India (15%), China (11%), Malaysia (4%) and the Philippines (3%). Most importantly, improved employment outcomes have been secured by traditionally disadvantaged groups. While labour market integration for all source countries had improved by 1999/2000, in the case of economic principal applicants from Eastern Europe, the Middle East/North Africa, India, the Philippines and China, the scale of this improvement had been dramatic. For example, 79 per cent of economic principal applicants from Eastern Europe had found work within six months of arrival by 1999/2000, compared to 31 per cent in 1993–95. The comparable rate for the Philippines was 76 per cent (versus 57%), with such gains further improving by the time of Australia's skilled migration review (2006).

Former international students had become strong program participants (as noted earlier, 52 per cent of the total within five years). By definition, they had self-funded to meet employers' English language and credential requirements, boosting the development of Australia's export education industry in the process. At the same time, the 2006 skilled migration review uncovered emerging problems in relation to student flows, which required addressing (Birrell, Hawthorne and Richardson, 2006).

From 1999 to September 2007, former students seeking two-step migration were exempted from English-language testing when applying for permanent residency, the assumption being that their English and acculturation levels would be strong by the time of migration (Department of Immigration and Multicultural Affairs, 1999). The skilled migration review provided compelling evidence that this was not always the case. A range of Australian providers appeared to have compromised their declared academic entry standards while developing international student flows — a finding endorsed by subsequent studies (Baas, 2006, 2007; Birrell, Healy and Kinnaird, 2007; Watty, 2007). Despite the majority of Australian universities publicising English entry levels of IELTS Band 6 or above for tertiary courses, post-course testing by the Immigration Department provided unambiguous evidence that many graduates fell well short of this standard (captured at the point of transition to skilled migration following a minimum of two years' Australian residence and tertiary study). In 2004–05, 43 per cent of recent international student graduates from China gained scores of IELTS Band 5, along with 36 per cent of those from Vietnam and 29 per cent from Thailand (Birrell, Hawthorne and Richardson, 2006). A year later the proportion of graduates scoring IELTS 5 rather than 6 or higher had become significantly worse, including an extraordinary 56 per cent of former students from South Korea, 51 per cent from Thailand, 47 per cent from Taiwan, 43 per cent from both China and Hong Kong, and 42 per cent from Bangladesh (see Table 7). The latest available data, derived from the 2006 Census, confirms just 22 per cent of 20- to 29-year olds had secured professional or managerial work in the first five years post-migration — the great majority of these certain to have been accepted as former international students (Birrell, 2008). This outcome stands despite the strength of the current labour market demand in the booming Australian economy.

In accounting for such outcomes, the skilled migration review identified serious risks in relation to Australia's export education industry, most notably the evidence of:

- *institutional conflict of interest*, leading to potentially compromised academic entry and progression standards;
- *unrealistic assumptions* concerning the speed and certainty of students' post-arrival IELTS gains (given the capacity of short English courses to deliver guaranteed access to degree and diploma courses via packaged visas);
- *inadequate surveillance or quality control* of the rapidly emerging registered training organisations providing training for the vocational sector; and
- *the high level of cultural and linguistic enclosure* experienced by many international students, particularly those located in the Sydney and Melbourne 'campuses' of select regional universities, who were at risk of academic segregation.

Table 7.   Language scores of former international students approved 2004–05 and 2005–06 (sub-class 880) by major country of origin

Source country	ESL points: 15 (IELTS 5) 2004–05 (%)	ESL points: 15 (IELTS 5) 2005–06 (%)	ESL points: 20 (IELTS 6) 2004–05 (%)	ESL points: 20 (IELTS 6) 2005–06 (%)	Total tested 2004–05	Total tested 2005–06
China	43	43	56	57	2,655	4,209
India	5	17	94	82	2,433	2,169
Indonesia	16	32	84	68	1,408	749
Malaysia	16	24	84	76	1,113	797
Hong Kong	17	43	83	57	863	683
South Korea	23	56	76	44	474	449
Singapore	10	18	90	82	440	258
Bangladesh	23	42	77	58	436	479
Sri Lanka	10	25	90	75	360	346
Japan	18	37	82	63	248	174
Taiwan	24	47	76	53	231	133
Pakistan	9	25	90	75	224	141
Thailand	29	51	70	49	200	175
Vietnam	36	33	64	67	200	152

Source: Adapted by Hawthorne from data provided in Birrell, Hawthorne and Richardson (2006), *Evaluation of the General Skilled Migration Categories*, Commonwealth of Australia, Canberra; and B. Birrell (2006), Implications of low English standards among overseas students at Australian universities, *People and Place*, 14(4), Table 5, p. 59.

Such results were the reverse of those anticipated by the Australian government in 1999. Moreover, a key finding of the 2006 review was that recent onshore applicants achieved significantly worse than off-shore principal applicants in terms of professional work. Despite near-identical proportions being employed within six months of arrival (82–83%), former students were found to be characterised by:

- annual salaries of around A$33,000 (compared to A$52,500 for offshore arrivals);
- average weekly earnings of A$641 (compared to A$1015);
- lower job satisfaction, with 44 per cent liking their work (compared to 57%); and
- far less 'often' use of formal qualifications in current work (46% compared to 63%) (Birrell, Hawthorne and Richardson, 2006, p. 97).

Since September 2007, decisive steps have been taken to address these issues. Exemption from English language testing is no longer allowed for former international students, given that it is impossible for the Department of Immigration and Citizenship to police education providers' academic entry and progression standards. International English Language Testing Scheme (IELTS) Band 6 has been declared the threshold 'competence' score for all economic migrants, across the four language skills[4] (significantly raised from Band 5). Liberalised access to post-course visas will facilitate former students' stays, allowing them an additional 18 months (if required) to 'gain skilled work experience; improve their English language skills; or undertake a Professional Year' related to their field of study. Only passport holders from the UK, Ireland, the US, Canada and New Zealand will be exempt from English testing on transition to economic migration, given the problem of defining which candidates should be waived. Significant bonus points will also reward 'proficient' English speakers (25 points for candidates rated IELTS 7 or above), a major determinant now of

---

[4] Speaking, listening, reading and writing; with the threshold score required for all four skills by independently validated language testing.

selection. The practices of educational providers will be better moni-
tored, in particular those operating in the fast-growing migration-driven
vocational training sector. Higher migration points will be provided to
Australian graduates who have completed postgraduate study, most
notably former students possessing doctoral degrees (25 points) or
three-year qualifications (15 points) (Department of Immigration and
Citizenship, 2007c).

Such steps are viewed as essential to maintaining the integrity of
Australia's skilled migration program. In terms of language measures,
they are justified by the review's finding that English language ability
represents the major determinant of professional employment outcomes:

> 'We conclude that in most dimensions of labour market success, the key is
> to have a level of English language competence that enables the respondent
> to report that they speak English at least 'very well'. [Those who do not]
> were much more likely to be unemployed; about half as likely as those with
> better English to be employed in a job commensurate with their skills; and
> about twice as likely to be employed in a relatively low skilled job' (Birrell,
> Hawthorne and Richardson, 2006, pp. 86–87).

5 INTERNATIONAL STUDENT MIGRATION: SELECT POLICY CHALLENGES

Despite the attractiveness of international students as skilled
migrants, a number of policy challenges clearly exist. First, the level of
future competition for students will be unprecedented — the US's
determination to expand foreign student recruitment is a prime
example, but one replicated across many policy sites.

Second, the stability of international students as a migration
source of supply must be questioned. In New Zealand, for example,
the number of Chinese students surged from 139 in 1998 to a peak
of 21,580 in 2004 (58% of the international student total). Demand
has since halved, at a reported cost to New Zealand's education
industry of US$500 million. This rapid reduction represents a skilled
migration setback as much as an export industry blow (Lasanowski
and Verbik, 2007).

Third, there is clear potential for migration-driven flows to rapidly distort international student enrolment by sector and discipline. For example, Australia's addition of multiple vocational fields to its 'Migration Occupations in Demand List' has led to extraordinary recent growth in demand for vocational and technical education courses (see Tables 8 and 9), at serious cost to university faculties that had expanded to address anticipated demand, e.g., in IT (Birrell, Hawthorne and Richardson, 2006; Australian Education International, 2007).

Finally, questionable educational providers may respond to migration-driven flows — for instance, select private training providers in Australia were described to the skilled migration review panel as 'wily entrepreneurial players who exist solely to funnel students into migration'. Education-linked migration policy requires vigilance, including the establishment and oversight of quality assurance systems adequately resourced for the task.

Unquestionably, in the period ahead, a growing number of APEC nations will choose to recruit and retain international students as skilled migrants. This process must involve:

- ongoing surveillance of export education and migration policies, in order to address distortions or abuses as they occur;
- developing pro-active measures designed to ensure that student flows have the capacity to address national workforce needs;
- factoring source-country demography into export education and skilled migration planning (for example, the rapid fertility decline occurring in key Asian source countries); and
- accepting the contemporary transformation of key migration-related international student markets to global export education providers (for example, China, Singapore and Malaysia).

Within the dynamic period of competition that lies ahead, there should be potential to maximise the promotion of 'brand APEC' while expanding the region's reputation for producing skilled, flexible and exportable global workers. Though the ethics of student migration remains a matter of debate, parents rather than source countries

Table 8. New international student commencements by Australian education sector (August 2006 and 2007)

Sector	August 2006	August 2007	Change (%)
Higher education	64,230	69,238	7.8
VTE	38,023	57,328	50.8
ELICOS	38,190	53,446	39.9
Schools	9,790	12,241	25.0
Non-award and other	20,608	21,224	3.0
Total	170,841	213,477	25.0
Higher education	64,230	69,238	7.8

Source: Monthly Summary of International Student Enrolment Data — Australia, Australian Education International, Department of Education Science and Training, September 2007 (Media Release).

Table 9. Visas issued by major occupation group and subclass of visa, 2005–06, General Skilled Migration Program (GSM) — Principal Applicant only

Occupation group	Visa 880, 881, 882 (onshore)	Visa 136 (offshore)	All other GSM visas	Total GSM visas issued
Accountants, auditors, corporation treasurers	6,595	2,619	488	9,702
Computing professionals	3,589	2,755	729	7,073
Building/engineering professionals	1,484	1,745	811	4,040
Food tradespersons	952	394	154	1,500
Nursing	229	1,136	107	1,472
Miscellaneous business/ information professionals	432	96	897	1,425
Mechanical engineering tradespersons	4	1,057	325	1,386
Sales, marketing and advertising professionals	186	94	779	1,059
Structural construction tradespersons	3	543	306	852
Other occupations	1,884	3,367	4,413	9,664
Total	15,383	14,593	9,400	39,376

Source: Adapted from Birrell (2006), Implications of low English standards among overseas students at Australian universities, *People and Place*, 14(4), Table 1, p. 54.

have typically funded these students' education. From an ethical perspective, their recruitment thus seems less problematic than the OECD migration norm — selection of mature-age professionals fully trained by their countries of origin.

REFERENCES

Appold S (2005). The weakening position of university graduates in Singapore's labor market: Causes and consequences. *Popul Dev Rev*, 31(1), 85–112.

American Council on Education Issue Brief (2006). Students on the Move: The Future of International Students in the United States. ACE Center for International Initiatives, October. http://www.acenet.edu/programs/international, 15 February 2008.

Australian Education International (2007a). Final Report on a National Symposium on International Students and English. Department of Education Science and Technology, Canberra, November.

Australian Education International (2007b). Monthly Summary of International Student Enrolment Data — Australia. Department of Education Science and Training, September (Media Release).

Australian Education International (2008). AEI International Student Enrolment Data 2008. Canberra, Australian Government, Commonwealth of Australia, http://aei.dest.gov.au/AEI/MIP/Statistics/StudentEnrolmentAndVisaStatistics/2008/20/08/2008.

Baas M (2006). Students of migration: Indian overseas students and the question of permanent residency. *People and Place*, 14(1), 9–24.

Baas M (2007). The language of migration: The education industry versus the migration industry. *People and Place*, 15(2), 49–60.

Beaverstock J (2002). Transnational elites in global cities: British expatriates in Singapore's financial district. *Geoforum*, 33, 525–538.

Beaverstock J and Boardwell J (2000). Negotiating globalization, transnational corporations and global city financial centres in transient migration studies. *Appl Geogr*, 20, 277–304.

Bedford R (2006). Skilled migration policy in Australia and New Zealand: Similarities and differences. In *Evaluation of the General Skilled Migration Categories*, B Birrell, L Hawthorne and S Richardson (eds.), pp. 219–246. Commonwealth of Australia, Canberra.

Birrell B (2006). Implications of low English standards among overseas students at Australian universities. *People and Place*, 14(4), 53–64.

Birrell B (2008). Some migrants not skilled enough. *The Age*, 30 April, p. 17.

Birrell B and Hawthorne L (1999). Australia's Skilled Migration Program Outcomes as of 1996. Commissioned research for the Review of the Independent and Skilled-Australian Linked Categories, Department of Immigration and Multicultural Affairs, Canberra.

Birrell B, Hawthorne L and Richardson S (2006). *Evaluation of the General Skilled Migration Categories.* Commonwealth of Australia, Canberra.

Birrell B, Healy E and Kinnaird B (2007). Cooks galore and hairdressers aplenty. *People and Place*, 15(1), 30–44.

Birrell B and Rapson V (2004). International students — Implications for Australia's immigration program and higher education system. Centre for Population and Urban Research, Monash University, October.

Borjas G (2002). An Evaluation of the Foreign Student Program. Harvard University, National Bureau of Economic Research (NBER), July, KSG Working Paper No. RWPO2-026.

Borjas G (2006). Immigration in High-Skill Markets: The Impact of Foreign Students on the Earnings of Doctorates. National Bureau of Economic Research, Working Paper 12085, Cambridge MA, March, 1–26.

Citizenship and Immigration Canada (2007). International student flows to Canada data, Ottawa.

Cotis J-P (2005). Challenges of Demographics. Keynote speech, Policy Network Spring Retreat, Warren House, Surrey, 11–12 March.

Department of Immigration and Multicultural Affairs (1999). *Review of the Independent and Skilled-Australian Linked Categories.* Commonwealth of Australia, Canberra.

Department of Immigration and Citizenship (2007a). Migration Program Planning Levels. Fact Sheet No 20, Australian Government. http://www.immi.gov.au/media/fact-sheets/20planning.htm, 15 December.

Department of Immigration and Citizenship (2007b). English Language Tuition for Adult Migrants. Fact Sheet No 24, Australian Government. http://www.immi.gov.au/media/fact-sheets/24amep.htm, 15 December.

Department of Immigration and Citizenship (2007c). Changes to General Skilled Migration (GSM) — Frequently Asked Questions. DIAC website, Australian Government, Canberra, 15 December.

Diaz-Briquets S and Cheney C (2003). Foreign scientists at the National Institutes of Health: Ramifications of US immigration and labor policies. *Int Migr Rev*, 37(2), 421–443.

Ferrer A, Green DA and Riddell WC (2004). The Effect of Literacy on Immigrant Earnings. Statistics Canada, Catalogue No. 89–552–MIE, No 12, Ottawa.

Finley D (2008). Attracting International Talent: Collaborating on Foreign Credential Recognition. The Honourable Diane Finley, PC MP, Minister of Citizenship and Immigration, Canada, Keynote Speech, Conference on Foreign

Credential Recognition, The Conference Board of Canada and Citizenship and Immigration Canada, Calgary, 22 April.

Finn M (2007). Stay Rates of Foreign Doctorate Recipients from US Universities: 2005. Oak Ridge Institute for Science and Education, Oak Ridge, TN.

Hawthorne L (2005). Picking winners: The recent transformation of Australia's skill migration policy. *Int Migr Rev*, 39(2), 663–696.

Hawthorne L (2007). *Labour Market Outcomes for Migrant Professionals — Canada and Australia Compared*. Full Report, Citizenship and Immigration Canada. http://www.cic.gc.ca/english/resources/research/2006-canada-australia.asp (accessed 10 June 2007).

Hawthorne L (2008). The impact of economic selection policy on labour market outcomes for degree-qualified migrants in Canada and Australia. *IRPP Choices*, 14(5).

Hiebert D (2006). Skilled immigration in Canada: Context, patterns and outcomes. In *Evaluation of the General Skilled Migration Categories*, B Birrell, L Hawthorne and S Richardson (eds.), pp. 177–218. Commonwealth of Australia, Canberra.

Hugo G (2007). Demographic Change in East and Southeast Asia and the Implications for the Future. Presentation to the 17th General Meeting of the Pacific Economic Cooperation Council, Sydney, 1–2 May.

International Centre for Migration Policy Development (2006). Study on Admission and Retention Policies Towards Foreign Students in Industrialised Countries. Vienna, October.

Jones FL (1989). The recent employment and unemployment experiences of immigrants in Australia. In *The Challenge of Diversity: Policy Options for a Multicultural Australia*, J Jupp (ed.), pp. 115–146. Australian Government Publishing Service, Canberra.

Lasanowski V and Verbik L (2007). *International Student Mobility: Patterns and Trends*. The Observatory on Borderless Higher Education, London.

Lowell L, Bump M and Martin S (2007). Foreign Students Coming to America: The Impact of Policy, Procedures, and Economic Competition. Institute for the Study of International Migration, Georgetown University, February.

Marginson S and van der Wende M (2007). Globalisation and Higher Education. Education Working Paper No. 8, Directorate for Education, OECD, Paris.

Matthews CM (2007). Foreign Science and Engineering Presence in US Institutions and the Labor Force. In *Trends in Higher Education*, Cruthers, JE (ed.), pp. 89–110. CRS Report for Congress, Congressional Research Service, JE Nova Science Publishers, New York.

National Science Foundation (2008). *Science and Engineering Indicators 2008*. National Science Foundation, Washington, DC.

Nesdale D *et al.* (1995). *International Students and Immigration*. Australian Government Publishing Service, Canberra.

OECD (2007). *Health at a Glance: OECD Indicators.* OECD, Paris.

Picot G, Feng H and Coulombe S (2007). Chronic low-income and low-income dynamics among recent immigrants. *Analytical Studies Research Papers*, Statistics Canada Research Paper Series, Catalogue No. 11F0019MIE, No. 294, Ottawa.

Regets M (2001). Research and Policy Issues in High-Skilled International Migration: A Perspective with Data from the United States. Discussion Paper No. 366, National Science Foundation, Arlington and 12A, Bonn.

Regets M (2007). Research Issues in the International Migration of Highly Skilled Workers: A Perspective with Data from the United States. Working Paper SRS 07–203, Division of Science Resources Statistics, National Science Foundation, Arlington VA.

Shanghai Jiao Tong University (2006). *Academic Ranking of World Universities 2005.* Institute of Higher Education, Shanghai Jiao Tong University, August.

Times Higher Education Supplement (2007). Top 200 Universities. November.

Watty K (2007). Quality in accounting education and low English language standards among overseas students: Is there a link? *People and Place*, 15(1), 22–29.

Zucker L and Darby M (2007). Star Scientists, Innovation and Regional and National Immigration. Working Paper 13547, National Bureau of Economic Research, October, Cambridge MA.

Business Models in Asia–Pacific Transnational Higher Education

Federico M. Macaranas

1 INTRODUCTION

1.1 Background

The Asia–Pacific hosts the world's most important and active transnational higher education (Huang, 2006). More countries in the region are aggressively promoting their net exporter/knowledge hub status/ goals as global markets expand and technologies reshape content and delivery systems. In response to the changing political, economic and social forces that impact on educational systems, various business models have been developed that affect the Asia–Pacific's regional integration as skilled workers, sharpened by global education services, are more mobile and contribute to the development of their home countries as well as to those attracting them as migrants.

This paper develops a typology of business models in transnational higher education to better understand the forces motivating the supply and demand sides of the markets, including those of providers, funders, students and other mobile inputs in the supply chain.[1] A brief discussion of business models is followed by an examination of higher education trends, including 'aid to trade' shifts, corporatisation of public universities vs. privatisation, public–private partnerships, the rise of corporate universities and research concerns, and GATS-related issues bearing on cross-border cooperation.

1.2 Typology of Business Models

As shown in Fig. 1, this paper integrates the three dimensions shaping the evolution of business models in transnational education: provision by the state vs. non-state actors, financing through public means vs. private/individual sources, and the development stages of cross-border activities from people to program to institutional mobility. The three evolved gradually and separately across the Asia–Pacific region, becoming more heightened in the last decade.

---

[1] *Business models* in education can be defined as the generic ways of *producing goods* (learning materials, research) *and services* (training) *using various inputs* (human resources such as faculty and administrative/support services, physical capital such as school buildings and laboratories, natural resources such as land for agricultural and forestry courses, information and knowledge as in library collections and electronic networks) *resulting in outputs* (graduates, research products) *and outcomes* (increased human welfare, prosperous and peaceful communities) *in a manner that generates private and/or social profits*. It generally looks at who owns the 'business'; who pays for which inputs, including the management that implements production; and other stakeholders, whose interests, including risk-taking, must be promoted and/or protected.

The *supply chain* in higher education further involves inputs such as faculty (issues in teacher training, advanced degrees), students (feeder schools, advanced placement credits, general quality of basic education), support staff (language proficiency, familiarity with global practices and standards), curriculum (philosophy of education, general education, specialist, professions, graduate), infrastructure (financing and risk sharing for construction of school buildings, laboratories, virtual and other physical facilities), research development and application (culture of science and technology, innovation policies, incentive schemes, industry linkages). Education outputs and outcomes are the subject of quality assurance systems.

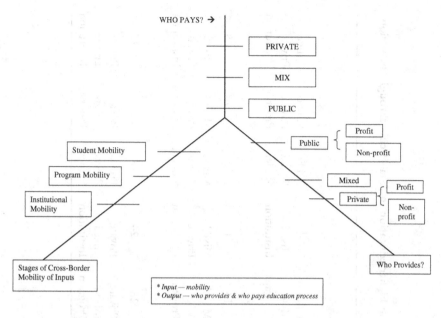

Figure 1. Three dimensions of a business evolution model in cross-border tertiary education

The two major factors in a business model are ownership/management (with correspondent vision/mission) and the source of financing.

As a public good, education is 'owned' by those who benefit from the activities (characterised by joint consumption and non-excludability at various levels of aggregation) and produced by the entity (or entities in the case of cross-border partnerships) that may be publicly or privately 'owned' in the sense of who initiates the concept and is responsible for overseeing the financing of the operations: the latter sense is adopted in the provider portion of Fig. 1 and the accompanying matrix presented in Table 1. Hence, national or local governments, religious authorities, stock or non-stock/for-profit or non-profit corporations, cooperatives, professional groups, chartered groups, etc., can be the initiator(s) that starts the process of gathering the various inputs for the educational entity and of

Table 1.   Provision vs. financing dimensions of business models in higher education in Asia–Pacific through the various stages of cross-border mobility

A: (Models 1–9)

	1	2	3	4	5	6	7	8	9
Provider	Public	Public	Public	Public	Public	Public	Public	Public	Public
Financier	Public	Public	Public	Mixed	Mixed	Mixed	Private	Private	Private
Mobility	Student	Program	Institution	Student	Program	Institution	Student	Program	Institution

B: (Models 10–18)

	10	11	12	13	14	15	16	17	18
Provider	Mixed	Mixed	Mixed	Mixed	Mixed	Mixed	Mixed	Mixed	Mixed
Financier	Public	Public	Public	Mixed	Mixed	Private	Private	Private	Private
Mobility	Student	Program	Institution	Student	Program	Institution	Student	Program	Institution

C: (Models 19–27)

	19	20	21	22	23	24	25	26	27
Provider	Private	Private	Private	Private	Private	Private	Private	Private	Private
Financier	Public	Public	Public	Mixed	Mixed	Mixed	Private	Private	Private
Mobility	Student	Program	Institution	Student	Program	Institution	Student	Program	Institution

operating the organisation directly or indirectly (e.g., outsourcing to a separate management group).[2]

Financing is dependent on the initiator's tax base, official donor sentiments, savings, retained earnings, or other assets for equity especially land, buildings, technology and industry-specific knowledge, and borrowing/fundraising capacity based on statutory provisions or market profitability prospects including target market ability or willingness to pay which is based on incomes or beneficiary user fees such as student tuition.[3]

The third major dimension of this business model is mobility, which globalisation has made more prominent in view of borderless transactions. Technological advances that include e-learning and IT-enabled services such as videoconferencing, and other non-bricks and-mortar institutions of higher learning have made possible truly global public goods out of education services through institutional mobility.

A matrix version of Fig. 1 presented in Table 1 shows 27 combinations of three factors in each of the three dimensions: host and partner providers in cross-border tertiary activities are public or private institutions or a mix of the two; sources of funding are purely public or private or a mix of the two; mobility is through students, faculty, researchers or others, or through programs/courses and institutions/providers.

---

[2] The growing public goods literature is both theoretical and is applied to different sectors and regions. For example, Neubauer (2007) discusses Asian inversions of public/private concepts resulting from different traditions of absolutism, the absence of sovereignty assignment to 'the people' and the inseparability of 'public' from government, the strong tradition of invested government bureaucracies, and the sense that 'the duties, rights and privileges' of the private sector have been delegated from governmental authority.

[3] No national databases compile industry-type information and hence only cross-border macro analyses of broad education indicators have been produced based on statistics collected by international groups such as UNESCO, OECD and the Institute for International Education (IIE). Only the Global Education Index collects information on specific education-related business entities, which is limited to publicly traded corporations in some stock markets. Hence, this study has compiled several dozen arrangements among Asia–Pacific tertiary educational institutions based on desk research, focus group discussions and personal interviews to identify some ownership/management and financing characteristics in cross-border cooperation.

In models 1–9 partners providing cross-border education activities are from the public sector (unilateral, bilateral, multilateral), 10–18 are mixed, and 19–27 are from the private sector (individuals, families, corporate, religious, community-based). Within each of the three, there are three alternative sources of funding (pure public for models 1–3, 10–12, 19–21; mixed for models 4–6, 13–15, 22–24; and pure private for models 7–9, 16–18, 25–27). Finally, for each of the provision–funding combinations, the three mobility types are considered.

The private provision–private financing cell in the matrix (models 25–27) is the current focus in market-oriented models zeroing in on alternative provider/institution and program mobility versus people mobility. However, given the nature of the transition economies in Asia, the public–private (models 7–9, 19–21) and public–public cells (models 1–3) in the matrix are of equal interest. Table 2 illustrates some of the examples across the 27 business models.

1.3 Evolution of Business Models

The prototype business models of Asian–Pacific universities are: (1) the French imperial university system, a centralised state-controlled system of two tiers — the *grandes écoles* to train the bureaucratic, military and technical elite, and the universities, renamed as faculties, educating the non-elite intellectuals (models 1–3); (2) the autonomous research-oriented German universities that trained scholars whose education revolved around seminars (models 1–3 also); (3) the civic society-based modern university in Great Britain, with an essentially private and non-state-interventionist approach (model 22 or 25); and (4) the American system initially built around the British model (models 19, 22, 25).[4]

---

[4] Among others, the mobility trends are reported in Knight (2007). She cites the various generic rationales for mobility from both the national and institutional perspectives, viz., at the country level: human resources development, strategic alliances, income generation, nation building and capacity building, social/cultural development and international understanding, while at the institutional level: research and knowledge production, student and staff development, income generation, international profile and reputation, quality enhancement/international standards, and strategic alliances.

Table 2. Examples of business models integrating provider, financing and mobility dimensions in transnational education

---

A. Models 1–9

Model 1   Australian public universities host Colombo Plan students from South and Southeast Asia's bureaucracy (post-World War II); Greater Mekong Subregion Phnom Penh Plan for Development short training programs funded by ADB and bilateral donors for middle and senior officials from Cambodia, China's western provinces, Laos, Myanmar, Northern Thailand and Vietnam (2003–current)

Model 2   Asian public universities host JICA researchers in program areas of interest to Japanese universities; World Bank Institute short courses for the general public or focus group discussions of communities of practice in development fields offered in public institutions across Asia–Pacific and paid for by local public funds or ODA money, delivered through videoconferencing facilities in the Global Distance Learning Network of the East Asia Pacific Area (2002–current)

Model 3   US state universities set up institutional research facilities funded by USAID in selected Asian countries to train local agriculturists and rural workers (1950s–1980s); International Center for MBA Education of Tianjin University of Finance and Economics set up by Oklahoma City University which awards the degree (originated from an MBA class in 1988) (Huang, 2006)

Model 4   Public universities in the US supported by private foundations, e.g., related to pharmaceutical companies, give teaching/research assistantships to foreign students (Purdue University, high-lysine corn research, 1970s)

Model 5   Public provider, funded by mixed public–private sources, course or program abroad

Model 6   Waseda University offshore degree course offered in collaboration with Nanyang Institute of Technology in Singapore from 2006 (Tsuruta, 2006); Ayala Corporation, with matching national government funds, sets up a technology park at the state-run University of the Philippines, to promote technology transfer including from expatriate scientists (2007)

Model 7   Public university in OECD hosts a private company trainee from a developing Asian country

---

(Continued)

Table 2.   (*Continued*)

Model 8	University of Wisconsin program at the University of the Philippines School of Economics funded by Rockefeller and Ford Foundations for training of government planning officers and potential faculty in various schools (mid-1960s–1970s)
Model 9	Industry association sets up a facility in a public university where foreign students/researchers are invited to team up with local experts

B. Models 10–18

Model 10	Government scholars are sent abroad to study in public or private universities or to tour facilities (US pensionado system for colonial Philippines, Hubert Humphrey fellowships)
Model 11	ODA-funded training or research programs in public or private universities
Model 12	Johns Hopkins–Nanjing University Center for Chinese and American Studies set up in September 1986, financed by both American and Chinese governments (Huang, 2006); Peking University–Yale University Joint Center for Plant Molecular Genetics and Agrobiotechnology in Beijing and Fudan–Yale Biomedical Research Center in Shanghai instigated by close personal relationships among scholars and scientists (Friedman, 2006)
Model 13	US professors lecture as Fulbright–SyCip fellows in public and private universities in the Philippines
Model 14	China–Europe International Business School Executive MBA Program set up in Shanghai in 1995 in cooperation with the EC (Huang, 2006)
Model 15	RMIT opens an offshore campus in rural Penang, Malaysia, (Adorna Institute of Technology) in cooperation with a local property development company in a 'ground-breaking initiative'; it closed down in 1999 as a result of the Asian financial crisis (Sugimoto, 2006). A first in China, University of Nottingham Ningbo, China campus set up in cooperation with Zhejiang Wanli University, which completely owns it (Huang, 2006)
Model 16	Public–private partnership model, private funding, individual
Model 17	PPP, private funding, program/courses
Model 18	PPP, private funding, institutional

(*Continued*)

Table 2. (*Continued*)

C. Models 19–27	
Model 19	Private universities host government scholars from other countries (Fulbright–Hays Program scholars in Ivy League schools)
Model 20	Corporations set up offshore research centres with some funding from local host government
Model 21	Private education service provider, funded publicly, to an individual from another country
Model 22	Private education service provider, funded by mixed public–private money, benefits an individual
Model 23	Private education service provider, funded by mixed source, benefits a program set up abroad
Model 24	Private education service provider, funded by mixed source, for an institution set up abroad
Model 25	Private education service provider, funded privately, for individuals who go abroad
Model 26	Private education service provider, funded by mixed public–private money, for a program abroad
Model 27	Temple University, USA, became the first foreign university in Japan when it was allowed to set up a branch campus through a provision on the recognition of home degree equivalent (Tsuruta, 2006); Microsoft Research Asia set up by Bill Gates in Beijing is allowed to grant postdoctoral degrees to its employees (Friedman, 2006) but loses its star Dr Kai-fu Lee to Google in July 2005 when it also sets up shop in China (Vise and Malseed, 2005)

The colonial experience in Southeast Asia embedded these European university systems there (see Box 1), but present-day cross-border education activities are now more influenced by globalisation forces.

1.4 State-led vs. Market-led Models

Cross-border tertiary education is influenced by the internationalism vs. globalisation strands of thought — i.e., state-led vs. market-led models — shaping various types of cooperation and competition.

Box 1. Colonial legacies

The Philippines is a latecomer in transnational higher education development partly because its higher education experience has been international and because its achievement levels in terms of quantity of professionals produced is relatively high for its level of development (Ong, Cheng and Evans, 1992). However, the content of education and quality issues critical in addressing competitiveness have been questioned over the past two decades as colonial legacies are made obsolete by globalisation.

The oldest university in Asia, the University of Santo Tomas was founded in 1611 by the Dominicans and was directly answerable to the Vatican to which the Spanish crown was obedient. It offered courses to a limited number of non-natives or those born in Europe who were to administer the archipelago and provided training for the religious hierarchy. Colleges and universities founded by various religious orders in major cities emulated this example.

However, by 1887 the curriculum in smaller towns included reading and writing and even the Spanish language which advocates of independence used, but not physics, chemistry, geography or agriculture (Corpuz, 1989).

During the American colonial period, the education system expanded, although it was seen by nationalists as an instrument of colonial policy (Constantino, 1967).

There are positive aspects of colonial legacies. The Philippines is the world's number one exporter of nurses and mariners, thanks in part to the experiences bequeathed by the public education system of colonial America and the practical shipbuilding skills from Spain during 17th century galleon trade. The sizeable English language training for Koreans now being conducted across the Philippines (making Korea the number one source of tourists by 2006) is a positive development in restraining the

(*Continued*)

Box 1. (*Continued*)

migration of highly skilled professionals, including those in the medical professions who train Korean professionals and young college students seeking admission to universities in the US or Europe. Even non-metropolitan cities attract thousands of Koreans, who come as tourists. Many extend their visas, and some eventually settle as small business owners, proving that regional integration can result from informal English education markets (interviews with Iloilo City Mayor Trenas, October 2007, and various officials of the Department of Foreign Affairs, December 2007–January 2008). Lee notes that this phenomenon of Koreans going abroad for short-term language training is a direct offshoot of foreign language ability being a *de facto* requirement by multinational companies in Korea (Lee, 2006, p. 96).

The British colonial policy for education likewise trained the bureaucracy to govern the various regions under its command, using the academic model and standards of the University of London as the bases for colleges and universities they set up in South Asia and the Malay Peninsula. Missionary churches (privately run, non-profit educational institutions) were also allowed in Asia. In principle, church and state were separately governed. But, like many state-founded schools, the religious school introduced new disciplines that eventually linked the segments of society with transnational economic interests, except in the humanities and social sciences where nationalist sentiments during the fight for independence or immediately thereafter spurred indigenisation.

Filipinos migrated in large numbers to the US following migration policy changes from the 1960s. This was assisted by the global integration of higher education and the formation of an international class of labour, which reduced the cultural and social barriers that had impeded such migration. This integration is

(*Continued*)

Box 1. (*Continued*)

most pronounced in the technical fields and, to a lesser extent, in the more quantitative social sciences, because the skills in these disciplines are not restricted by cultural content, and the technical terms they depend on are used transnationally. This internationalisation of professions biases global migration towards the technically and scientifically trained as it overcomes many of the barriers, both cultural and social, between Asia and the West (Ong, Cheng and Evans, 1992).

Industrialised countries such as the US have built an advanced technological base because their large economies foster a diversified labour force that enables specialised research and development and the creation of highly specialised professionals who have access to a high-quality research and development environment that is supported by the state. Countries such as China are now building their own advanced technological base and opening up their educational system (Ong, Cheng and Evans, 1992).

The former is 'aligned with the spirit and agenda of neo-colonial and traditional geo-political dynamics typical of the old world order' while the latter is defined by the 'emerging agenda of global competitiveness, mass culture, and high technology' (Bernardo, 2003, p. 223).

The business models under the internationalism strand (models 1–9 if based on the business model dimension of provision, and models 1–3, 10–12, 19–21 if based on the financing dimension) enhance the international character or quality of students, programs and institutions for related educational or general development goals. In contrast, the second cluster — open market transnational education (models 19–27 if based on provision, and models 7–9, 16–18, 25–27 if based on the financing dimension) — anchored on opportunities afforded by increasing economic globalisation (Bernardo, 2003, pp. 223–233). The ethical basis for the former is a communitarian approach to economic relations while the latter is a utilitarian model. At the extremes, the education 'aid to trade' shift is seen in models 1–3 (provider and financier both public) moving to models 25–27 (provider and financier both private).

In the evolution of business models, it is instructive to study the differences between market-rational vs. plan-rational states because they shed light on factors that promote or impede education partnership across borders that promote the competitiveness of nations.

1.5 International Competitiveness

A more recent trend affecting transnational higher education started in the market-dominated 1990s even among transition economies in Southeast Asia — the growing recognition of how firms and nations compete and how human resources and innovation variables, among others, influence the allocation of investment funds across countries.[5]

Where general education indicators are weak, and where economic performance indicators are relatively low, 'aid'-type business models of cooperation (models 1–3) may be suitable for boosting competitiveness, e.g., the 2006–08 Aid for Trade projects of CIDA for APEC EIP in education institutions in Indonesia, Lao PDR, the Philippines, Thailand, Vietnam, and the Colombo Plan-type intervention of the ADB Phnom Penh Plan Program in the Greater Mekong Subregion. Here the internationalism business model is dominated by public funding from abroad for programs but provision is through a local facility that makes use of a mix of local and foreign trainers. Where innovation indicators and knowledge transfer variables are weak, the appropriate models may be public–private partnerships (models 10–18), but where they are relatively strong they may be pure private types (models 19–27).

---

[5] The three most important works on these are the Institute of Management Development's (IMD) *World Competitiveness Yearbook* for 55 countries, the World Economic Forum's *World Competitiveness Report* for 125 economies, and International Finance Corporation's *Doing Business* series for 178 economies.

The plan-rational state operates economic enterprises, including educational institutions, to promote its competitiveness. On the other hand, the market-rational state rarely has an industrial policy. Domestic and foreign policy will stress reciprocal concessions and rules, and foreign policy, which subordinates trade policy, will be used to reinforce political relationships rather than to gain economic advantages (Chalmers, 1982).[6]

The observations on rules and reciprocal concessions are relevant to the negotiations on the four GATS modalities, other market-oriented models (models 19–27) and some of the mixed public–private models where formal partnerships have been effected in the name of international competitiveness (models 10–18).

The international competitiveness of nations is being worked out in the context of global division of labour as multinational investors exploit worldwide supply chains to achieve targets, e.g., profits or market share (models 7–9, 16–18, 25–27 where financing is private), especially model 27 where corporations set up knowledge-creating activities or institutions for their own use or for suppliers and business partners.

The trend over the past 20 years has been towards models that relate to the emerging global environment of open markets (shift from models 1–9 and 10–18 to 19–27) in what were models based on internationalism, e.g., student mobility, faculty exchange and development, research collaboration, internationalisation of curricula, and international networks of higher education institutes (especially in models 1–9) (Bernardo, 2003). These models are now based on distance education (cross-border or locally supported), twinning programs, articulation programs, branch campuses, franchising arrangements, or quality assurance and standards in internationalising curricula. New issues include offshore operations as an indicator of a host country provider's loss of credibility as its overseas programs and campuses reportedly accept inferior students, e.g., Australian institutions in Singapore, Malaysia and Hong Kong, or as qualified faculty are

---

[6] Curiously, in *Globalization and Quality in Higher Education*, Singh (2002) views the planned regulatory framework for the import of higher education to Malaysia as similar to the more free-market-oriented Hong Kong.

stretched thin in cross-country travel and mentoring. These are general concerns as business models shift from student mobility to program and provider mobility (Sugimoto, 2006).

The various forms of transnational education mobility based on models for capacity building in new economies respond to the needs of 1.5 billion additional workers who entered the global labour force from once-closed countries such as China, India and the USSR. These workers have been denied opportunities to fulfil their potential but are trainable in the new processes and technologies (Friedman, 2006) that are now effected through business models that directly cater to the needs of the invisible market of poor people such as through university partnerships with industry (Posadas, 2007).

2 ISSUES ARISING FROM VARIOUS MODELS

2.1 Public Provision and Funding: Corporatisation and Privatisation

The shift from models 1–9 to models 19–27 represents privatisation that includes increased private provision of domestic or cross-border education or private sector buy-out of public institutions. These should be contrasted with the shift from models 1–3 to models 4–9, representing more autonomy for public universities that are being corporatised (Adireksarn, 2003).

---

[7] Data are for 2003, with the total education expenditure shares second only to Iceland. The authors also describe the stages of Korea's educational development, which embrace (1) a government-initiated approach, first in 1948–60 as a national infrastructure was being set up with foreign assistance, and next in 1960–80 as traditional higher education was strengthened with private resource mobilisation, followed by (2) a partial market approach although still government-led in 1980–2000, enhancing lifelong learning through the creation of a diversity of higher education institutions, the development of highly skilled human resources in national strategic fields such as IT and biotech, and the introduction of a credit bank system (long-term loans with low interest to private schools at all levels), and further to (3) a government–market coordinated period from 2000 focusing on human resources innovation, quality and productivity, relevance and regional dispersal (New University for Regional Innovation in 2004), and through government restructuring and infusion of support through Brain Korea 21 (pp. 107–133).

There appears to be more corporatisation in Asia–Pacific than privatisation as most countries prefer a mix of public and private institutions. Even the US envisages that private education will supplement rather than displace public education systems, and New Zealand recognises that a reduction in education trade barriers 'will not erode core public education systems and standards' (Larsen, Martin and Morris, 2002). Where there is a history of a more dominant public presence, corporatisation is the preferred response for easier regulation or continued pursuit of internationalism objectives by the older states while the route of instituting more private universities is the choice in developing economies to meet the surging demand as well as to spur competition.

The recent corporatisation trend in public tertiary education in Asia–Pacific, which makes it easier to partner with foreign education providers, started with the national budgetary squeezes in the latter part of the 1990s that forced many public universities to become autonomous. The classic case is Indonesia after the Asian financial crisis of 1997. In July 1999, the government invited the four most established universities to submit plans for autonomy. Changes in regulations allowed these universities to exist as separate legal entities yet not be privatised and hence remain eligible for block grants. In 2000, the four universities were given a five-year transition to allow them to transfer non-land assets and personnel and set up new budgeting and control systems (Brodjonegoro, 2003).

Even a transition economy such as Cambodia has re-created its public higher education institutions (HEI) as more autonomous public administration institutions (PAI) after allowing the charging of fees in 1997. Three publicly funded universities now have PAI status and can go beyond traditional academic partnerships and cooperation schemes with foreign partners (Chet, 2006).

Privatisation and corporatisation will have different impacts across Asia–Pacific education systems and economies depending on how the program mobility (models $2 + 3j, j = 0, \ldots 8$ in Table 2) and the institutional mobility models (models $3k, k = 1, \ldots 9$) are executed. While Asia and the Pacific have the world's most active transnational higher education, the various models became common in the region only in the 1990s (see Table 3).

Table 3. Select market opening in transnational higher education in Asia–Pacific

Country	Year	Law/Registration
A. Southeast Asia		
1) Cambodia	1997	Government policy re private participation in economic development leads to more private higher education institutions.
	2003	Royal Decree No NS/RKT 03/03/129, establishing the Accreditation Council of Cambodia (ACC), makes it mandatory for all local and foreign HEIs in Cambodia to obtain accreditation status from ACC to confer degrees.
	2004	Rectangular Strategy #4 focuses on capacity building and human resource development with a clear role for higher education services.
2) Indonesia	2003	National Education System Act #20 stipulates that only an accredited foreign university can offer a program (including distance education) in collaboration with a local university.
	2005	Ministry of Trade regulations for foreign universities limits their presence to Medan, Jakarta, Bandung, Bogor and Yogyakarta; requires them to collaborate with local institutions, invest in infrastructure and involve local staff in their operation; and forces them to comply with National Standards and Regulations, including a mutual recognition agreement.
3) Laos	1995	Prime Minister's Decree on Private Education promotes investment in education and establishes a regulatory framework within the context of the national education system for the operation of private schools.
4) Malaysia		Government regulation allows local public HEIs to recruit international academic staff and to allocate places in the non-competitive undergraduate academic programs to international students.
		Legislation creates the Committee of Competitiveness and Marketing of Higher Education and encourages local HEIs of world-class standards to establish

(Continued)

Table 3. (*Continued*)

Country	Year	Law/Registration
		branch campuses overseas (three have done this — INTI College, Informatics and APIIT). Malaysian Qualifications Framework (MQF) allows universities to establish MRAs with other countries under GATS.
	1996	Private Higher Educational Institutions Act (amended 2003) re the establishment and upgrading of private universities and university colleges encourages foreign universities to set up branch campuses in Malaysia. Government regulation restricts the proportion of international students to a maximum of 5 per cent of total student population per public university.
5) Philippines	2001	CHED Memo #32 grants autonomous status to private HEIs including the privilege to establish branches or satellite campuses without prior CHED approval; this permits extension classes and distance education courses and programs to expand access to higher education and to establish affiliation with recognised foreign HEIs.
6) Singapore	1985/ 1991	Act provides for more stringent entry requirements for foreign students, requiring them to sign a bond to live and work in Singapore for at least three years after graduation. Policy of Internationalization as outlined in the Strategic Economic Plan provides for developing Singapore into an international centre of learning.
	2002	Ministry of Education allows programs of bona fide overseas universities to be subject to market forces.
	2003	Government program 'Global Schoolhouse' increases intake of international students, which will grow to 20 per cent of undergraduate enrolment.
7) Thailand	1999	National Education Act B.E. 2542 (as amended by B.E. 2545–2003 Private Higher Education Act) stipulates all reform programs on education in Thailand.

(*Continued*)

Table 3. (*Continued*)

Country	Year	Law/Registration
	2005	Thailand–Australia Free Trade Agreement (TAFTA) specifies that HEIs operated by Australia in Thailand must specialise in science and technology (covering life sciences, biotechnology, nanotechnology) and be situated outside Bangkok and metropolitan areas; half of the members of the University Council must be Thais; restricts equity participation for Australia to 60 per cent; and specifies that Thai secondary and higher education can operate in Australia in all modes of supply except commercial presence.
8) Vietnam	1994	The Ministry of Education and Training (MOET) allows the establishment of centres for distance learning in HEIs*.
	2000	Decree #06/2000/ND-CP provides incentives for foreign investment in several areas, including education and training, which leads to the establishment of the first university with 100 per cent foreign investment — the Royal Melbourne Institute of Technology (RMIT)–International University Vietnam with three campuses (Ho Chi Minh City, 2001; Hanoi, 2005; and South Saigon).
B. Australia and the Near East		
1) Australia	1979	Government introduces visa fee (Overseas Student Charge), charging private overseas students a part of their university costs; new Overseas Student Policy (1985) opens the higher education market to full-fee paying overseas students.
	After 1990	Government policy stops subsidising overseas students, forcing many universities to become more entrepreneurial.

(*Continued*)

*Nine universities and colleges in Vietnam conduct distance learning programs: Hue University, Da Nang University, VNU-HCM, Hanoi Pedagogic University, Hanoi University of Technology, Dalat University, Ho Chi Minh Open University, VNU-H's College of Foreign Languages and Binhduong People-Founded College.

Table 3.   (*Continued*)

Country	Year	Law/Registration
	2000	Education Services for Overseas Students Act (ESOS) regulates the provision of education services to international students.
	2000	The Australian Universities Quality Agency (AUQA) establishes a non-profit company to conduct institutional audits of offshore campuses.
2) China	1995	The Contemporary Regulation on Operation of Higher Education Institutions in Cooperation with Foreign Partners pushes the expansion of transnational education by encouraging foreign institutions to operate in China.
	1998	The Interim Provisions for Chinese Foreign Cooperation in Running Schools issued by the State Education Commission (renamed the Ministry of Education) requires cooperation with or involvement of foreign institutions with Chinese institutions located in China to provide transnational education and that the number of local Chinese members of the Board or any governing body of the offshore institution to be at least half of the total, with the presidency held by a Chinese citizen living in China.
	2003	State Council regulations on Chinese–Foreign Cooperation in Running Schools (i) affirms the Ministry of Education provisions re Chinese members of the Board of Trustees and nationality of the president or the principal administrator; (ii) encourages transnational programs in higher education, in cooperation with renowned foreign institutions, to improve quality and to introduce quality foreign educational resources, and no longer restricts profit-making activities; (iii) the introduction of foreign higher education services and joint degree programs results in an increase in foreign degree programs in Chinese campuses, mostly in Beijing and Shanghai universities, with a focus on graduate education.

(*Continued*)

Table 3. (*Continued*)

Country	Year	Law/Registration
3) South Korea		Ministry of Education regulations allow joint programs and curricula with foreign institutions in the fields of basic science, high technology, international studies and specialised fields, with foreign teachers taking responsibility for half of the total number of classes. Two-thirds of the members of the Board of an educational institution must be Korean, except when the contribution of a foreign national or institution goes beyond half of the total appropriations. However, there is a restriction in the institution's enrolment capacity, specifically for graduate schools and institutions that train teachers and doctors, and on the location of new institutions (which must be outside Seoul and its suburbs). This latter regulation was relaxed in 2007 in order to attract foreign HEIs to set up campuses in South Korea.
4) Japan		Japan's ministerial ordinances allow the establishment of offshore degree programs that can be recognised under the Japanese educational system (MEXT). Educational reforms in Japan include the incorporation of national universities and increasingly competitive funding mechanisms. MEXT has also relaxed the regulations concerning the provision of education through e-learning and offshore branch campuses.
	2001	E-learning through the Internet is recognised, including offshore off-campus (distance) education.
	2004	MEXT regulations strictly follow the territorial principle for offshore on-campus education, which means that a foreign university's branch campus cannot be recognised as an HEI in Japan unless the institution meets the standards under the Japanese chartering system. The education provision of foreign institutions

(*Continued*)

Table 3. (*Continued*)

Country	Year	Law/Registration
		not recognised as HEIs in Japan (while validated by their home institutions) is not treated as being equivalent to that of their home institutions. Similarly, Japanese institutions providing educational services outside Japan (including those with locally validated degree courses) are not recognised within the Japanese educational framework, particularly entire offshore degree programs run by Japanese universities.
	Late 2004	Ministerial ordinances revised effective December 2004 for foreign institutions and April 2005 for Japanese institutions, to enable a Japanese university to establish its school, department or other organisation outside Japan to provide a whole or part of an educational program leading to a degree. Branch campuses of foreign institutions in Japan can confer degrees or credits equivalent to their home institutions under certain conditions (their establishment as a branch campus and their educational programs must be authorised as part of their home institutions in their original countries, their degrees/credits must be equivalent to those of their home institutions and they must be recognised in Japan as educational institutions with courses of foreign universities, validated under the school education system and/or by bona fide licensing/accrediting bodies of their original countries).
	2006	New IT Reform Strategy provides the development of training programs and teaching materials at universities in collaboration with the government and industry as well as distance education using ICT (such as the Internet) by 2010.
5) Hong Kong	1996	Non-Local Higher and Professional Education Ordinance, legislated in 1996 but not coming into force until December 1997, provides for a code of practice for non-local courses, requiring

(*Continued*)

Table 3.   (*Continued*)

Country	Year	Law/Registration
		any overseas institution to gain accreditation or other formal permission from the Education and Manpower Bureau before commencing operations. All exported courses conducted in Hong Kong, leading to the award of non-local higher academic qualifications (sub-degree, degree, postgraduate or other post-secondary qualifications) or professional qualifications must be properly registered or be exempted from registration. There is no direct regulation in terms of quality of transnational HE, which is left to market forces. Purely distance learning courses conducted through mail and the media are exempted from registration, although the operators are encouraged to apply for registration to show that they fulfil the registration criteria.
6) Taiwan	2002	Government issues the 'Initiative to Promote International Competitiveness in Colleges and Universities' wherein a large amount of funds is allocated to encourage colleges and universities to engage in activities advancing international academic linkages/exchanges, to set up twinning programs and seek international accreditation in various professions.
		The Procedural Rules Governing Distance Learning at Junior Colleges and Higher Levels stipulate that credits earned via distance learning can only apply to a maximum of one-third of the total credits required for graduation.
		Foreign organisations are allowed to set up educational institutions in Taiwan based on local laws and regulations governing private schools and colleges. Requirements for colleges and universities to obtain recognition by the Ministry of Education are specified in the Standards for the Establishment of Private Schools of all Kinds and Levels.

(*Continued*)

Table 3. (*Continued*)

Country	Year	Law/Registration
	1974	The Private School Law provides that both the chairman of the board and the principal or president of a private university must be Taiwan nationals. However, the nationality clause for the university president position has been amended recently. Foreigners are not allowed to set up schools or colleges to educate their nationals within Taiwanese territory.
	2004	The Taiwan Scholarship program offers a monthly stipend of up to NT$30,000 to each qualified foreign student pursuing studies at a university or college in Taiwan. Foreign students are also allowed to stay and work in Taiwan after graduation. Taiwan has a 'five-no's' policy when it comes to programs in mainland China — no faculty recruited outside the Taiwan territory; no non-Taiwanese students; no expenditures introduced from Taiwan; no curriculum advocating Taiwan–China reunification or communist ideology; no pressure from China to add or delete any part of the curriculum for ideological reasons.

China allowed foreign partners into its higher education institutions in 1995 and by 2002 had 657 cross-border joint programs. Malaysia relaxed its 1969 regulation barring foreign universities to set up branch campuses in 1996 and by 1997 had 497 transnational programs in 122 private institutions. In 1996, Australia implemented a three-year reduction in higher education funding with the result that many universities sought further foreign students and the establishment of offshore programs, which by 2003 numbered 1569, mainly in China, Malaysia and Singapore (Huang, 2006).

With its opening to the West, the two-way flow of academics and students, especially the UK, US, Germany and France, helped to modernise Japan. Beyond student mobility (models $1 + 3i$, $i = 0, \ldots 8$), however, internationalisation or *kokusaika* became part of post-war Japan's major reforms and now includes recognition of overseas bases and branch campuses under its education system (see model 6 in Table 2), as well as recognition of degrees or credits offered by branch campuses of foreign institutions in Japan as equivalent to those offered by home universities (model 27).

A rare exception to market opening in education is the Philippines, where constitutional provisions prohibit foreign ownership of educational institutions beyond minority shares and place caps on foreign student population in each educational institution. Similar to Indonesia, though, it has foreign providers who are able to skirt domestic laws and have a domestic presence.[8]

The Australian experience with raising funds from private fees demonstrates how business models evolve with policy shifts. Australia started its internationalisation policy in the form of development assistance exemplified by the Colombo Plan, launched in July 1951 to train overseas students mainly from South and Southeast Asia. This passed some costs onto private overseas students in the form of a visa fee and later an overseas student charge (model 1 in Table 2). A policy change in 1985 made education a revenue-generating exportable commodity with the acceptance of full-fee paying foreign students, in effect shifting from 'educational aid' to 'educational trade' (model 7). Nine of the top 10 providers of overseas students to Australia in 2004 were from Asia, with the region accounting for 82 per cent of international students (Sugimoto, 2006).

Like privatisation, corporatisation may shake up the whole education structure. Since the landmark decision in 2004 to make Japanese national universities more autonomous by freeing them from government administration, their numbers have decreased through mergers,

---

[8] Restrictions have been relaxed in certain cases via presidential fiat, e.g., Asian Institute of Management in Makati, Metro Manila, where more than the allowed one-third of degree students are from outside the Philippines. A study on liberalising Philippine education services was conducted for the Philippine Services Coalition in preparation for GATS negotiation (Macaranas, 2004).

but at the same time local public and private universities have increased — including for-profit companies in special deregulated business zones (moving away from models 3 and 6 to model 27) (Tsuruta, 2006). Korea has a similar policy of attracting world-class educational institutions to locate in its Free Economic Zones irrespective of its GATS stand, although it reverted to a less liberal attitude in September 2005 (Lee, 2006).

The dangers of fee-driven institutions under both privatisation and corporatisation models arise from inequities across economic class, geography, disciplines and quality, but can be minimised with public–private partnership models (models 10–18) (Hawkins and Ordonez, 2007). Even the largest fee-based private universities in the Philippines (already infused with Filipino–Chinese Taipan funds) have to 'partner' with government regulatory agencies concerning tuition fee increases. This is true only if regulation is viewed as a partnership as in the co-opetition model, rather than seeing this sovereign act as one that restricts competition (Brandenburger and Nalebuff, 1996).[9]

Foreign education institutions preference to partner in either or both provision and financing with public vs. private institutions is important because institutions may set up greenfield operations, i.e., independent of any partner, when locating in economic processing or free trade zones where domestic regulations do not impede educational institutions from bringing in their own programs, faculty, etc.

2.2 Program and Institutional Mobility

Different program and institutional cross-border tie-ups exist in terms of the provider-financing mix across models 1–27. How, rather

---

[9] The authors stress the capture of value by a firm in any economic activity from its cooperative relationships with not only its suppliers and complementors — regulators, in the case of education institutions — but also competitors and customers. Business model changes can be thought of as responses to changes in the players, added values, rules, tactics, and scope in the game of maximising value creation.

than why, they ally with transnational providers will now be explained.

Public providers in host countries can partner with private, public or mixed institutions from abroad. However, differences in national vision shape policies towards transnational higher education. China's policy, introduced in 1995, requires foreign institutions to cooperate with domestic institutions in any transnational education and 'shall not seek profits as the objective' (Huang, 2006, pp. 23–24, quoting SEC, 1995). This reflects the primacy of social over economic objectives as China adjusts to its market socialist economy, although since 2003 the profit-making objective has been relaxed for overseas institutions of higher learning running courses in China (Yang, 2007). In contrast, Hong Kong's free-market policy merely insists that domestic and transnational education providers supply consumers with sufficient information to enable them to make informed choices (Yang, 2006).

Japan's 2004 neoliberal reforms transforming national universities into independent administrative corporations allows for more diverse, flexible and global academic activities, a response to the post-bubble economy that led to economic stagnation in the 1990s.[10] The higher education supply was expected to have matched the ageing population's demand by 2007, but even by 2005, the shortage of new entrant students had been felt in private universities (160 out of 542 institutions) as well as in junior colleges (158 out of 383 institutions), hence the need to attract quality foreign students.[11] However, revenue purposes are not driving Japan to further attract foreign students. Its internationalism heritage in transnational higher education is reflected in official development assistance programs, especially in the Greater Mekong Subregion (models 1, 2, 10, 11 in Table 2) (Tsuruta, 2006; Lee, 2006).

---

[10] Elsewhere, differing levels of autonomy alter prospective partner perceptions of their joint ability to create value in any business model.

[11] Korea's current oversupply situation, which began in 2002 and is in part the result of a professed shift to a technology-driven knowledge economy, is also felt in both national/public as well as private universities.

Private providers in host countries can also forge links with foreign partners that are private, public or mixed. However, the set of issues may be no different from those of public providers although they typically start from a management perspective that is radically different from public institutions dependent in part on government funding.

Hence, while there is more autonomy in Australia, there is more expensive (especially staff time) regulation, reporting and review because most universities are public institutions established by state governments, with the federal government providing the majority of funding. While local governments provide no funding, they can constrain facilities expansion for cross-border programs through planning delays (Loxton, 2003).

It is evident that no joint venture will be undertaken by partners unless there are mutual benefits. Supply-side advantages may include design, pre-testing, implementation, evaluation and monitoring for quality assurance of curriculum; learning materials; faculty; administrative support, especially in e-learning environments; facilities; and land for further expansion. On the demand side is the recruitment of students and the final users of knowledge in the firms benefiting from the training.

Typically, a local host has the facilities and the land while the foreign partner has the curriculum, learning materials and faculty. Risk sharing is thus shaped by these initial input endowments.

Alternative infrastructure construction business models now enrich the options of transnational education partners, allowing them to pass on various risks to subcontractors, financing institutions and donors for specific programs with a variety of private participation schemes. These can be done through arrangements such as the traditional design-and-build option; operate and maintain; a turnkey operation; lease–purchase; lease or own–develop–operate; build–operate–transfer; or build–own–operate. Such private participation in education inputs extends to outsourcing techniques in the management of institutions where owners do not have to worry about the day-to-day operations of programs or institutions through various education contracts, e.g., contracts dealing with inputs, processes, outputs, or input/output bundle (Patrinos and Sosale, 2007).

Examples of such outsourcing are public–private partnerships and other affiliation/network-type arrangements that are becoming more prominent in the Asia–Pacific (models 10–18 in Table 2). The World Bank Institute (WBI) partners with both public and private higher education institutions in delivering short-term courses in the region that used to be delivered only in Washington DC, and has convinced Japan to establish its own Tokyo Distance Learning Center to complement the satellite-based videoconferencing system housed in its US headquarters. Here the business model consists of cosharing infrastructure costs with the WBI and local partner universities (which are expected to be independent in the long term from WB funding). Eventually courses are to be either fee-paying through private individuals or firms and/or funded by other bilateral/multilateral donors. The value creation premise is that Asia–Pacific developing countries need to have a cost-effective delivery mechanism for courses on a shared and timely basis.

2.3 Mutual Benefits from Partnerships: 'Make or Buy' Decisions

The decision-making framework for a local institution to partner with a foreign provider can be adapted from the classic 'make or buy' business model. Here, the 'buy' decision is to purchase a franchise, attract a branch campus from abroad, or partner a foreign provider/funder in a program or institutional mode, rather than to 'make' or provide the course or degree itself.

The local institution's decision-maker must assess whether the outside market gives an alternative to vertically integrating within the existing set-up, e.g., funding internal expansion with new or updated curriculum, retooled faculty, new facilities and learning materials, sometimes called organic growth. Outside market opportunities may be more beneficial or cost-effective if:

- There are economies of scale that cannot be achieved internally.
- Foreign providers have better execution abilities than in-house providers owing to hurdled learning curves, better/more resources

and so on. These outside market opportunities range from purchase of course materials, faculty and administrative support systems in franchising models, as in model 17 in Table 2, to the increasingly popular twinning and articulation programs of the variety of +1 or +2 years abroad with variants of joint degree offerings now common reflected in models $2 + 3i$ ($i = 1, ... 8$) variants, e.g., models 5, 8, 11, ... 26 (Besanko *et al.*, 2007).

If the outside market does not give the decision-maker an alternative, the local institution will have to do the work, or support a quasi-independent supplier through a joint venture (+1, +2 variants in all models of program mobility) or strategic alliance (such as franchising or setting up a branch campus). If the outside market offers alternatives to organic growth, the local institution decision-maker must determine whether the market relationships will be impeded by information, coordination or 'hold-up' problems.

In the absence of such problems, the local institution should partner with the foreign provider. However, if they are present, the local decision-maker must determine if these problems can be prevented through a well-written contract with the foreign provider or through organic growth.

Southeast Asian countries that are relatively late in providing higher education for their population because of competitiveness and national development purposes include Malaysia, Thailand and Indonesia. These countries are likely to benefit from purely 'buy' business models from the leading suppliers such as the US, Australia and the UK who 'make' programs, while NIEs such as Singapore, Hong Kong, Taiwan and Korea are in better positions to adopt joint alliances models in between the purely 'buy' or 'make'. This model is sometimes referred to as tapered integration, i.e., between vertical integration and market exchange.

2.4 Supply Chain and Value Chain: Primacy of Quality Outputs/Outcomes

Input-based decision-making is only part of the partnership strategy formulation. The new challenge to universities is centred on output- and outcome-based education as quality issues become the focus of policy-making even with regards to cross-border activities. Such outcome-based education forces the issue of value creation in any business model where total benefits are derived for both the producer (producer surplus on top of profits) and the consumer (with a consumer surplus in addition to welfare/utility from payments made) (Hawkins and Neubauer, 2007, citing Sanyal and Martin).

The Porter value chain model is a useful tool for understanding where partners (including consumers and producers) can mutually benefit. It starts from inbound logistics, then moves to production/operation, outbound logistics, marketing and sales, and finally after-sales service. Each of these value-creating primary activities requires firm-level support such as finance and accounting, human resources management, technology development, and procurement. In the global market economy, local partners may find it more difficult to move as they progress through the value chain without the assistance of foreign institutions. Of course, partners need to identify where they have comparative advantage along the value chain to maximise their contribution in any joint venture.

As countries learn from partnerships, the inevitable question is what part of the value chain will migrate from the originator country. This forces continuous strategising in blue rather than red oceans bloodied by competition in old products, and hence the focus on lifelong learning for every participant in transnational education partnerships.

However, partnership for moving through the value chain more efficiently may be valid only for countries that envision themselves to be global knowledge hubs. Few Asia–Pacific economies profess to educate primarily for outside markets (Australia, Japan and Singapore plan to remain net exporters, while Malaysia and Singapore, although net importers from Australia and the UK, are positioning themselves to be on the positive side of the trade ledger with their ventures in Thailand and Vietnam) (see Table 4 for program and provider mobility in Southeast Asia, Australia and the Near East).

A major policy issue for countries that are unable to absorb graduates domestically (e.g., 85 per cent of Filipino nurses work abroad; slow-growing regions in the Philippines also push engineers to work internationally) relates to education liberalisation primarily to

Table 4.   Program and provider mobility in higher education, 2006

	Cambodia	Malaysia	Laos	Philippines	Indonesia	Singapore	Thailand	Vietnam
A. Southeast Asia								
Program Mobility								
a) Franchise		✓		✓				
b) Twinning		✓		✓		✓	✓	✓
c) Double/Joint degree	✓	✓	✓	✓	✓	✓	✓	✓
d) Articulation	✓	✓		✓		✓	✓	✓
e) Validation (accreditation)	✓	✓		✓	✓	✓	✓	
f) E-learning/Distance education	✓	✓		✓				✓
Institutional Mobility								
a) Branch campus	✓	✓		✓		✓	✓	
b) Independent institution		✓				✓		
c) Acquisition/merger								
d) Study centre/Teaching site	✓	✓	✓	✓	✓	✓	✓	✓
e) Affiliation network								

(Continued)

Table 4. (*Continued*)

	Australia	South Korea	Taiwan	China	Japan	Hong Kong
B. Australia and the Near East						
Program Mobility						
a) Franchise					✓	
b) Twinning	✓		✓		✓	✓
c) Double/Joint degree	✓			✓	✓	
d) Articulation		✓			✓	
e) Validation (accreditation)				✓	✓	✓
f) E-learning/Distance education	✓	✓	✓			✓
Institutional Mobility						
a) Branch campus	✓			✓	✓	✓
b) Independent institution	✓					✓
c) Acquisition/merger						
d) Study centre/Teaching site	✓	✓				
e) Affiliation network	✓			✓	✓	✓

Source: UNESCO SEAMEO, *Higher Education in Southeast Asia*, 2006.

complement domestic resources for graduates to compete more effectively in global markets. A second policy issue concerns the brain flow when such countries are desperate to retain high-level manpower that is increasingly attracted by advanced nations through selective migration policies (Maskus, Mobarak and Stuen, 2007).

2.5 Independent Private Initiatives

2.5.1 *Education-related publicly traded stocks*

Companies traded on the stock exchange broadly interested in postsecondary education include firms operating for-profit universities (model 26), companies that run multicampus colleges internationally (models 24 and 27), IT training companies in higher education (model 27), e-learning and related firms (model 26) and multinational publishing houses (model 27).

The Observatory on Borderless Higher Education (2003) created a Global Education Index from 50 such companies. Share prices were tracked from January 1993 based on a 10-year perspective covering the e-education bubble of early 1997 to early 2000 as part of the dotcom bubble. An initial study compared the stock prices and financial results of the firms with those of two broad stock market indices (Dow Jones Industrial Average (DJIA) and Standard & Poor's 500) and found that bricks and-mortar education firms operating physical campuses made significant progress following the dot-com crash as did the three publishing giants in the GEI. Conversely, e-learning firms languished at half their original value by 2003 because of excessively high valuations for initial public offerings during the dot-com boom, a fate met by IT software and consultancy firms as well as IT training companies in the GEI.

If these globalisation-induced education industry financial products are to be traded in open markets, the underlying goods and services and financial consumer sentiments will shape future products, i.e., secondary market issues such as derivatives and other cocktails of financial instruments from which further capital can be generated, thus adding a new risk dimension to the operations of transnational higher education. Whether governments will be willing to rescue educational institutions the way the housing industry and the general financial industry have been bailed out remains an open question. Lim (2007) notes that the classic strategy of leverage and mismatched funding to maximise yields characterises both the current subprime debacle and the savings and loan association problem 20 years ago, but the new element is the securitisation and distribution model that has dispersed and broadened financial risk.

2.5.2 *Corporate and research universities*

The same decision/issue tree can be used to understand the business models where the new providers of knowledge 'make' rather than 'buy' education goods and services from the outside market. In this instance, however, the reason for in-house provision may be due to significant coordination problems and possible leakage of information. Two of Microsoft's four research centres are in Asia (Beijing and Bangalore) and were set up to solve relationship-specific coordination problems. The Chinese government gave Microsoft Research Asia the right to grant postdoctoral degrees to stringently screened Chinese workers who show excellent capabilities within two-year contracts (Friedman, 2006).

Other examples of these are the in-house training programs of corporate universities that reorient stakeholders to knowledge-intensive innovation strategies and retool technical and administrative support staff for adoption of global standards wherever they operate (Macaranas, 2007).[12]

Coordination of firm-specific on-the-job requirements with curriculum offered by traditional colleges and universities is becoming more difficult in the fast-changing global environment of business and technology. While advisory boards and curriculum development committees with members drawn from the business sector have been

---

[12] The TI partnership enabled the firm to win the Philippine Quality Award, the equivalent of the Malcolm Baldrige Award for overall excellence.

set up in some universities, the technology transfer and application of concepts are conditioned by many factors best served by in-house training. Hence, the popularity of corporate universities.

By acting as educational entities assisting the parent organization achieve its goals through cultivating both individual and organizational learning and knowledge, corporate universities have a growing presence in Asia–Pacific. However, they remain unable to replace traditional colleges and universities, most of whom partner with them (Allen, 2002). Partnership for research is different from partnership for training, which is more common in corporate universities because of investment decisions based on different reasons. Strategic decisions in untradeable or hard-to-market physical assets, resources and capabilities call for a sequential analysis of commitment-intensive choices in the case of partnership for research (Besanko *et al.*, 2007).

IBM's Services Sciences, Management and Engineering approach to innovation for productivity and quality improvement addresses such sequential analysis of choices in partnership, as the services component of GDP has overtaken agriculture and industry percentage shares in most Asia–Pacific economies. IBM is initially partnering with key universities in China and Thailand in the development of this new field of education, believing that 'without dramatic change, it is unlikely that institutions of higher learning will keep pace with the dynamic nature of work' (Braim, 2007, p. 3).

The corporate partnership with higher education has proved successful in the major research universities in Asia–Pacific, particularly for global production networks in the electronics, biotechnology, automotive and logistics industries, while public research institutes have complemented university-based research (Yusuf, Altaf and Nabeshima, 2004; Posadas, 2007).[13] Business model issues include

---

[13] Such infrastructure and institutions are only part of the larger policy framework for global competitiveness. Also vital are openness to foreign direct investment, human capital that absorbs, assimilates and diffuses imported technology, competition-based industrial policies vs. Schumpeterian-type monopolies, and mobility of workers domestically and from overseas especially among expatriate nationals (Yusuf, Altaf and Nabeshima, 2004, pp. 356–7).

niche market needs rather than broad cross-border education partnerships (Yusuf, Altaf and Nabeshima, 2004), and vertical vs. horizontal value chain creation, which represent economies of scope versus scale in both education/research and technology commercialisation.

Knowledge creation/transmission/preservation outside the traditional university has been greatly assisted by the convergence of the 10 flatteners of the new world, especially the combination of the PC, the microprocessor, the Internet and fibre optics — resulting in a shift from a vertical to a more horizontal chain of command for value creation, as typified by innovations in companies such as Hewlett Packard, where different teams collaborate even with competitor firms (Friedman, 2006).[14]

2.5.3 *GATS issues and business models*

GATS modalities seem to be neither necessary nor sufficient to explain the growth of various business models in transnational higher education, GATS itself being the result of earlier global trends. These include the persistence of the four non-mutually exclusive approaches to cross-border higher education — mutual understanding or the internationalism strand, skilled migration, revenue generation, and capacity building (OECD, 2004).[15]

Moreover, the four GATS modalities are not mutually exclusive, and hence any business model must integrate relevant modalities for cross-border arrangements. For example, online learning (Mode 1) may have to start with some commercial presence (Mode 3); before corporate universities are set up (Mode 3), consumption abroad for face-to-face training of trainers in the source country (Mode 2) or movement of natural persons for similar training (Mode 4) may have to be arranged.

---

[14] Friedman (2007) elaborates on the 10 flatteners. The classic HP example is its co-opetition partnership with Cisco and Nokia in developing a camera cell phone that beams its digitized pictures to an HP printer (p. 208).

[15] These four approaches can also be considered as both the vision/mission of entities in various business models, and the rationale at both macro and micro levels for cross-border cooperation.

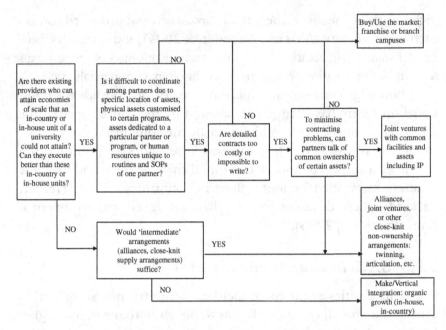

Figure 2. Issue tree for various mobility models in transnational higher education.

Source: Adapted from Besanko *et al.* (2007). *Economics of Strategy*, 4th Ed., p. 131. John Wiley & Sons, USA.

The other major concerns for business models related to GATS include (1) national treatment regarding public universities' granting of scholarships or grants which have to be extended to foreign students, professors, researchers, etc.; (2) the application of the most-favoured-nation principle to the mutual recognition arrangement for higher education institutions accredited by various international bodies; and (3) the bottom-up negotiation approach that recognises different national concerns that do not necessarily overlap, as illustrated in Fig. 2.

3 CONCLUSION

The evolution of transnational higher education business models to more 'trade-oriented' GATS-type arrangements has not precluded 'aid'-type assistance of OECD countries to the developing countries of the Asia–Pacific region. In both systems, however, there has been a shift towards acceptance of more private universities as well as more autonomous public universities as national budgets are increasingly constrained by structural shifts from ageing populations (with the shortage of university students in OECD countries that has led to student mobility models and distance learning approaches) or growth of services sectors (requiring business and management skills as well as science and technology expertise to serve global production chains in the developing nations, which has led to openness to program and provider mobility models, as well as corporate universities).

A key issue in building an Asia–Pacific community is the consideration of education as a global public good that must be funded by the global public for the mobile segment of the population (not only in the physical sense of mobility but in being able to contribute to global production processes). This pushes the theoretical concern onto aggregating national and regional public goods into 'preferential' or 'free' trade areas in education services while waiting for a global services negotiation in GATS to reach some meaningful result.

Consequent to this is the question of who are likely to remain the net exporting countries in such a second-best solution. Even the developing countries that have opened up to newer forms of cross-border cooperation are moving to the transition economies of the region as providers and funders of education-related projects, either in tandem with development cooperation partners, purely as a private sector initiative, or in mixed public–private partnerships.

The value capture and risk sharing that varies across business models suggest that market-led versions will focus on long-term quality issues for both final consumers and the funders. In internationalism-motivated projects, where donor country taxpayer funding is ultimately the issue, the perceived benefits on political, socio-cultural and non-economic dimensions of regional relations are likely to be weighed against the costs in more open systems, especially on the major issue of redressing the brain drain.

This last concern is likely to persist as the 'skimming' of the best and the brightest of developing countries continues through the selective migration policies of OECD countries, and as the individual benefit–cost calculus diverges from the social. This is a core issue in developing a true community in the Asia–Pacific. The business of education may deepen and broaden that understanding.

REFERENCES

Adireksarn P (2003). Opening Address for the International Conference on University Autonomy: Making it Work. Nakhon Ratchasima, Thailand, 29 July.

Allen M (ed.) (2002). *The Corporate University Handbook*. AMACOM, New York.

Bernardo A (2003). International higher education: Models, conditions and issues. In *Education and Globalization*, TS Tullao Jr (ed.), p. 223. Philippine APEC Study Center Network and the Philippine Institute for Development Studies, Makati, Philippines.

Besanko D, Dranove D, Shanley M and Schaefer S (2007). *Economics of Strategy*, 4th ed. John Wiley & Sons Inc. http://asia.news.yahoo.com/070523/5/singapore277897.html (accessed 26 March 2008).

Braim S (2007). Keynote Address, National Conference on Improving Competitiveness Through S&T Human Resource Development, Republic of the Philippines, Department of Science and Technology, Science Education Institute, 28 March.

Brandenburger A and Nalebuff B (1996). *Co-opetition*. Doubleday, New York.

Brodjonegoro SS (2003). Higher Education Reform in Indonesia. Paper presented at the International Conference on University Autonomy, Thailand, 29 July.

Chet C (2006). *Higher Education in Southeast Asia*. UNESCO Asia and Pacific Regional Bureau for Education, Bangkok.

Constantino R (1967). The miseducation of the Filipino. In *History of the Filipino People*, TM Agoncillo and OM Alfonso (eds.), pp. 443–449. Malaya Books, Quezon City.

Corpuz OD (1989). *The Roots of the Filipino Nation*, Vol. II, pp. 64–65. AKLAHI Foundation Inc., Quezon City.

Friedman T (2006). *The World is Flat: A Brief History of the Twenty-First Century*. Farrar, Straus and Giroux, New York.

Hawkins J and Ordonez V (2007). Higher Education in Asia: An Overview. Paper presented at the International Forum on Education 2020, September.

Hawkins J and Neubauer D (2007). Globalization, Quality Assurance and Higher Education: Trends in Asia Pacific. Paper presented at the International Forum on Education 2020, September.

Huang F (ed.) (2006). *Transnational Higher Education in Asia and the Pacific Region.* International Publication Series No. 10. http://en.rihe.hiroshima-u.ac.jp/tmp_djvu.php?id=68332 (accessed 28 March 2008).

Huang F (2006). *Transnational Higher Education in Mainland China: A Focus on Foreign Degree-conferring Programs.* International Publication Series No. 10. http://en.rihe.hiroshima-u.ac.jp/tmp_djvu.php?id=68332 (accessed 28 March 2008).

Institute of Management Development (IMD) (2006). *World Competitiveness Yearbook.* IMD, Lausanne.

International Finance Corporation. *Doing Business.* World Bank, Washington, DC.

Knight J (2007). Cross-border tertiary education: An introduction. In *Cross-border Tertiary Education: A Way towards Capacity Development,* Centre for Educational Research and Innovation (ed.). OECD/World Bank, Paris.

Larsen K, Martin JP and Morris R (2002). *Trade in Educational Services: Trends and Emerging Issues.* OECD Working Paper (revised).

Lee MH (2006). *Transnational Higher Education of Korea: The Task and Prospects.* International Publication Series No. 10. http://en.rihe.hiroshima-u.ac.jp/tmp_djvu.php?id=68332 (accessed 28 March 2008).

Lim M (2007). Old Wine in New Bottles: Subprime Mortgage Crisis — Causes and Consequences. Paper presented at the 32nd Federation of ASEAN Economic Association Annual Conference, Bangkok, 8 December.

Loxton J (2003). Autonomy in Australian Universities and the Three R's. Paper presented at the International Conference on University Autonomy, Thailand, 29 July.

Macaranas FM (2004). *Competitiveness Study on Education Services.* Department of Foreign Affairs: Philippine Services Coalition, the Philippines.

Macaranas FM (2007). Lifelong Learning in the Philippines. Working Paper 13, ILO Subregional Office for South-East Asia and the Pacific.

Maskus K, Mobarak AM and Stuen E (2007). International graduate education and innovation: Evidence and issues for East Asian technology policy. *Asian Economic Papers,* 6(3), 78–94.

Neubauer D (2007). The Public Good and Public Goods in Higher Education. Paper presented at IFE2020, East-West Center, Honolulu, September.

OECD (2004). *Internationalisation and Trade in Higher Education: Opportunities and Challenges.* OECD, Paris.

Ong P, Cheng L and Evans L (1992). Migration of highly educated Asians and global dynamics. *Asia Pacific Migration Journal,* 1, 543–567.

Posadas D (2007). *Rice and Chips: Technopreneurship and Innovation in Asia.* Prentice Hall/ Pearson Education South Asia, Singapore.

Patrinos HA and Sosale S (eds.) (2007). *Mobilizing the Private Sector for Public Education.* World Bank, Washington DC.

Singh M (2002). Globalization and quality in higher education. In *Globalization and the Market in Higher Education,* S Uvalic-Trumbic (ed.). Brookings Institution Press, New York.

Sugimoto K (2006). *Australia's Transnational Higher Education in the Asia-Pacific Region: Its Strategies and Quality Assurance.* RIHE International Publication Series No. 10, March.

Tsuruta Y (2006). *Transnational Higher Education in Japan.* International Publication Series No. 10. http://en.rihe.hiroshima-u.ac.jp/tmp_djvu.php?id=68332 (accessed 28 March 2008).

UNESCO (2006). Higher education in South-East Asia. http://unesdoc.unesco.org/images/0014/001465/146541e.pdf (accessed 28 March 2008).

Vise, DA and Malseed M (2005). *The Google Story.* Bantam Dell, New York.

World Economic Forum (2007–2008). *Global Competitiveness Report.*

Yang R (2006). *Transnational Higher Education in Hong Kong: An Analysis.* International Publication Series No. 10. http://en.rihe.hiroshima-u.ac.jp/tmp_djvu.php?id=68332 (accessed 28 March 2008).

Yang R (2007). China Case Study. Paper presented at the APRU–PECC Project Meeting, Sydney, December.

Yusuf S, Altaf MA and Nabeshima K (eds.) (2004). *Global Production Networking and Technological Change in East Asia.* World Bank, Washington DC.

Forms of Privatisation: Globalisation and the Changing Nature of Tertiary Education

William G. Tierney

1 INTRODUCTION

Only a little more than a decade ago, if one person said he worked at a private university and a second person said she worked at a public university, it was relatively clear where the two individuals worked, who attended the institutions, who taught at the institutions and, most importantly, for the purposes of this paper, who financially supported the institutions. The individual at the public university was a public servant and, if on the faculty, most likely worked full-time, students were predominately of the traditional age range of 18–24 and generally full-time, and the government supported the institution. A private university may also have had full-time faculty and traditionally aged students who were predominately full-time, but the employees were not government workers and the university did not utilise government funds, instead largely relying on tuition paid by students and the largesse of donors and alumni. The delineation of differences between a public and a private university, then, was quite clear—either an individual worked at a public or a private institution.

What one means, however, by terms such as 'private university' and 'public university' in the first decade of the 21st century is undergoing a sea change (Marginson, 2007). The stark delineation between the two has been replaced with a matrix of how to think of private and public higher education. Those institutions that were once entirely public entities now use diversified funding schemes that look more like those of private institutions. The meaning of a private institution is also remarkably diverse. Various for-profit and non-profit forms of private colleges and universities are rapidly increasing to meet the demand for tertiary education. Higher education is a growth industry and thus the either–or dichotomy between public and private has faded. Correspondingly, the motives and behaviours of public and private higher education actors (e.g., policymakers, officials) are becoming ever more variable and complex.

In this chapter, I analyse these changes and place them within larger transformations that are taking place primarily because of globalisation. There are multiple issues tangentially related to this topic, such as the privatisation of public universities or the creation of rogue institutions that are unaccredited and exist simply to make a profit and bilk the customer, but one text can cover only so much. Accordingly, I have two discrete purposes. The first is the transformations that are occurring, particularly in the different funding and governing strategies that finance and maintain private higher education, with Malaysia used as a case study. The second is what these trends mean for the well-being of higher education and what the implications are for the larger society with regard to private and public benefit in a system that has become more private and competitive.

2 GLOBALISATION AND THE MOVEMENT TOWARDS PRIVATISATION

No one can convincingly argue that public institutions have become more private solely because of globalisation. Such an assertion gives globalisation a definitional strength that attributes to it virtually all change that occurs. Nevertheless, the two terms are interrelated and the rise of privatisation has occurred during the development and expansion of globalisation. Globalisation here pertains to broad economic, technological, and scientific trends that deal with people, goods, and capital moving beyond defined, stable state borders. As Simon Marginson (2008, p. 2) notes, 'globalization refers to processes of convergence and integration on a world or meta-regional (continental) scale'. Globalisation with regard to higher education touches on many of the key assumptions about the term — the importance of the international flow of ideas and knowledge, the closer economic integration of countries through the increased flow of goods, services, capital and labour, and the cross-border movement of people (Stiglitz, 2006, p. 4).

The transformations in the world economy are not entirely new and the ways that academic institutions respond also have historical roots (Altbach, 2004). Migration and trade, for example, have always played a role in human history, and nations have sent their students to other countries for an education and welcomed foreign students to their own institutions. Part of the definition of the modern 20th century professor suggests that what he or she studied was transnational, and that the creation, development and expansion of knowledge occurred through the faculty's scholarly analysis and evaluation in journals that supposedly transcended national borders. Indeed, some universities have had long-standing relationships with other institutions or campuses in foreign countries.

What is currently taking place, however, is unprecedented because of its size and scope. Whereas only a handful of universities claimed the mantle of international prominence, today many countries desire to have their institutions ranked in the top 100 of the world. As Philip Altbach (2003, p. 5) has observed, 'everyone wants a world-class university'. The increase in the number of students taking courses and degrees in other countries has been phenomenal. By 2005, close to 2.7 million students participated in tertiary education outside their country — an increase of approximately 60 per cent in half a decade. Although 70 per cent of study abroad historically has been in five developed countries (United Kingdom, United States, Australia, Germany and France) that percentage is shifting; Japan, Canada, Malaysia, China and Singapore also seek to increase their market share of students (Verbik and Lasanowski, 2007).

For-profit higher education has existed for over a century, primarily as proprietary institutions offering vocational and technical training, but for-profit education is now the fastest growing tertiary sector. Companies such as Apollo and Laureate more closely parallel multinational companies with franchises throughout the world than they do a traditional single campus public or private institution. The demand for increased levels of knowledge and training has broadened the number of providers as traditional institutions are unable to respond sufficiently to these marketplace demands. The result is a movement towards the privatisation of tertiary education.

As Guilbert Hentschke (2006, p. 17) has pointed out, 'in most cases privatization involves both public (government) agencies and private (non-profit or for-profit) businesses — each providing a wide and overlapping array of goods and services'. Such an observation is a useful starting point for determining what privatisation actually means during a time of globalisation. As I discuss below, there is no one form of privatisation with the term meaning only that what was once a (strictly) public entity is now a (strictly) private one. Instead, we see types of privatisation where government resources are given to a private entity to offer courses, government resources are provided to the consumer rather than the institution so that students might choose the purveyor, the purveyor provides the service but the government remains responsible for the service, or private for-profit arms of a non-profit public institution are created. Each of these types of privatisation has similarities and differences, and the forms that an institution takes frequently overlap.

The increase in institutions has raised questions about the quality of the goods that are provided as well as who should judge that quality. Whereas accreditation once was in the domain of a specific country (or a specific region within a country), the ability of a company to have headquarters in one country and offer courses in several others has raised the same sort of questions and concerns that other multinationals have created. This rise of new organisations and the transformation of traditional colleges and universities into hybrids of what they once were has been so swift that even to provide a taxonomy of the higher education providers has proved difficult.

3 FORMS OF POSTSECONDARY PROVIDERS

There are nine forms of postsecondary providers, and although various forms have existed for quite some time, over the last two decades we have seen a great deal of transformation within one form, as well as the creation of new forms. Regardless of institutional form, postsecondary providers are largely defined by these six characteristics:

(a) ownership refers to who has legal control and authority of the organisation and how it is governed;
(b) funding arrangements pertain to how the organisation supports itself and what it does with the income (e.g., an organisation is either a for-profit entity seeking to make money for its partners, a not-for-profit entity independent of the state government, or a not-for-profit entity that is part of the public sector);
(c) organisational purpose delineates the single or multiple functions of the organisation;
(d) curriculum pertains to what kind of teaching and learning takes place;
(e) clientele; and
(f) faculty highlights what kinds of students attend the institution, who the faculty are, and what is expected of them.

These nine models of institutions have overlapping as well as distinct purposes (see Tables 1 and 2). I employ these models as ideal types of

Table 1.   Characteristics of postsecondary providers in Malaysia

	Ownership and governance	Funding	Organisational purpose	Teaching and learning	Clientele	Faculty
Traditional university	Non-profit, state appointed and administered	State funded	External and centralised decision-making	Traditional format and curricula	18–24 years old, full-time, local	Full-time, mostly doctorate
Traditional private university	Non-profit, independent administration	Tuition fees and donations	Internal and centralised	Traditional format and curricula	18–24 years old, full-time, generally local	Full-time, mostly doctorate
Virtual university	Non-profit or for-profit, independent administration	Tuition fees	Internal and centralised	Virtual format and employment/ skills-driven	Adult, part-time, international, and local	Part-time, mostly master's degree
Franchise university (traditional)	Non-profit or for-profit; independent or franchise controlled	Tuition fees	External and centralised	Traditional format with focus on employment skills	18–24 years old, full-time, local and adult, part-time, local, and international	Part-time, mostly master's degree
Franchise university (twinning)	Generally non-profit	Tuition fees	Externalised and centralised	Traditional format with focus on employment skills	18–24 years old, full-time, local and adult, part-time, local, and international	Mostly part-time, mostly master's degree

(Continued)

Table 1. (Continued)

	Ownership and governance	Funding	Organisational purpose	Teaching and learning	Clientele	Faculty
Publicly supported private universities	Non-profit or for-profit; partial involvement of state	Tuition fees and state funds	Internal and centralised	Traditional format and curricula	18–24 years old, full-time, local	Part-time, mostly master's degree
Corporate university	Component of human resources unit or equivalent	Corporation support provided by government or private corporation	Internal and centralised	Traditional format with job-related training	Employees and potential employees	Staff of the corporation
For-profit institutions	Company-owned or publicly traded corporation	Tuition fees	Internal and centralised	Traditional and non-traditional format with focus on employment skills	18–24 years old and adult, full-time and part-time, international and local	Part-time, mostly master's degree
Other forms of institutions	Non-profit or for-profit	Tuition fees or subsidy from provider or state	Centralised, external	Non-traditional	Adult, part-time, local, and international	Part-time

Note: These types of institutions are described in more detail in the text of this paper.

Table 2. Characteristics of specific postsecondary institutions in Malaysia

	Ownership	Funding	Organisational purpose	Curriculum	Clientele	Faculty
Universiti Sains Malaysia (traditional university)	Direction from Ministry of Higher Education (MOHE)	Funded by Federal Government through MOHE	Centralised power with vice-chancellor and external influence from MOHE	Traditional format and curricula	About 95% Malaysians, full-time, 18–24 years old	Full-time, about 60% with doctorate
Universiti Tunku Abdul Rahman (traditional private university)	Non-profit, independently administrated, politically affiliated	Tuition fees and donations	Internal and centralised	Partly traditional, partly employment-driven	Mostly Malaysians, full-time, 18–24 years old	Full-time, minimal with master's degree
Wawasan Open University (virtual university)	Non-profit, independently administrated, political affiliated	Tuition fees and donations	Internal and centralised	Employment-driven with web-based learning	Mostly working adults, part-time	Part-time, minimal with master's degree
University of Nottingham, Malaysia Campus (franchise university)	For-profit, collaboration of host institution and local corporations	Tuition fees	Strong directive from host institution	Employment-driven	Mixture of locals and international, full-time and part-time, 18–24 years old, and adult	Full-time, about 53% with doctorate

(Continued)

Table 2. (*Continued*)

	Ownership	Funding	Organisational purpose	Curriculum	Clientele	Faculty
Taylor's University College (franchise university)	For-profit, part of an education group	Tuition fees	Centralised and strong influence from partner university	Employment-driven	Mixture of locals and international, full-time and part-time, 18–24 years old, and adult	Full-time and part-time
Curtin University of Technology Sarawak Malaysia (publicly supported private university)	For-profit, collaboration of host institution and state government	Tuition fees and state funds	Strong directive from host institution	Employment-driven	Mixture of locals and international, full-time and part-time, 18–24 years old, and adult	Full-time and part-time, about 31% with doctorate
Universiti Teknologi PETRONAS (corporate university)	Owned by PETRONAS Malaysia's national oil company	Support from PETRONAS	Internal with strong directive from PETRONAS	Skills-driven for oil industry	Majority of students supported financial by PETRONAS	Full-time, about 50% with doctorate

(*Continued*)

Table 2. (*Continued*)

	Ownership	Funding	Organisational purpose	Curriculum	Clientele	Faculty
INTI International University College (for-profit institution)	For-profit corporation	Tuition fees	Internal and centralised	Employment-driven	Mixture of locals and international, full-time and part-time, 18–24 years old, and adult	Full-time and part-time
AIMST University (other forms of institutions)	Non-profit, independently administrated, politically affiliated	Tuition fees and donations	Internal and centralised	Employment-driven	Mostly Malaysians, full-time, 18–24 years old	Full-time, about 55% with doctorate*

Note: These institutions are described in more detail in the text of this paper.
*Excluding faculty from Medical and Dental school.

the current system with the recognition that each is in a period of transition as a result of the pressures of globalisation. Some institutions of a particular model are in direct competition with one another whereas others have carved out a distinct niche. Some institutions have the potential to capture the clientele from another group of institutions while many are in competition for the services of the same faculty. These forms may be found in many countries but may not have existed only a decade ago. Further, as privatisation expands, additional models will be created and/or unique arrangements will arise within a country because of its specific regulatory environment. Different types of institutions have unique characteristics — accreditation, for example, is a critical characteristic for some providers and taken as a given at others; research is a defining characteristic for what I call 'traditional private' institutions, but irrelevant for many other colleges and universities.

Is such an amalgamation of institutional types that are essentially unregulated in a country's best interest, or might a better system prevail? Governments, of course, routinely ask this about all private businesses. Although all countries have different versions of similar types of providers and regulate these providers differently, the similarities are greater than the differences in countries that seek to expand their higher education offerings. Malaysia will act as a case study of the type of providers in the tertiary education market and their characteristics.

The postsecondary sector in Malaysia is undergoing rapid change in large part because of globalisation coupled with the country's recent rapid economic growth. It thus provides an example of how a nation grapples, successfully it seems, with the forces of globalisation. About 60 per cent of the population is under 30 years of age, and 10 per cent of 18–24-year-olds are enrolled in universities (Perkinson, 2007). In 1985, over 85,000 students attended public institutions; 20 years later, this had increased to over 300,000 (see Table 3). The number of Malaysians studying at overseas colleges and universities has shrunk in relation to the overall percentage of students attending postsecondary education. In-country private institutions have seen the largest growth. In 1985, only 15,000 students attended private

Table 3.   Total number and percentages of students in higher education institutions in Malaysia, 1985–2006

	1985	1990	1995	2001	2006
Public	86,330	122,340	189,020	304,628	331,025
(%)	51.0%	53.0%	51.5%	44.8%	46.7%
Private	15,000	35,600	127,594	270,904	323,787
(%)	8.9%	15.4%	34.7%	39.9%	45.7%
Overseas	68,000	73,000	50,600	103,726	53,924
(%)	40.1%	31.6%	13.8%	15.3%	7.6%
Total	169,300	230,940	367,214	679,258	708,736

Sources: Lee (2004c) and MOHE (2007).

colleges and universities; in 2006, that number had increased to over a quarter of a million, a growth from just 8.9 per cent of the total student population to 45.7 per cent. The overall number of students attending all types of postsecondary institutions more than doubled from 169,330 in 1985 to 708,736 in 2006 (see Table 3). The overwhelming percentage of students in private institutions are non-Malay Malaysians (predominately Chinese and Indians) who have been excluded from public universities and have chosen to study at home rather than abroad (Ahmad and Noran, 1999).

The increase in students, of course, has presaged a remarkable growth in public and private postsecondary providers with varying purposes. In 1985, Malaysia had six public institutions; in 2007, this had risen to 20. The Ministry of Higher Education (MOHE) has designated four institutions as research universities, one or two of which will become 'apex' universities, ranking among the world's great research universities. The government's aim is to have at least one of those institutions ranked in the top 100 by 2010 (MOHE, 2007c).

In addition to public universities, the public postsecondary education sector includes polytechnics and community colleges. There are currently 24 polytechnics and 37 community colleges located in all 13 states in Malaysia, with the exception of the Federal Territory. Polytechnics offer certificate and diploma courses, graduating

Table 4. Breakdown of graduates according to level of qualifications, 2001–2006

	2001	2002	2003	2004	2005	2006
Public universities						
Diploma	92,809	67,807	69,157	62,136	60,911	67,628
Bachelor	182,649	184,190	192,288	194,470	209,148	223,968
Postgraduate diploma	430	433	530	439	546	330
Master	24,884	25,527	27,316	30,711	28,877	30,347
PhD	3,856	3,882	5,068	6,222	7,639	8,752
Sub-total	304,628	281,839	294,359	293,978	307,121	331,025
Private institutions						
Certificate	91,542	93,393	88,632	84,212	50,672	68,442
Diploma	117,090	129,929	131,947	130,265	101,311	123,937
Bachelor	59,965	67,062	90,631	105,325	101,395	124,071
Master	2,176	4,019	3,048	2,981	4,849	6,477
PhD	131	197	86	108	598	860
Sub-total	270,904	294,600	314,344	322,891	258,825	323,787
Polytechnics						
Certificate	26,614	27,442	26,082	30,573	33,159	33,421
Diploma	25,225	25,456	27,410	33,809	40,675	48,624
Sub-total	51,839	52,898	53,492	64,382	73,834	82,045
Community colleges						
Certificate	1,108	3,207	6,424	8,945	9,873	11,273
Total	628,479	632,544	668,619	690,196	649,653	748,130

Source: Malaysia Ministry of Higher Education (MOHE), (2007a).

about 51,000 students in 2001 (Department of Polytechnic and Community College Education [JPPKK], 2008) and more than 82,000 in 2006 (see Table 4). Community colleges graduated 1000 students in 2001 and more than 11,000 in 2006. The ultimate aim of the government is to establish a community college in each of the 222 parliamentary constituencies.

The rise in private institutions has been even more dramatic. As Jane Knight (2007, p. 138) has observed, 'The increase in worldwide demand for higher education has resulted in a diversity of providers delivering education across borders.' In 1992, there were around

156 private institutions in Malaysia; by 2007, there were over 500. However, the 1992 figure is only approximate as the market was then virtually unregulated and there was no accurate account of the number of private tertiary institutions nor of the courses they offered.

This rise in institutions and student enrolment reflects my earlier points about globalisation and tertiary education. On the one hand, as Muhammad *et al.* (2006, p. 4) have noted, 'like many developing countries across the globe, education, particularly at [the] tertiary level, is seen as an instrument of social mobility'. The assumption is that a high school qualification is no longer sufficient for gainful employment. On the other hand, the larger economic pressures and fiscal crises of the late 1990s in Southeast Asia forced Malaysians who otherwise would have sent their children abroad to find low-cost alternatives within Malaysia (Ahmad and Noran, 1999). The development of technology that enabled distance learning as well as similar pressures being faced throughout the world to generate capital has created opportunities that did not exist 10 years earlier. The Australian government, for example, had begun to privatise their tertiary education system; these newly privatised universities quickly began looking beyond Australia to capture revenues to compensate for the loss in government funding.

The Malaysian government also recognised that the demand for tertiary education exceeded their capacity to provide public higher education solely through the traditional mechanisms of taxation and appropriations. They acknowledged the benefits — primarily increased international prestige and increased revenues — of foreign students studying in Malaysian institutions. Even though some private institutions have relationships with political parties or state governments, once one group started a private university, others followed. Malaysia has become a dynamic example for understanding the changes that are taking place worldwide both within and across segments of the higher education system. I will first discuss the lineaments of the generic form and then flesh this out with a current example from Malaysia.

3.1 The Traditional Public University

The majority of the world's universities have been, and remain, public. Although the manner in which they are governed differs from country to country, the control for the institution ultimately resides with the state or federal body that has granted the university its charter. Frequently, the governing authority is the state itself or a governing board appointed by the state. Although the faculty has some role in the governance of the institution, in general, public institutions outside the United States and Latin America are centralised entities with a hierarchical decision-making structure.

Until recently, most public institutions received approximately 90 per cent of their funding from the state. Student fees were low or null, revenue from donors or corporations was meagre, and capital investments were virtually non-existent. The student body consisted primarily of students of the nation, most of whom were of a traditional college-going age (approximately 18–24 years). As students attend university in large part to be trained for employment, the curriculum is aimed at the professional workplace as well as the arts and humanities. The manner in which teaching and learning occurs is not very different from what occurred a century ago. Faculty members provide lectures or advanced students have small seminars where a professor leads a discussion. The faculty is professionally trained and, over time, at the better institutions, all faculty members hold doctoral degrees.

3.1.1 *Universiti Sains Malaysia*

Universiti Sains Malaysia (USM), established in 1969, is the second oldest public university in Malaysia and considered one of the best. It has 24 academic schools, 14 centres and 7 research units. Of its approximately 22,000 students, 25 per cent are studying for a master's or doctoral degree. It has 1500 academic staff spread over three campuses (USM, 2008).

USM fits the prototype of a traditional public institution. As with all public universities in Malaysia, it is regulated under the University and College Act of 1995. The vice-chancellor is its chief executive officer, appointed by the Minister of Higher Education (Lee, 2004a). The governing body is the board of directors, comprising the chairperson, vice-chancellor, and six representatives drawn from the local community, the government and the private sector. However, even though it is the governing body, the board has limited jurisdiction and matters pertaining to policies and regulations remain under the purview of the Ministry of Higher Education and related government departments. The university receives roughly 90 per cent of its funding from the ministry and that support is expected to continue. In short, USM is a publicly funded institution through the Ministry of Higher Education and is administered as a hybrid of the bureaucratic and entrepreneurial models of public universities with strong government intervention and control (Lee, 2004b). Although the ministry has acknowledged the need to provide greater autonomy to universities, by 2008 little had changed. Faculty members regard themselves as public employees, with no right to academic freedom or vigorous participation in governance.

The conventional methods of instruction — lectures and tutorials — continue to be delivered by the faculty. About 60 per cent have doctoral degrees, the remainder hold master's degrees. Malaysian students account for more than 95 per cent of the student body, although the university has been encouraged to increase the number of foreign students, especially at the graduate level where the language of instruction is primarily English. Malaysian students are predominantly admitted after graduating from secondary school and sitting an examination that gauges aptitude for academic work. Students apply to a centralised system run by the Ministry of Higher Education, and thus the ministry decides which students attend which institutions. Other essential areas, such as the student's area of study and tuition fees, are under the purview of ministerial departments.

3.2 The Traditional Private University

Traditional private universities have a long history; in some countries, such as Venezuela, they actually outnumber public institutions.

The traditional private institution in general parallels the public university with regard to student body, curriculum and faculty. They often have a distinct tradition: some are religious or single-sex, others have a unique pedagogical focus delivering instruction through small seminars or a narrow curricular focus in a particular field of study (e.g., law, medicine, engineering). Nevertheless, traditional-aged students and doctoral-holding faculty members are involved in a teaching and learning experience more similar than different from the public institution.

Ownership and funding arrangements are what separates the institution from a public university. A traditional private university is a non-profit organisation with a governing board that is separate from the state government. In most countries, the state has granted the organisation the right to offer courses as a university, but the organisation exists as any non-profit organisation rather than receive direction and authority from the state. The funding scheme relies on student tuition and, quite frequently, the donations of wealthy alumni and benefactors. Many private universities also receive funding through research grants and community-based projects, but the bulk of the income derives from student tuition and fees.

The organisation may be centralised or decentralised, but the direction the university takes is decided by the board. That is, the faculty may have a significant say in the governance of the institution, or their power may be circumscribed, but the organisation does not receive centralised direction from a ministry or government. Vice-chancellors tend to have more authority in traditional private universities than in public institutions, primarily because their role is akin to that of a chief executive officer of a private company rather than that of a senior administrator of a government ministry-controlled public university.

3.2.1 *Universiti Tunku Abdul Rahman*

The Malaysian Chinese Association (MCA), a Chinese political party that is in the current ruling coalition of the Malaysian government, established the Universiti Tunku Abdul Rahman (UTAR) in 2002, naming it after Malaysia's first prime minister (UTAR, 2008). The founding of the university resembles the founding of Catholic institutions in the United States — a particular population excluded from participation in mainstream institutions founds separate institutions that cater to the needs of that population.

UTAR is the second higher education institution established by the MCA. It is a non-profit institution with three primary forms of fiscal support: (a) the MCA, (b) the Chinese community and (c) student tuition and fees. The immediate past president of the MCA currently chairs the UTAR Council, which acts as the board of directors for the university. The university president is the chief executive officer in control of university operations. Though the university was established by a political party, the institution is autonomous from the Ministry of Higher Education and is governed similarly to other private institutions in Malaysia. What will happen to the UTAR if the MCA dissolves is entirely unclear. Although the political party has provided relatively little funding, the ability to work with the government and generate fiscal support has been vital to the university's existence (UTAR, 2008).

The university's long-range plan is to provide a comprehensive range of courses within eight schools or faculties. To date, four faculties (located on separate campuses) offer 38 degree programs. The main campus, which began operation in June 2007, has 16,500 students (16,300 undergraduates and 200 postgraduates). All faculty members have at least a master's degree. Admission requirements are similar to those for public universities (UTAR, 2008).

3.3 Virtual Universities

The newest form of postsecondary institutions delivers most, if not all, of its academic programs online. Virtual universities may be non-profit organisations or for-profit corporations that seek to generate income for investors. The board of either the non-profit or for-profit institution exerts a great deal of control and, since the vast majority of these institutions are private, the state's role is limited to granting a charter, enforcing contracts and ensuring that the law is followed.

Indeed, a virtual university has the potential to know no geographic boundaries. Although certain institutions may cater to a particular national entity, the reality is that, as the strength and capability of the internet and web-based servers gain strength, the potential for a virtual university to extend its reach throughout an entire region and even the world is significant.

The curriculum of these universities is more practice-focused; courses that demand laboratory work or recitation are generally not provided. Most courses qualify for practice-based certificates (associate's level) or bachelor's degrees. Graduate education is generally confined to professional master's degrees such as business or teacher education. Students and faculty are largely part-time. The student population is generally older than that of public institutions, and the faculty consists predominately of retired public university instructors or junior faculty gaining work experience. Because the faculty is mostly part-time, its role in governance and decision-making is minimal. The organisation, whether non-profit or for-profit, relies almost entirely on student tuition and fees for its income. Since research is non-existent, the organisation does not generate income from foundation or government grants. In addition, since most of these institutions are too young to have an alumni donor base, they generally do not collect charitable donations. Virtual universities fall within the category of cross-border education because where students take their classes is irrelevant. The potential for the growth of these institutions is considerable, although such virtual universities still capture a small share of the overall market.

3.3.1 *Wawasan Open University*

Wawasan Open University (WOU) promotes itself as the first private, not-for-profit, open learning institution in Malaysia with an aim to promote a lifelong learning community without borders (WOU, 2008). The Parti Gerakan Rakyat Malaysia Party (Gerakan), another Chinese political party in the current ruling coalition of the Malaysian government, established WOU in 2006. The main campus is geographically based in Penang with regional centres in four other cities throughout the country, although location is relatively unimportant as most of the learning takes place online.

The executive authority of the university is the council, appointed by the board of directors of the Wawasan Education Foundation.[1] The vice-chancellor heads the administration of the university, assisted by the academic senate and the corporate management board. WOU has a Center of Graduate Studies and three academic schools — Business and Administration, Science and Technology, and Foundation and Liberal Studies. The curriculum is structured on the credit system and the teaching/learning methodology includes tutorials and continuous assessments (e.g., tutor-marked assignments, short tests, quizzes, projects and participation in online forums) (WOU, 2008).

The main function of the 11 full-time faculty at WOU, half of whom possess doctoral degrees, is the development of curriculum and assessment. The vast majority of teaching is undertaken by part-time faculty or tutors. The current student population is about 2000 with significant projected growth over the next decade. The initial source of funding for WOU was from the Yeap Chor Ee Charitable Trust, in addition to donations from private individuals. The five-year strategy is that WOU will support itself through tuition by 2013 (WOU, 2008).

3.4 Franchise Universities

In an organisational world with confusing terms and evolving arrangements, the forms that a franchise university may take are multiplying and many sub-forms exist under this umbrella term. Indeed, not so long ago, a branch campus might have been regarded as a form of a franchise. I consider two forms that franchises currently take.

---

[1] The Wawasan Education Foundation (WEF) was established by Gerakan on 21 March 2000 under the Companies Act 1965 with the primary aim of receiving and administering funds for the promotion of education, charitable purposes, and scientific activities (adapted from the Gerakan web site at http://www.gerakan.org.my, accessed 29 February 2008).

The idea of a standard franchise still exists. An organisation in one country enables a provider in another country to offer its courses, provided that certain basic commitments are met. As franchises exist in various regions, particular attention is paid to local customs and norms. Hence, an individual franchise of a university modifies its product based on the location. A franchise university may offer a business degree, but the curriculum may vary, depending on its exact and unique location in a region or a nation.

A franchise has to generate a profit. A business plan might exist whereby the host will agree to provide fiscal support, but at some point the franchise has to turn a profit for the franchisee and the franchisor if it is to survive. Franchises are either for-profit or non-profit entities, but income — entirely through tuition — plays a significant role in both. The norm is that universities in developed countries create a franchise in a developing country as a way of generating revenue for the home institution.

Depending on the courses that are offered, a franchise may be quite similar to a standard traditional university with full-time students and faculty. More common, however, is that the curriculum attracts part-time students and demands less expensive part-time faculty. Regardless of the arrangement, the role of the faculty in the governance of the institution is generally quite minimal, and the control of the organisation is highly dependent on the vice-chancellor and the board. Ultimately, however, the authority remains in the hands of the host institution. These sorts of arrangements have been increasing rapidly, especially in Southeast Asia. One-fifth of the 80,000 foreign students enrolled in Australian universities, for example, were at offshore campuses in the late 1990s, with the numbers increasing by the year (Bennell and Pearce, 1998).

Variations of a simple franchise are 'twinning' and 'joint degree' arrangements. While these are quite different from a franchise, they share similarities with one another. Two organisations in two (or more) countries agree to an academic collaboration. Twinning enables the two countries to offer a degree that generally is awarded by one country with courses taken in both countries. Joint degrees have a similar arrangement but the academic degree is awarded by both countries.

Both arrangements may have similar curricula, student bodies and faculties. The strength of twinning is that it has the potential of cutting costs — a service provider in one country uses the service provider's faculty in the other country rather than spending money on hiring new faculty or transporting the host country's faculty to the new country. Again, however, the main purpose of these arrangements relates to the need for such courses in a country, and the ability of these courses to attract consumers and net revenue.

Why do twinning or dual degree programs succeed? Why, for example, does a traditional public institution not offer the specific degree, thereby meeting the market need, and do so at a lower cost? The answer is twofold. On the one hand, the capacity of traditional public institutions to respond to the overwhelming demands of the market is not possible since they offer their services at below-market value, primarily because the government subsidises the institutions. As a result, some consumers are shut out of traditional public institutions or are unable to take courses at a convenient time and location. On the other hand, some consumers want the cachet of taking a program from a foreign institution with an international higher education brand name. The assumption is that the quality of a foreign country's offerings may provide greater market value than a course at a domestic public institution. Thus, domestic students in developing countries such as Malaysia are willing to pay significantly more for a program that is twinned or is offered jointly with a university in a developed country.

3.4.1 *University of Nottingham*

An example of a traditional franchise is the University of Nottingham Malaysia (UNM), one of the two branch campuses of the University of Nottingham outside the United Kingdom. Established in 2000, UNM currently provides higher education to over 2700 students from 50 countries (UNM, 2008). The campus is an incorporated company partnership between the University of Nottingham, UK, and two leading publicly listed companies in

Malaysia — Boustead Holdings Berhad and YTL Corporation Berhad (Sirat and Kaur, 2007).

UNM's chief academic and administrative officer is the vice president, who is responsible to the vice-chancellor, senate and the university court at the home campus. The vice president is supported by five offices and two services centres in the administration of the Malaysian campus. The three faculties and one graduate school, assisted by the Academic English and Learning Support Unit, provide 19 degree programs and 17 postgraduate programs, with several disciplines for research and doctoral degrees. The Malaysian campus has 116 faculty members, over half of whom have doctorates.

A unique feature of the Nottingham program is that students who study at the Malaysian campus pay local tuition fees even though they are substantially lower than that of the home campus. The student diplomas give no campus location, thus, the same degree costs approximately half as much in Malaysia as in the United Kingdom. The per annum tuition fee for a business degree at UNM, for example, is approximately 25,000 MYR or £4000; the same courses and degree on the main campus have variable costs, with the lowest being 57,000 MYR or £9000.

3.4.2 *Taylor's University College*

Another example of a franchise is Taylor's University College (TUC), a standalone organisation that markets its own programs but also offers degrees with other brand names from other universities. TUC originated from Taylor's College, which was established in 1969 and received university college status in 2006. More than 50,000 students have graduated from TUC (TUC, 2008).

TUC provides British, Australian and Canadian pre-university studies, and degree courses with partner universities from Australia, the UK, France and Malaysia. For the degree programs, TUC and the partner universities have twinning arrangements, with the exception of the Bachelor of Architecture program, which is offered solely by TUC. Students have the flexibility to pursue the degree on a '3 + 0', '2 + 1', or '1 + 2' basis — students study at TUC for three, two or one year(s) and then, if necessary, at the partner institution. The degree derives from the partner institution. The curriculum and final exams are standardised according to the degree-awarding university. The teaching — through conventional lectures, tutorials, and in-class quizzes — remains the responsibility of TUC (TUC, 2008). The courses offered are often market-driven (Fuller, 1999).

On the administrative and governance front, TUC is part of Taylor's Education Group, which is composed of three private international schools. The university college is led by the president, whose responsibilities resemble that of the chief executive officer of a private corporation. The financial sustainability of the institution is generated from student tuition revenues.

The academic structure of the university college revolves around the fields of study as well as the country of the partner university. Most of the faculty is part-time. Fuller (1999) notes that Taylor's also reflects the model of a corporation and a for-profit college with the importance of shareholders' dividends. Such an observation reflects yet again the overlapping forms of private institutions in the Malaysian higher education sector.

3.5 Publicly Supported Private Universities

State and federal governments have long supported public universities, as shown in the above example of the Universiti Sains Malaysia. The United States is an example of a state helping to develop and sustain publicly supported universities such as the University of California and the University of Michigan. Governance derives from a public charter with a significant amount of institutional funding coming from state coffers.

A relatively new form of privatisation, however, is public monies being provided for a privately operated postsecondary institution. As with any private company, the state has to grant permission for the private entity to function, but in this example it also financially supports the private entity. As it is a private corporation, the state has no say in what the university will develop or offer other than through its fiscal support. In effect, the state is a major supporter of the private university, as any investor would be of a private for-profit company. However, the to the state in this instance are not fiscal but educational and social for its citizens. This type of higher education has obvious overlaps with other forms and is a variation of a franchise, with the significant difference that the funding comes from a public state, not another organisation. Corporate universities may also receive public funding, but the actual relationship exists with the corporation, not the state.

This is a departure from the idea of education as a public good that not only derives from public monies but is administered as a public entity. Education remains a public good as the funding is largely public, but the purveyor is private. The assumption is that it is irrelevant whether the purveyor is private or public; what matters is the outcome for the citizens. However, why does a public entity such as a university not offer courses and degrees for the same or less cost than the private entity and provide similar or better quality?

3.5.1 *Curtin University*

At the invitation of the Sarawak State Government, Curtin University of Technology Sarawak Malaysia (CUTSM) began operation in 1999. It is the first offshore campus of Curtin University of Technology (CUT), Western Australia (CUTSM, 2008), and the first foreign university located in East Malaysia (Borneo Island).

In 1998, the Western Australian Minister of Education proposed an amendment to the Curtin University of Technology Act to allow CUT to enter into business arrangements in the midst of setting up CUTSM. The four-year strategic plan (2007–2010) reflects the for-profit element of the branch campus, whereby increasing revenue and strengthening financial security is one of the five major areas. CUTSM conducts research and development and was the first foreign university in Malaysia to receive access to the Intensification for Research in Priority Areas (IRPA) grants from the Ministry of Science, Technology, and the Environment in 2001; the branch campus has since been awarded numerous research grants by the state government and the industry (CUTSM, 2008).

CUTSM is led by the pro-vice-chancellor, the chief executive for the Malaysian campus. It comprises schools of business and engineering and science as well as a department of mass communication and a pre-university section. Of the 84 faculty members in the three degree-awarding schools and sole department, 26 have a doctorate. It has about 1500 students and intends to increase the student body by 8 per cent over the next five years. Tuition fees per annum in Australia for a business degree are A$18,200 or 54,000 MYR, while the same degree taken on the Malaysian campus is A$5367 or 15,700 MYR. Without the considerable subsidies provided by the state, it is unlikely that the institution could exist (CUTSM, 2008).

3.6 Corporate Universities

Companies have long had training programs for their employees, but over the last generation, the number of corporate universities has risen and 'there are now about 1600 corporate universities, up from only 400 10 years ago' (World Bank, 2002, p. 34). Although the majority specialise in continuing education for company employees, some programs offer degrees, and a few open their courses to outsiders. In general, these universities are small and, if only for that reason, usually do not compete directly against the other organisational forms. Students who want to attend a traditional public or private institution or a franchise from another country are usually not interested in, or able to take, a program at a corporate university.

A corporate university may also derive from a public source — the government. Government-linked companies are one way a university can function. An obvious comparison exists with publicly supported private universities, with the distinction that the company has an intermediary role. The alternative is that the corporate university is a privately held corporation. Whether the company is private or public, the university's focus is generally the same — to educate its employees. Thus, they function in an entirely different manner from the other forms discussed here. Faculty usually work for the company, providing training or teaching as a component of their employment.

Faculty involvement is non-existent in the functioning of the institution, and the fiscal arrangement exists solely within the organisation. The university may be an arm of the organisation and different units may pay tuition to the university, or the costs may be subsumed and the university not regarded as a revenue centre. A corporate university generally does not have a governing board but is administered by a division (e.g., human resources) of the company. A successful program is measured by the management's belief that either their employees are learning the requisite job skills to improve their performance, or potential employees are brought up to an acceptable skill level before they begin employment. Accordingly, the curriculum is tied to explicit learning outcomes in a manner that often is absent in traditional postsecondary education. The assumption is that a corporate university can offer courses more closely tied to corporate needs than any other provider.

3.6.1 *Universiti Teknologi PETRONAS*

Petroliam Nasional Berhad (PETRONAS), the national oil company of Malaysia (PETRONAS, 2008), established the Universiti Teknologi PETRONAS (UTP) in 1997, specialising in engineering and technology programs at both undergraduate and postgraduate levels. The university has produced close to 1500 graduates (UTP, 2008).

UTP is governed by the PETRONAS education division. The top governing body of the university is the eight-person board of directors, including the PETRONAS company secretary. The chief executive is the rector, who is assisted by the management committee and senate to handle matters pertaining to administration and academic affairs. The Academic Advisory Council (AAC), Industry Advisory Panel (IAP) and International External Examiners (IEE) provide external consultancy support. The curriculum focus of the university is geared towards meeting the needs of PETRONAS as the nation's major oil company, specialising in chemical, civil, electrical and mechanical engineering (UTP, 2008).

Although postsecondary students can attend UTP, PETRONAS sponsors about three-quarters of the students with the assumption that these students will work for the corporation or one of its sub-sidiaries upon graduation. Unlike typical corporate universities, UTP's faculty is employed as academic staff of the university and not of PETRONAS. About half of the 270 full- and part-time faculty hold doctoral degrees (UTP, 2008).

3.7 For-Profit Universities

Another fast-growing form of tertiary education is the for-profit university. The curriculum, students and faculty may not differ greatly from some of the other forms — students tend to be adult, faculty tends to be part-time. The curriculum is practice-based and the ability of students to gain employment is critical. Instruction may be delivered by standard lecture- and seminar-based classes, but for-profit universities have also been at the forefront of virtual education.

What separates for-profit entities from the others is in their title — for-profit. Ultimately, these institutions exist to generate net revenues for their investors, which may be either a privately held or publicly traded company. The faculty has little say, if any, in the governance of the institution. The chief executive officer is the individual who runs the company for the board. Finances are derived from student tuition, which may or may not be subsidised by their families, their current employer or the state; they conduct no research and generate no revenue from donors. The business plan of a for-profit company is critical and the manner in which the institutions function is entirely different from that of a traditional public or private university, or even a franchise or twinning arrangement. The organisational purpose is to generate net revenue through growth in scale and/or profit margins. Such a single-minded focus changes the organisation in ways quite distinct from that of its counterparts.

3.7.1 INTI International University College

INTI International University College (INTI-UC) began as INTI College in 1986 (INTI-UC, 2008). The college gradually expanded into 11 branch colleges in Malaysia and elsewhere. In 2006, the main campus was upgraded to a university college and became INTI-UC, comprising eight associated colleges throughout Malaysia and two branch colleges, one each in Indonesia and China. In February 2008, INTI Universal Holdings Berhad, a publicly listed company and the major shareholder of the institution, sold 51.2 per cent of its stake to Laureate Education, Inc., although the acquisition has exceeded the current regulation on foreign equity of only 49 per cent (Sirat and Kaur, 2007; Soo, 2007; Tan, 2008). The latter is the largest operator of private international universities and a brand name of an international network of universities with over 30 institutions. This acquisition resembles the model of for-profit institutions that INTI-UC was operating previously and will continue under the network of Laureate Education, Inc.

The board of governors provides the corporate direction of the institution while the board of academic advisors offers external advice on academic matters. The associated colleges are led by principals, who play the role of chief executive officers in their respective colleges; the INTI-UC is led by the president, who is also a member of the board of governors. The board of governors functions similarly to the board of directors in a corporation, insofar as the major stakeholder in the institution is a publicly listed company. The institution is expected to be profit-driven and tuition fees are expected to be the major source of revenue.

INTI-UC comprises five faculties, four academic schools and four centres, which altogether offer programs from pre-university and foundation levels to postgraduate studies. Of its 27 degree programs, 7 are offered entirely by INTI-UC and the remaining are twinning or credit transfer programs with foreign universities. Since the inception of INTI College two decades ago, the institution has produced over 18,000 graduates. Full- and part-time faculty teach one or two courses (INTI-UC, 2008).

3.8 Other Forms of Universities

I have outlined the dynamic environment in which postsecondary education currently exists. Although the forms are relatively standard from country to country, new forms continue to be developed. Publishing companies, libraries, K-16 education systems, and a host of other organisational forms are beginning to experiment with offering postsecondary education. One unique example in Malaysia has already been considered — an institution owned by a political party.

3.8.1 *Asian Institute of Medicine, Science and Technology*

Three of the four major component parties in the current ruling coalition — the Malaysian Chinese Association (MCA), the Malaysian Indian Congress (MIC), and the Chinese-dominated Gerakan Party — have established institutions of higher education. The objective of these institutions generally is to create wider access to tertiary education for the racial and ethnic groups of interest to these parties. The result is that about 95 per cent of the enrolment in private institutions is made up of non-Malay Malaysians (Ahmad and Noran, 1999).

In 2001, the Asian Institute of Medicine, Science and Technology (AIMST) was established by MIC and officially upgraded to AIMST University in 2007 (AIMST, 2008). This university has four faculties and two centres. The chief executive officer is the vice-chancellor, who reports to the board of directors, with the International Academic Advisory Council providing external advice on the direction of development of the university. The board of directors functions as the highest governing body of the university and oversees its development. Similar to other institutions founded by a political party, the major funding comprises financial support from the party, donations and tuition fees. The university is free from government influence and is governed as a private university.

Students at AIMST are admitted based on the same criteria as those who attend a traditional public university. Of the 122 full-time staff members, more than 60 per cent are assigned to the medical and dental schools. Among the non-medical faculty, 55 per cent have doctorates. Although tuition is higher than at a traditional public university — AIMST fees are about 9300 MYR per year whereas public university fees are about 1200 MYR per year — financial aid makes it more affordable (AIMST, 2008).

4. PRIVATISATION AND THE FUTURE OF HIGHER EDUCATION

What can be made of such a dynamic market other than to acknowledge how fast the system is evolving and how many different players are involved in these changes? More importantly, what suggestions might be made about the worth of these changes for a nation such as Malaysia? I conclude with three observations that respond to these questions.

4.1 Privatisation and New Providers Will Increase

All of these changes are possibly little more than new players trying to enter a market. Eventually only a few providers will remain and the market will return to previous norms. From this perspective, the gold rush that many believe exists in the education market is merely a flash in the pan. Another possibility is that either a government will revert to the previous stance and restrict new entrants, or that a fiscal crisis will force fledgling companies to close and/or not attempt new ventures. Although these scenarios are, of course, possible, I do not believe they are likely. That is, a country such as Myanmar might be able to close its borders, but in a globalised world developing countries can no longer simply restrict goods, services, capital and labour if they wish to prosper. Globalisation, as with all systems, has winners and losers. Although the path to winning is by no means clear, closing off from others is not likely to bring success. Further, the timeframe over the last 20 years has been long enough to demonstrate that education is indeed a growth market. As noted at the outset, globalisation suggests that developing countries need an educated workforce, and the public sector cannot meet the increased demand by itself. While every region will have periods of economic growth and recession, the trajectory is clear: the long-term demand for postsecondary education is not going to recede.

Thus, one might more accurately predict that more entrants will try to gain a toehold in the tertiary education market, rather than fewer. It is entirely plausible that, if I were to update this article a decade from now, additional forms of privatisation would be categorised. The either–or dichotomy of public or private is an artefact of the 20th century and there are likely to be new entrants to meet the needs of specific niche markets. In particular, as technology improves, the potential for virtual universities that know no geographic boundaries is considerable. The public sector must determine which markets it is to serve. Then it needs to make an argument as to why it, rather than institutions in the private sector, can better serve those markets. After all, why would a nation spend tax dollars for a service that the private sector can provide at the same or lower cost? However, the increase of new providers raises specific concerns that any government needs to consider.

4.2 Data About Consumer Participation and Organisational Performance Need to be Improved

The provisional framework offered here necessitated an intellectual treasure hunt for verifiable data that was often contradictory and confusing. There are three critical reasons to collect systematic and verifiable data.

First, without trustworthy data there is no way of knowing who is participating in tertiary education and who is not. This is important for any country concerned about educational equity for and is key to the idea of transparency as essential for good government. It is likely, for example, that some sectors of society have greater educational opportunities than others. Without an awareness of why different sectors are participating at a lower rate than others, the country cannot create policies that increase participation among all constituencies.

Second, the institutions in the forms outlined above educate students for different kinds of employment. Some lead to blue-collar jobs whereas others lead to professional employment. Without data to track the success of employment for an institution's graduates, a nation will not know if an institution is actually doing what it promises. Further, as with the earlier point, some groups are more likely to attend institutions that place them on one sort of career path while other groups end up on another career path. If a nation espouses educational equity, it will want to know if groups are being tracked for lower-skilled jobs so that they might develop ways to overcome such problems.

Finally, no one benefits if a student does not complete the intended degree or certificate. Certainly the reasons for non-completion are multi-faceted and frequently the onus falls on the individual student. However, not all institutions are similar and some do a better job than others of supporting students towards degree completion. All institutions exist because the state has granted them permission. If an institution fails to meet its goals, then the government should have that data to determine which institutions to support.

4.3 Quality Assurance Mechanisms Need to be Put in Place and Measured

Because globalisation is a relatively new term, there are no hard and fast rules about how a nation should respond with regard to education and privatisation. I have suggested here that privatisation is likely to increase and the number of providers likely to expand, and that to revert to strict market control or to believe that the trends will reverse is a mistake. What, then, is the role for the government other than to continue monitoring traditional public institutions in the same way? The answer is twofold.

On the one hand, the movement towards privatisation and the erosion of the traditional public institutions market share suggests that the government needs to provide greater autonomy and leeway to public universities, allowing them to compete more successfully against their private counterparts. Privatisation in the marketplace means that competition is a given. For an organisation to compete successfully, the focus and goals of the institution need to be driven by those closest to the decision-making rather than be managed from a distance. A concomitant point is that each institution has to distinguish itself with regard to purpose and constituency. Malaysia, for example, currently has 20 public universities. If the government takes seriously the suggestions offered here, they will provide greater autonomy to each institution, but the Ministry of Higher Education will ensure that each institution has a distinctive niche in the higher education marketplace rather than all 20 trying to be similar.

On the other hand, the government's role is to ensure that the product of any entity is of the highest possible quality, whether that entity is public or private. The consumer needs enforceable protections to ensure that an organisation actually delivers what it promises. The government needs to protect the citizenry from fraud and its many ramifications. Simply stated, individuals are at risk of losing their income if their money is not well spent because of the low standards or false claims of an institution.

Further, education is more than simply a product such as food. To be sure, if dumplings are tainted and individuals get sick, then a government needs to oversee the recall of the dumplings and deal with the local or foreign producer to ensure that they improve their quality. Education, however, affects more than an individual's physical well-being. In a globalised world, a nation will not prosper if it does not have the assurance that the system providing the educational goods and services is of the highest possible standard. In the 21st century, whether the provider is private or public is of less importance. What matters is that the provider turns out a product that will enhance the well-being of the individual and the nation, and this should be the focus of government.

ACKNOWLEDGEMENTS

Chang Da Wan was a Research Officer at IPPTN at University Science Malaysia when I wrote this paper and he was extremely helpful in collecting the data pertaining to Malaysia; he is currently a PhD student in Education at Oxford University. Comments on an earlier draft by Lisa Garcia, Morshidi Sirat, Jane Knight, Peter Kell, Simon Marginson, Tony Welch and Gib Hentschke were also very helpful.

REFERENCES

Ahmad MA and Noran FY (1999). Business of Higher Education in Malaysia: Development and Prospects in the New Millennium. Paper presented at ASAIHL Conference on The New Millennium: Business and Higher Education in the Asia–Pacific, Auckland Institute of Technology, New Zealand, December.

Altbach PG (2003). The costs and benefits of world-class universities. *Int High Educ*, 33, 5–8.

Altbach PG (2004). Globalisation and the university: Myths and realities in an unequal world. *Tert Educ and Manag*, 10, 3–25.

Asian Institute of Medicine, Science and Technology University (AIMST) (2008). http://www.aimst.edu.my (accessed 3 March 2008).

Bennell P and Pearce T (1998). Internationalisation of Higher Education: Exporting Education to Developing and Transitional Economies. IDS Working Paper No. 75, Institute of Development Studies, University of Sussex, UK.

Curtin University of Technology Sarawak Malaysia (CUTSM) 2008. http://www.curtin.edu.my (accessed 14 March 2008).

Department of Polytechnic and Community College Education (JPPKK) (2008). http://jppkk.mohe.gov.my (accessed 28 February 2008).

Faculty of Computing and Information Technology (FOCIT), INTI International University College (2007). http://focit.intimal.edu.my (accessed 4 March 2008).

Fuller T (1999). For-profit colleges divide Malaysians. *International Herald Tribune*, February 15. http://www.iht.com (accessed 3 March 2008).

Hentschke GC (2006). Privatization in education: Myths, realities, prospects. *USC Urban Ed*, Fall/Winter, 17–19.

International Medical University (IMU) (2007). http://www.imu.edu.my (accessed 28 February 2008).

INTI International University College (INTI-UC) (2008). http://www.intimal.edu.my (accessed 4 March 2008).

Knight J (2007). Crossborder education — Changes and challenges in program and provider mobility. In *New Arenas of Education Governance: The Impact of International Organizations and Markets on Educational Policy Making*, K Martens, A Rusconi and K Leuze (eds.), pp. 136–154. Palgrave Macmillan, Basingstoke, Hampshire.

Lee MNN (2004a). Malaysian universities: Towards equality, accessibility and quality. In *Restructuring Higher Education in Malaysia*, MNN Lee (ed.), pp. 16–23. School of Educational Studies, Universiti Sains Malaysia, Penang, Malaysia.

Lee MNN (2004b). The corporatisation of a public university: Influence of market forces and state control. In *Restructuring Higher Education in Malaysia*, MNN Lee (ed.). pp. 29–37. School of Educational Studies, Universiti Sains Malaysia, Penang, Malaysia.

Lee MNN (2004c). Private higher education in Malaysia: Expansion, diversification and consolidation. In *Restructuring Higher Education in Malaysia*, MNN Lee (ed.), pp. 47–62. School of Educational Studies, Universiti Sains Malaysia, Penang, Malaysia.

Malaysia Ministry of Higher Education (MOHE) (2007a). *Jumlah enrolmen pelajar di institusi pengajian tinggi, tahun 2001–2006* [Chart showing breakdown of graduates according to level of qualifications, 2001–2006]. http://www.mohe.gov.my/web_statistik/statistik_pdf_2008/data_makro_1-2.pdf (accessed 25 February 2008).

Malaysia Ministry of Higher Education (MOHE) (2007b). http://www.mohe.gov.my (accessed 25 February 2008).

Malaysia Ministry of Higher Education (MOHE) (2007c). *National Higher Education Action Plan 2007–2010.* http://www.mohe.gov.my/transformasi (accessed 5 June 2008).

Marginson S (2007). The public/private divide in higher education: A global revision. *High Educ*, 53, 307–333.

Marginson S (2008). *The External Dimension: Positioning the European Higher Education Area in the Global Higher Education World.* Unpublished manuscript.

Muhammad J, Chan HC, Suhaimi S and Suzyrman S (2006). *Enhancing Quality of Faculty in Private Higher Education Institutions in Malaysia.* National Higher Education Research Institute, Penang, Malaysia.

Perkinson R (2007). Public and private higher education: A growing global enterprise. In *The Europa World of Learning*, 57th ed., A Gladman (ed.). Routledge, Oxford.

Petroliam Nasional Berhad (PETRONAS) (2008). http://www.petronas.com (accessed 3 March 2008).

Sirat M and Kaur S (2007). Transnational Higher Education in Malaysia: Trends and Challenges. Paper presented at the meeting of the Association of Southeast Asian Institutions of Higher Learning (ASAIHL) Conference, Perth, Australia, December.

Soo A (2007). Malaysia's INTI Universal receives takeover offer from Laureate Education. *AFX News Limited*, 18 September. http://www.forbes.com (accessed 24 June 2008).

Stiglitz JE (2006). *Making Globalization Work.* WW Norton, New York.

Tan K (2008). Laureate gets controlling stake in INTI Universal. *The Edge Daily*, 20 February. http://www.theedgedaily.com (accessed 4 March 2008).

Taylor's University College (TUC) (2008). http://www.taylors.edu.my (accessed 29 February 2008).

Universiti Sains Malaysia (USM) (2008). *Prospectus 2008.* Universiti Sains Malaysia Public Relations Office, Penang, Malaysia.

Universiti Teknologi PETRONAS (UTP) (2008). http://www.utp.edu.my (accessed 3 March 2008).

Universiti Tunku Abdul Rahman (UTAR) (2003). http://www.utar.edu.my (accessed 3 March 2008).

University of Nottingham Malaysia Campus (UNM) (2008). http://www.nottingham. edu.my (accessed 3 March 2008).

Verbik L and Lasanowski V (2007). *International Student Mobility: Patterns and Trends.* The Observatory on Borderless Higher Education, London.

Wawasan Open University (WOU) (2008). http://www.wou.edu.my (accessed 29 February 2008).

World Bank (2002). *Constructing Knowledge Societies: New Challenges for Tertiary Education.* World Bank, Washington, DC.

Research and Collaboration in an Expanding Higher Education Market in the Asia–Pacific: The Experiences of Malaysian Universities

S. Morshidi, Ahmad Farhan Sadullah, Ibrahim Komoo, Koo Yew Lie, N.S. Nik Meriam, A. Norzaini, Y. Farina and W. Wong

1 INTRODUCTION

It has long been recognised that universities contribute to society by improving the level of human capital and overall human development (Pyle and Forrant, 2002). However, the context within which universities play this important role has changed significantly in the last decade (Newman, Couturier and Scurry, 2004). Notably, in recent years, competition for a greater share of the global economy has led governments to think much more strategically about the economic significance of academic knowledge production/creation and dissemination. In this connection, Newman, Couturier and Scurry (2004) note that universities that were accustomed to an established place in their segment of higher education and in their geographic area now find that the competition crosses both these boundaries.

It is important to note that, within the swiftly changing context noted above, national government strategies and policies in developing countries continue to be the key factors influencing the higher education environment, which in turn shapes the role that individual institutions will play within that environment (Task Force on Higher Education and Society, 2000). National governments in developing countries such as Malaysia have a major influence on other players in the higher education market in areas including research funding and assessment. It follows that the status and prestige of individual higher education institutions are determined by the quality and quantity of their research and other output.

In view of this, higher education institutions are reorganising themselves to meet these new challenges. Interestingly, options to do this include collaboration with other institutions at both the global and national levels. International higher education and increasing student mobility, together with the emerging education market in important regions of the world, are generally regarded by many countries as something to capitalise on (see Verbik and Lasanowski, 2007). Higher education institutions find themselves in the midst of a complex set of relationships. Their destiny is increasingly dependent on a particular set of changing circumstances, not all of which are within their control. The transnational and global nature of knowledge and work, the cultural production of knowledge, and communications in space–time, which is highly compressed, add to the complex challenges of higher education.

It is generally agreed that globalisation and the internationalisation of higher education necessarily gives rise to competition among countries, for the institutions are continuously working towards improving the international competitiveness of the higher education sector. This, in turn, enhances the international competitiveness of the national economy (van der Wende, 2004). Lee (2004) notes that the corporatisation of public universities is very much in line with the global trend of changing universities into enterprises and developing in them a corporate culture and practices that enable them to compete in the marketplace. However, this paper will proceed on the basis of several premises. First, the internationalisation and expansion of the higher education market in the Asia–Pacific region presents countries in this region with numerous opportunities for collaborative research that in the medium to longer term will result in a win–win situation for all involved. Denman (2002) notes that globalisation opens up opportunities for international university cooperation. It is envisaged that there will be a dense network of collaboration and cooperation in research activities, with substantial mobility of researchers and research students, which will contribute to the development of a simultaneously competitive and/or synergistic national, regional and global system of innovation for participating countries. Research and innovation should, however, be appropriately sustainable, contextualised and linked with the ways of being and ways of knowing and learning in universities and communities.

Second, it is argued that the development and smooth operation of innovation systems depend on the fluidity of knowledge flows — among enterprises, universities and research institutions. OECD (1996) notes that innovation is the result of numerous interactions by a community of actors and institutions, which together form what are termed national innovation systems. It is important to note that increasingly these innovation systems are extending beyond national boundaries to become international. Arguably, the fluidity of knowledge flows noted earlier rests on collaboration and cooperation rather than on competition between countries and institutions. The mechanisms for knowledge flows include joint industry research, public/private sector partnerships, technology diffusion, and movement of personnel (OECD, 1996). This is an important lesson learned.

This paper, therefore, is an attempt to detail the opportunities taken and the challenges arising from internationalisation of the market for education services, in particular as these are related to research and teaching, international research cooperation, and development of the national system of innovation. Of particular importance in this context is to establish through specific experiences of higher education institutions how these links, once established, can be further strengthened through research exchanges, collaboration and cooperation. Ultimately, the output of the paper is the formulation of an Asia–Pacific higher education framework for regional cooperation in research and innovation.

It is important to note at this juncture that the links among research universities, various R&D centres, public research organisations and industry must be encouraged and facilitated to enhance the commercialisation of R&D. Tighter collaboration and networking must also be extended internationally, where appropriate, to ensure better outcomes and to attract foreign talent, research opportunities, and funding.

Ideally, the above assertions and propositions can be illustrated and verified through an analysis of the experiences of different types of higher education institutions and research institutes in the Asia–Pacific region, particularly among institutions that have presented themselves as lynchpins or movers of regional cooperation in research and innovation. However, for lack of time and space, this paper will concentrate only on the experiences of research universities in Malaysia.

The Malaysian Government has recently designated four universities — Universiti Malaya (UM), Universiti Sains Malaysia (USM), Universiti Putra Malaysia (UPM) and Universiti Kebangsaan Malaysia (UKM) — as research universities. Each of these institutions has specific strengths in terms of exploiting opportunities created by the expanding education markets in the Asia–Pacific region. In this paper, we examine the experiences of three of these four universities: UM, USM and UKM. The experience of Monash University Sunway Campus is included primarily to showcase the specific and unique experiences of a foreign university operating within the Malaysian higher education system. This approach will provide an interesting comparative perspective with respect to the responses of higher education institutions in Malaysia to the opportunities and challenges presented by the expanding education market in the Asia–Pacific region.

2 DEFINITION OF RESEARCH IN THE MALAYSIAN CONTEXT

The definition of research is broad, and in the context of research universities in Malaysia it covers the whole spectrum of activities related to research, innovation and commercialisation. Research is defined as the discovery, development, application and preservation of all forms of knowledge, be it scientific, humanistic or social scientific. Currently, all research universities in Malaysia focus on three types of research:

1) basic and fundamental research for the advancement of knowledge and knowledge generation;
2) applied research for problem solving and application for society and industry; and
3) developmental research for product and process development, prototyping and output for commercialisation.

2.1 Research Collaboration

Research collaboration in all universities in Malaysia, particularly research universities, takes many forms, including research links, networks and partnerships. Research collaborations frequently consist of networks, which are characterised by horizontal exchanges of information and activities. As these lack a hierarchy, they can develop into long-term arrangements. The majority of research collaborations involve smart partnerships between researchers in planning, conducting, managing and facilitating research activities that enable the production or the application of scientific knowledge. Research collaborations are expected to contribute to the research and innovation processes in terms of academic mobility, joint postgraduate supervision, co-authorship of publications, joint product development in relation to commercialisation of research products, and technology transfer.

2.2 Research Collaboration: Objectives, Modes and Forms

2.2.1 *Objectives*

The internationalisation of research and academic researchers has been on the agenda of research universities in Malaysia (Sarjit, Morshidi and Norzaini, 2007), and was further emphasised in the recently released *Pelan Strategik Pengajian Tinggi Negara Melangkaui Tahun 2020* (*National Higher Education Strategic Plan Approaching 2020*) and the accompanying document, *National Higher Education Action Plan 2007–2010*. It is argued that the transnational engagement of researchers is expected to position Malaysian university researchers strategically within the global knowledge societies. The growing importance of worldwide or international rankings of universities, generally based on research criteria, has also changed the scope and nature of research (and publications) in Malaysian universities. In addition, Malaysia's higher education policy, which has been realigned to accord with the objective of creating 'world class' research universities (Kementerian Pengajian Tinggi Malaysia, 2007), has presented Malaysian universities with the opportunities to position themselves accordingly. This objective is to be achieved through a systematic and sustained effort at making research more responsive to the requirements and challenges of internationalisation. Towards this end, it is immediately acknowledged that efforts must be directed towards international research cooperation and cross-border networking.

Thus, research universities' engagement in collaborative research, be it bilateral or multilateral, is increasingly important to Malaysia's position in the global knowledge economy. The quality and impact of internationalisation of research should be mapped in terms of international networking and linkages, leadership and representation in international professional bodies, competitive international research grants, and quantity of international postgraduate students (Kementerian Pengajian Tinggi Malaysia, 2007).

2.2.2 *Modes of collaboration*

The common platform for cooperation is the desire to develop academic exchange programs and cooperation in teaching and research to further the advancement and dissemination of learning. This may include various modes that are designed to suit the width and spread of collaborative activities agreed by the partners. These measures include the following activities commonly practised by many universities in Malaysia: exchange of staff and students in teaching and research programs, exchange of scientific materials, publications and information, joint curriculum development, and research collaboration.

2.2.3 *Forms of collaboration*

In practical terms, there are two forms of collaboration:

1. A Memorandum of Understanding (MoU) — the general format is based on an intention to create a relationship with no specific obligations for the parties involved, and thus is not legally binding.
2. A Memorandum of Agreement (MoA) — this entails a detailed format of cooperation with specific obligations for the parties involved, and thus is considered legally binding.

The procedures for MoUs/MoAs are, by and large, fairly well established in all universities in Malaysia, including research universities. The process would normally involve a critical phase of institutional 'matching', whereby intentions are created and parties get together to discuss and identify areas of common interest. This is then followed by official approval by top university management and the University Senate, if necessary. There have been occasions when formal representations by Malaysian government officials and the diplomatic corps were deemed necessary to highlight ventures of significance not only to Malaysian universities but also to Malaysia.

Suffice to say that in all Malaysian universities, guidelines detailing the necessary work process to facilitate collaborative efforts are available.

2.2.4 *Academic staff mobility programs*

A number of mobility schemes have emerged in recent years in the Asia–Pacific region, some related to students and their study abroad, others related to professional mobility (Lenn, 2004). The exchange programs for staff in most Malaysian universities include both academic and administrative staff. Among the mobility programs that are currently available for academic staff are:

- sabbatical leave,
- post-doctorate training,
- fellowships,
- research attachment,
- foreign lectureships, and
- foreign consultation.

The following case studies of higher education institutions in Malaysia serve to highlight the outcomes or experiences with respect to links to research and research-related matters. It has to be stated that universities in Malaysia operate within the guidelines as laid down by the government. While there is some degree of administrative autonomy, most universities, including research universities, remain financially heavily dependent on the government (Abdul Razak, Sarjit and Morshidi, 2007). In this respect, therefore, what has been possible and feasible in the past in terms of exploiting the expanding markets has been severely constrained by government policies. The future may be somewhat different and more promising for these universities based on the strategies and approaches noted in the recently released *National Higher Education Strategic Plan Approaching 2020*.

3 CASE STUDIES

3.1 Universiti Malaya (UM)

3.1.1 *The need for collaboration*

UM's top management has acknowledged that a strong national and internationally connected science, education, research and innovation capacity will result in a more sustainable and vigorous intellectual environment, provide valuable global skills, and introduce new perspectives to students and staff. In addition, the nation will see the development of highly qualified and globally aware talent to fuel labour market demands and the growing knowledge economy. Indeed, meaningful collaboration will result in the development of new business for UM.

In the final analysis, collaborations will add value to UM's standing and reputation as the premier higher education institution in Malaysia. The choice of partners for UM cuts across all sectors of the education system, both core and peripheral. Notable partners include public and private institutions of higher learning and research, other government agencies and the private sector and, last but not least, multilateral forums such as UNESCO and WHO.

UM seeks to engage partners at both the national and international levels, with the following reasons as the main drivers for international collaboration:

- philosophical — education is for the betterment of nations and humanity;
- formal — one of the key performance indicator targets set by the Government of Malaysia to UM; and
- practical — internationalisation will lead to increased quality and competitiveness and will enrich the learning experience of students.

Table 1 provides the latest summary list of MoUs by country with UM. It is evident that collaborations with UM are spread across the

Table 1.   UM: Summary list of international
MoUs by country

Country	No. of collaborations
Argentina	1
Australia	8
Austria	1
Brunei	1
China	5
Chile	1
Egypt	1
France	2
Germany	1
Hong Kong	1
Indonesia	14
Ireland	1
Italy	2
Japan	18
Korea	14
Netherlands	7
New Zealand	4
Norway	1
Philippines	1
Russia	1
Singapore	2
Sweden	1
Syria	1
Thailand	5
United Kingdom	15
US	6
Vietnam	2
Yemen	2
Zambia	1
Others	7
Total	**127**

globe, and that this institution continually reaches out to more partners, with a current leaning towards the US in order to improve its
presence in the Americas. In the past, Japan and Korea were the main
source countries for collaborative research work.

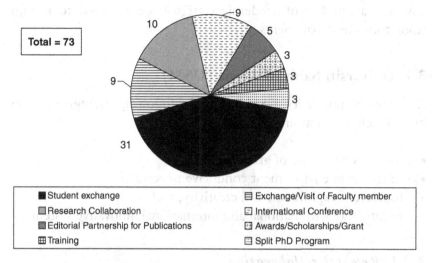

Figure 1. UM: Number of international MoUs with activities

UM is fully aware that MoUs should lead to concrete activities and not remain as collaborations that look good on paper. Thus, serious efforts have been and are being made to ensure full realisation of MoUs. Figure 1 shows the number of MoUs with concrete activities to date, with a substantial majority of these activities being in the area of student exchange.

UM collaborations with international agencies include those with the National Institute of Health (US) on HIV-related studies in Malaysia, the National Institute of Infectious Diseases (Japan) on genotyping of pathogens and emerging protozoans, the Korea Ocean Research & Development Institute (KORDI) on marine science, and Seegene Inc. (Korea) on a dengue virus genotyping kit and detection of chikungunya virus.

3.1.2 *Academic staff mobility*

UM is intensifying its efforts to attract high-calibre foreign academic staff, and had a target to increase international faculty by 180% in 2007. Staff sabbaticals overseas have always been encouraged and in any year a number of academic staff will be attached to foreign laboratories or departments.

3.2 Universiti Sains Malaysia (USM)

As a research university, USM has set the following strategic goals for itself to achieve its aspirations:

- to act as an engine of growth;
- to create an environment conducive to research;
- to nurture exploration and creativity; and
- to integrate with national and international innovative systems.

3.2.1 *Research collaboration*

Collaboration can be initiated either by USM, as a top-down exercise, or bottom-up by individual researchers, research groups or research centres. A top-down initiative would normally be backed by USM in terms of funding, management and organisational support. These are usually collaborations that are deemed to be of great potential, and are in line with the niche, vision and mission of USM. Nevertheless, equal importance is given to other forms of collaboration, as USM has had successes in making such researcher-initiated links into a university-wide effort, involving researchers from across all three campuses of USM. It is a USM practice that an MoU with any institution should open up opportunities for collaboration university-wide, and is not exclusively for the initiator of the collaboration. It is also the practice of USM to have MoAs attached to these MoUs to ensure that these collaborations are always active.

Organisations that have links with USM (active since 2000) are wide-ranging. Table 2 lists the nature of the collaborations and the institutional level by country for the Asia–Pacific region (details are provided in Appendix 1). The success of this networking and cross-border relationships may be further supported by the number of grants received as well as the mobility of researchers and students between partnering nations. Since 2000, 81 projects have been established with

Table 2.   USM: Collaborators by country
(active from 2000 onwards)

Country	No. of collaborators
Australia	9
Canadian	2
China	9
Cuba	6
Indonesia	9
Iran	3
Japan	15
Korea	3
New Zealand	1
Pakistan	1
Palestine	1
Singapore	2
Sri Lanka	1
Thailand	1
The Philippines	2
USA	5
Vietnam	1
Other regions	25
Total	**96**

35 organisations from 12 countries, amounting to US$3 million, and involving 56 USM researchers.

3.2.2 *Collaborations with the private sector/industry*

USM has been collaborating with private industry for some time, with its collaboration with the global electronic flagship INTEL the foremost. USM and INTEL's co-location in Penang has made this collaboration possible for the last 20 years. Furthermore, the establishment of USM's private arm — USAINS Holding Sdn Bhd — under the corporatisation of Malaysian universities in the late 1990s has made collaborations and joint ventures with the private sector possible.

3.2.3 *Innovation at USM*

USM has always viewed innovation as a key factor in attaining its mission, and is therefore serious about positioning itself in the global higher education landscape, exploiting its innovation to give it competitive advantage. Following an 'out-of-the-box' approach to research and innovation, the USM Innovation System was formulated to advance the innovation agenda of the university. Because it intends its research agenda to go beyond the normal domain, USM has included the entire innovation nexus of Research–Development–Commercialisation–Enterprise plus Park (P). This nexus (RDCP) represents the complete innovation cycle as formulated by USM; Fig. 2 is a diagrammatic representation of this cycle.

USM believes that facilitation is critical in ensuring that as many products as possible will go through the R–D–C journey. The innovation park concept was created to ensure that there is a place for incubation and for new ventures to be conceived, nurtured and ensured of success. The innovation system is a framework to ensure that the university will assist all to excel. Importantly, the system

Figure 2.   USM as a research-intensive university

Source: Dzulkifli and Ramli (2005).

acknowledges the contribution of all players, whether they are doing fundamental research, or providing intangible contributions to product innovation. In addition, the innovation system stresses the need to collaborate: amongst the players in USM, partners from outside, and especially players within industry. The Innovation Park is the place to nurture future talents, realise endeavours, seal partnerships and develop/commercialise products. In the final analysis, this whole set of integrated activities is expected to bring benefits and economic returns to the university. In other words, the innovation system provides a closed-loop and clear investment returns to the university.

It is noteworthy that USM's innovation park embodies its aspiration of catering for research in both the arts and the sciences. This park, appropriately called the Science and Arts Innovation Space (SAINS), will complete the ingredients of the USM Innovation System. With the established procedures, facilitators and a custodian, in the form of the Innovation Office, USM hopes that the innovation drive will help elevate USM to the next level of success.

Figure 3 depicts conceptually the ways in which the USM Innovation System will provide clear links and returns both for the teaching and the career path of academic staff. It illustrates clearly the nature of output required of academic staff to realise the USM model. More importantly, the innovation system emphasises the important role of linking with global and national institutions, private industry and the community at large.

3.3 Universiti Kebangsaan Malaysia (UKM)

3.3.1 *Research collaborations*

As the national university of Malaysia, UKM's main aim is to contribute to the advancement of knowledge in the social sciences and humanities, religion, and science and technology through the Malay language as the official medium of instruction (UKM, 2000). UKM offers a wide range of undergraduate and postgraduate programs and undertakes a large share of the scientific research in the country,

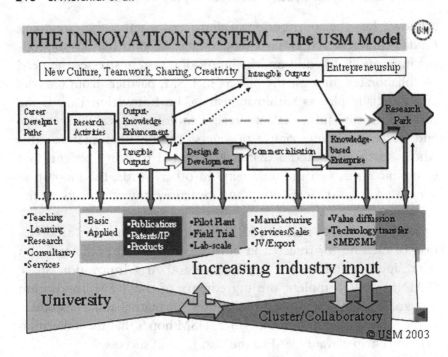

Figure 3.   The USM innovation system

Source: Dzulkifli and Ramli (2005).

as well as activities involving cultural dissemination and the preservation of national heritage, for which it is responsible. The UKM Strategic Plan (2000–2020) emphasises the requirements of an internationalised university. One of the general objectives of the internationalisation strategy for research is to develop networks focusing on research, consultancy and publication at regional and international levels and to identify UKM research centres as referral centres at the international level (Universiti Kebangsaan Malaysia, 2000).

Before its establishment as a research university, many of UKM's research collaboration activities were built on existing personal relationships and friendships. These casual links primarily involved individual academics who worked together informally on similar research projects without any funding.

However, with the setting up of the Centre for Public and International Relations (PUSPA) in 2002, formal collaborative relationships were established in the form of MoAs or MoUs signed by the university and/or the Ministry of Higher Education. Many of the collaborative programs focused on research capacity building that provided pathways for UKM academics to improve their research skills, in turn strengthening their research capacities.

3.3.2 *Research collaborations in the Asia–Pacific region*

UKM has been active in expanding its research activities and has signed MoUs with universities and institutions in Asia and the Pacific, with East Asia topping the list (Table 3). (Details are provided in Appendix 2.)

While science and technology and medicine were important fields and niche areas for research collaborations between UKM and institutions in the Asia–Pacific region, research areas in the social sciences and humanities are becoming increasingly important.

Table 3. UKM: Number of MoUs and research collaboration in the Asia–Pacific region

Region	No. of MoUs and research collaborations
East Asia	31
Southeast Asia	27
Australia & New Zealand	17
Americas	18

3.3.3 *Postgraduate student mobility program*

The postgraduate student exchange program in UKM was set up in 2002 by the Department of International Relations, PUSPA. Under this program, a student may spend up to three months undertaking research in a foreign laboratory. These students are viewed as UKM's ambassadors to enhance collaborative research with

Table 4. UKM: Postgraduate student mobility programs 2002–2006

Year	No. of students	University/Institution
2002	2	• University of Canterbury, New Zealand
2003	9	• Australian National University, Australia • University of Cape Town, South Africa • University College Cork, Ireland • Universitaet Maastricht, The Netherlands • Institut Teknologi Bandung, Indonesia • Hussian Ebrahim Jamal (HEJ) Research Institute of Chemistry, University of Karachi, Pakistan
2004	6	• Hussian Ebrahim Jamal (HEJ) Research Institute of Chemistry, University of Karachi, Pakistan • Stockholm Universiteit, Sweden • Institute Teknologi Bandung, Indonesia • Cambridge University, UK • University of Reading, UK • The Royal Botanic Gardens, Kew, UK
2005	7	• Beijing University of Chemical Technology, China • Hussian Ebrahim Jamal (HEJ) Research Institute of Chemistry, University of Karachi, Pakistan • University of Cologne, Germany • The Royal Botanic Gardens, Kew, UK • University of Queensland, Australia
2006	3	• National University of Chonbuk, Korea • University of Colorado Science Centre, USA • University of New South Wales, Australia

the university they visit. The number of students involved and university/institutions visited are given in Table 4.

3.3.4 *Chairs and visiting professor program*

UKM has obtained endowment funds from the private sector to set up special professorial chairs of research and training in faculties and institutes. About US$2.7 million has been donated by outside corporations and foundations for the five chairs of excellence, as indicated

Table 5. UKM: Professorial Chairs and Visiting Professor
Programs funded by the private sector

Name of Chair	Year established
Noah Foundation Chair	1995
Pok Rafeah Chair	1997
Rashid Hussain Group Chair	1997
Tun Ismail Ali Foundation Chair	2001
Abdulaziz Palace Foundation Chair	2002

in Table 5. It is interesting to note that most of the chairs are held by leading scholars from the Asia–Pacific region.

In view of the development of an Asia–Pacific Framework for research and innovation, it is important at some stage to examine the areas of strength of lead scholars in the Asia–Pacific and to explore their contributions in terms of multilevel, multisectoral and interactive synergies with industry, civil society and the university.

3.4 Monash University Sunway Campus, Malaysia

3.4.1 *Research collaborations*

Monash University Sunway Campus established its presence in Malaysia on 23 February 1998 in Bandar Sunway, Selangor, upon the invitation of the Malaysian Government. Monash University sees itself at the forefront in terms of engaging with society and the community. Through building links with government, business and the local community, the university hopes to contribute to national and regional development through education, research and philanthropic endeavours and thereby become an integral part of Malaysia.

Industry and government linkages are important elements of the campus strategy to make significant contributions to the nation and the region. Monash University has engaged with industry, government and organisations and important 'think tank' institutes in the region. These collaborations have taken the form of research cooperation, technological partnership, sharing of resources (expertise, equipment and software) and industry-sponsored postgraduate scholarships.

Monash Malaysia has undertaken several initiatives to enhance its engagement with the community, including government (such as the National Information Technology Council, Multimedia Commission and the National Economic Action Council) and local professional societies (such as the Institute of Engineers Malaysia and Institute of Banks Malaysia).

A network has also been established with government and quasi-government agencies or bodies, corporations (industry), other institutions of higher learning, and non-government organisations (NGOs). (Details are presented in Appendix 3.) This engagement enables Monash Malaysia to contribute to the review and development of standards of professional practice, national higher education policy, and socio-economic policies in Malaysia and the ASEAN region.

Monash Malaysia was allowed access to government funding in late 2004 for the Intensified Research in Priority Areas (IRPA) from the then Ministry of Science, Technology and Environment. Within a short period, the campus had secured its first IRPA funding. This funding was frozen in 2005, and in 2006 it was restructured into three new grants. Monash Malaysia's Medical School at the campus has also successfully garnered a number of grants from the Ministry of Health. Access to such funding options has proven beneficial for both researchers and the government of Malaysia to achieve the country's benchmark for research and development through measures used by the Malaysian Science and Technology Information Centre (MASTIC), such as bibliometric study and research innovations and commercialisation.

Internal research funding increased by 15% and external funding by 54% between 2006 and 2007. External collaborations increased in tandem with increased funding as well as research events sponsorship (Table 6).

Table 6. Monash University Sunway Campus: Breakdown of externally funded projects by collaboration partners

No. of projects	No. of projects with public institutions	No. of projects with private institutions	No. of projects with industry partners	No. of projects with international institutions/industry partners
34	14	2	3	9

Note: Some projects do not have external collaborations.

3.4.2 Research collaboration areas

Monash Malaysia has five schools: the School of Arts and Sciences, School of Business, School of Engineering, School of Information Technology, and the Tan Sri Jeffrey Cheah School of Medicine. Research collaboration at the campus involves diverse categories, but emphasises science, technology, and medicine and health.

3.4.3 Research plans

Monash's future direction is driven by two plans developed to achieve research excellence by 2010: the Campus Operational Plan 2008–2010 (COP) and the Research and Research Training Plan 2006–2010 (Table 7).

4 UNDERSTANDING RESEARCH CULTURE: THE MALAYSIAN CONTEXT

In Malaysia, conducting research of the highest quality is central to the mission of all research universities (Morshidi, 2007). University researchers must understand that research requires development as a continuous process measured against new challenges and stated objectives that the university should set, review, renew and resource in a given period of time. In the pursuit of a research culture and excellence, all research universities have instituted a research strategy

Table 7. Monash University Sunway Campus: Research and research training plan strategies 2006–2010

RRTP	Strategies
Research excellence	Manage academic staff profile to achieve national research leadership
	Address national and international multidisciplinary research priorities
	Align investment in research infrastructure and support to achieve national research leadership
Impact through research training	Provide HDR students with high-quality supervision, infrastructure and support
	Increase the quality and number of HDR students
	Increase staff with postgraduate qualifications on all campuses
Impact through engagement and collaboration	Enhance the ability for industry, government and the community to engage with Monash Malaysia researchers
	Increase collaboration with leading international research institutions
	Increase collaboration with national research institutions

and operational policy to provide direction and vision for the development of research. These include:

1) coordinating and encouraging 'team research' based on research clusters and groups;
2) planning and facilitating the research direction of research teams/groups based on strengths and a comprehensive action plan;
3) monitoring team research performance and team leaders based on set key performance indicators;
4) providing an assessment of the quality of research as a means of selectively allocating research funding; and
5) providing appraisal, reward and remuneration systems to nurture and develop research excellence.

Accordingly, effective management structures and mechanisms are regarded as fundamental components of the research environment capable of generating the desired culture as well as research quantities and quality outcomes.

5 WHAT INHIBITS RESEARCH CULTURE: PUTTING STRATEGIES IN PLACE

There are many challenges for the newly established research universities in Malaysia. The change from the old paradigm of individual research to group research with a direct relevance to the university research trust or priority areas is slowly taking place. The demand for interdisciplinary and integrated research also poses great challenges to some of the faculties and research institutes. These faculties and institutes have been traditionally organised with units encompassing similar disciplines. The lack of fit and the difficulty in communicating and collaborating across disciplines need to be addressed. Another constraint is the shift of emphasis from research input and processes to the management of research products or output. Based on research quality indicators, measurable research output increasingly determines the performance and quality of research. The challenge is to encourage university researchers to produce tangible output from their research so that what they use (input), do (process) and produce (output) in research will add measurable value to the nation and society. These new demands are clearly reflected in USM's Innovation Plan.

6 DISCUSSION AND CONCLUSION

The way forward in enhancing university collaboration in research and student exchange in the Asia–Pacific region has been in place for some time. For the Malaysian research universities discussed in this chapter, membership in international associations has helped expand their networks of linkages. These associations hold regular meetings to discuss general and specific issues pertinent to higher education and related matters. Many seminars have focused on how to further enhance research collaborations as well as to improve research management. As trust between partners is a prerequisite in any collaboration, potential partners may be secured by participation in such networks. UM, USM and UKM became members of the ASEAN University Network (AUN) in part through their research activities in the ASEAN–European Union University Network Programme (AUNP).

The European Commission developed AUNP to build long-standing, high-level political dialogue with the Association of Southeast Asian Nations (ASEAN). A total of €7.7 million was allocated to fund programs over a five-year period beginning in 2002. There were two major components in the program: partnership projects and network initiatives. The partnership projects provided funding for many areas of mutual interest. The network initiatives aimed at strengthening education-based networks in Southeast Asia through dialogue, round table meetings and Rectors' conferences. The research strand under AUNP not only enhanced networking between ASEAN and EU universities but also provided a platform for intra-ASEAN research networking. AUNP dialogues promoted the expansion of membership of the ASEAN University Network. Research collaboration can only be enhanced if membership into other specialist networks is also expanded. Many research and university associations in the Asia–Pacific region can act as springboards for meaningful collaboration.

What lessons can be learned from the case studies presented above? Can we build and sustain the extant models and adopt the experiences of Malaysian universities as points of entry to discuss the issues relating to the development of an Asia–Pacific framework for research and innovation?

Research universities in Malaysia are actively seeking international collaborations within the Asia–Pacific and beyond. Monash Malaysia is trying to embed itself locally, which may not be surprising as it sees itself as 'global', being an Australian import. Broadly, the case of Monash Malaysia could be employed as a point of departure to examine why large numbers of foreign students find this type of university 'a mobile commodity', and to look at the ways in which providers, including lecturers, design curricula and programs as mobile commodities within the discourse of global economies, politics, migration and security. Further, given what is reported here, there is an urgent need to examine the ways in which Australian global higher education has been mediated in terms of the local Malaysian partnership to leverage research and innovation. How, for example, have the Australian guidelines on teaching, learning and governance been used for the Malaysian campus? How have the Malaysian campus and its ways of doing in the Malaysian context informed Monash Australia, if at all?

Each research university discussed has specific strengths where strategic links to research (at the international level) are evident. UM is looking to the West, but UKM and USM are emphasising the Asia–Pacific. As far as can be determined from the reports submitted, postgraduate and staff mobility are still low, although Malaysia is increasingly viewed as an important player in the higher education market with a new group of learners from the Middle East and Southeast Asia. In view of the significance of the learner in knowledge production, economic wealth creation and labour movement within a rapidly expanding higher education market in the Asia–Pacific, the opportunities have not been fully exploited. At the same time, research universities need to examine learner mobility closely as it increases and multiplies, particularly in relation to work, migration, security and world citizenship issues.

It is important to conceptualise an Asia–Pacific framework for research and innovation, building on the extant models shown here as case studies. In terms of establishing a sustainable research and innovation framework, USM's model may be used (among other existing national and regional models) as a point of entry to compare and build an Asia–Pacific framework where multiple stakeholders identify and work with multiple and plural pathways across private–public–civil–industry sectors to translate research into teaching, commercialisation and community collaboration.

Although the earlier section of this paper discussed the organisational structures of research collaboration and innovation, it did not touch directly on the specifics of research strands. It would, however, be important for an Asia–Pacific framework on research and innovation to identify and compare significant areas of research within and across contexts (regionally and locally).

Underpinning collaborative research, a complex negotiation of the plural cultures, languages and knowledge of the Asia–Pacific for the sciences and the arts and social sciences is imperative if the local in the global is to be sustained. UKM's research strategy in terms of developing Malay as a medium of knowledge for science and the arts and humanities could be reflexively examined as a point of entry for building a sustainable Asia–Pacific framework for research and innovation.

Next, in terms of a sustainable Asia–Pacific framework for research and innovation, the link between research and teaching is an important area to investigate. USM's model of innovation has developed as a dynamic research–innovative system. This could be analysed for the Asia–Pacific framework, with regional cooperation as its building block and the expanding market for education as its driving force. Insofar as the link between research and teaching is concerned, future discussion should focus on the dynamics and mechanisms of how research informs teaching–learning and is in turn informed by teaching–learning. Current theories on learning and teaching in higher education do not see a clear divide or a unilinear relationship between research and teaching. Indeed, they see teaching and learning as a research focus in its own right, with an equal interactive relationship with research.

In terms of a viable future, stakeholders would need to re-evaluate the dominant discourse around international ranking that has led in part to accelerated efforts in international collaboration and research, but with competition lurking in the background.

REFERENCES

Abdul Razak A, Sarjit K and Morshidi S (2007). Restructuring of university governance: The case of Malaysia. In *Higher Education in the Asia Pacific. Challenges for the Future*, P Kell and G Vogl (eds.), pp. 61–83. Cambridge Scholars Publishing, Newcastle.

Denman B (2002). Globalisation and its impacts on international university cooperation 1. http://www.globalisation.icaap.org/content/v2/04_denman.html (accessed 12 March 2008).

Dzulkifli AR and Ramli M (2005). Implementing research assessment in institutions of higher learning: The case of USM. Global University Network for Innovation in Asia and the Pacific 2005 Conference, Kuala Lumpur, 6–8 December.

Kementerian Pengajian Tinggi Malaysia (2007). *Pelan Strategik Pengajian Tinggi Negara Melangkaui Tahun 2020*. Kementerian Pengajian Tinggi Malaysia, Putrajaya.

Lee MNN (ed.) (2004). *Research Assessment in Institutions of Higher Learning.* Penerbit Universiti Sains Malaysia, Penang.

Lenn MP (2004). Quality Assurance and Accreditation in Higher Education in East Asia and the Pacific. World Bank Paper Series, Paper No. 2004–6, August.

Morshidi S (2007). Envisioning and Imaging of the Malaysian Universities Towards Achievements of Regional Hub Status: Are Academics Being Marginalised and Deprofessionalised in the Process? Report of COE International Seminar on 'Constructing University Visions and the Mission of Academic Profession in Asian Countries: A Comparative Perspective', Research Institute for Higher Education, Hiroshima University, February.

Ministry of Higher Education Malaysia (2007). *National Higher Education Action Plan 2007–2010*. Ministry of Higher Education Malaysia, Putrajaya.

Newman F, Couturier L and Scurry J (2004). *The Future of Higher Education. Rhetoric, Reality, and the Risks of the Market*. Jossey-Bass, San Francisco.

OECD (1996). *The Knowledge-Based Economy*. OECD, Paris. http://www.oecd. org/dataoecd/51/8/1913021.pdf (accessed 25 January 2008).

Pyle JL and Forrant R (2002). Globalization, universities and sustainable human development: A framework for understanding the issues. In *Globalization, Universities and Issues of Sustainable Human Development*, JL Pyle and R Forrant (eds.), pp. 3–28. Edward Elgar, Cheltenham.

Sarjit K, Morshidi S and Norzaini A (eds.) (2007). *Globalisation and Internationalisation of Higher Education in Malaysia*. Universiti Sains Malaysia Publisher and Institut Penyelidikan Pendidikan Tinggi Negara, Penang.

Task Force on Higher Education and Society (2000). *Higher Education in Developing Countries: Perils and Promises*. World Bank, Washington, DC.

Universiti Kebangsaan Malaysia (2000). *Pelan Strategik UKM 2000–2020*. Universiti Kebangsaan Malaysia, Bangi.

van der Wende MC (2004). Higher Education Institutions Responses to Europeanisation, Internationalisation and Globalisation: Developing International Activities in a Multilevel Policy Context. Final Report, December. http://www. utwente.nl/cheps/documenten/heigloupdate.doc/index.html (accessed 12 March 2008).

Verbik L and Lasanowski V (2007). *International Student Mobility: Patterns and Trends*. The Observatory on Borderless Higher Education, London.

Challenges and Opportunities in the In-Employment Education Market: A Singapore Perspective

Jayantee Mukherjee Saha and David Ang

1 INTRODUCTION

Education is a liberating force as it has the capability to empower people to think differently and to look at a world of possibilities. Education changes the face of the economy, transforms civilisations and revolutionises thought processes. The impact of education has become more prominent in the current knowledge era. For an economy to prosper, flourish and maintain sustainable growth and development, it needs to be driven by an adequately educated workforce.

As a small island with no natural resources, Singapore has had to emphasise the skills of its population to be economically competitive. From the time of independence, the government has stressed education and training, thus this English-speaking cosmopolitan city-state has thrived on international trade, finance and foreign investment.

The Singapore economy has the second highest per capita GDP in Asia, after Japan (US & Foreign Commercial Service and US Department of State, 2004).

This paper provides an overview of the Singapore education market and looks at the country's 'in-employment' education market. It then considers the major challenges and issues, the Singapore Model, quality assurance, and the role of the corporate sector.

2 OVERVIEW OF THE SINGAPORE EDUCATION SYSTEM WITH SPECIAL REFERENCE TO IN-EMPLOYMENT EDUCATION

In 2000, Singapore's then Minister of Education Teo Chee Hean expressed his ambition to make Singapore the 'Boston of the East' (Teo, 2000). The education industry already formed an integral part of Singapore's economy, contributing 3 per cent of the GDP in 2000; by September 2001, there were some 50,000 foreign students on student visas. The Economic Review Committee 2002 identified education as one of the services industries to be developed and promoted, not only to cater to local needs but also to the large number of international students studying in Singapore.

2.1 The Education System in Singapore — The Genesis

After Sir Stamford Raffles of the East India Company founded Singapore in 1819, a dual education system developed between English-language schools and vernacular schools that taught in the mother tongue (Chinese, Malay and Tamil).

In the 1860s, the colonial state abandoned its non-interventionist policy, initiating a small number of English-language primary and secondary schools and providing free Malay-language primary education. However, grants-in-aid to non-government schools were irregular until 1920 (Gopinathan, 1974). The Winstedt Committee on Industrial and Technical Education (1925) was more forward-looking and highlighted the pressing demand for English-speaking clerks of works, assistant surveyors, road overseers and marine engineers

(Wong and Ee, 1971). The Straits and Federated Malay States Government Medical School had been established in 1905 using funds raised largely by the Chinese community in Singapore and Penang. In 1921, the school was expanded and renamed King Edward VII College of Medicine. In 1929, Raffles College was established to offer courses in the arts and sciences.

After World War II, the colonial education policy took a dramatic turn in the wake of riots and agitation, particularly among the Chinese, for an end to colonial rule. The Ten-Year Program, adopted in 1947, was based on three principles: (1) education should be aimed at fostering the capacity for self-government and the idea of civic loyalty and responsibility; (2) equal opportunity for all; and (3) free primary education in English, Chinese, Malay and Tamil (Gwee, 1969).

In 1948, several businessmen advocated that a polytechnic be established to train technicians and craftsmen. The Report of the Committee on a Polytechnic Institute for Singapore (1953) recommended such a move on four grounds:

- the obvious lack of technical expertise;
- the breakdown of the traditional apprenticeship system;
- the return of many European engineers to their countries after the war; and
- the difficulty in recruiting technicians from the region because immigration laws restricted immigration to highly paid foreign workers (Tan, 1994).

Singapore Polytechnic was established the following year.

On attaining government, the People's Action Party based its education policy on the All-Party Committee Report of 1956. However, a power struggle within the party between the Chinese-educated leftists and the English-educated moderates led to an acrimonious split in 1961. In addition, Malay was declared the national language in preparation for the merger with Malaya in 1963. Because of irreconcilable differences, Singapore left the federation in 1965.

With the consolidation of power within the People's Action Party, the English-educated professionals continued the colonial emphasis on English-language schools for another reason: to prepare Singapore for the needs of an industrial society.

In 1962, the Singapore division of the University of Malaya became the University of Singapore. Full government recognition of the degrees conferred by Nanyang University came in 1968. In the same year, the degree courses at Singapore Polytechnic were transferred to the University of Singapore, leaving the polytechnic to concentrate on diploma courses and, from 1969, certificate-level courses. Meanwhile, the Ngee Ann Kongsi (a foundation involved in educational, cultural and welfare activities in Singapore) established Ngee Ann College in 1963.

In 1979, a Council for Professional and Technical Education under the chairmanship of the Minister for Trade and Industry recommended a substantial increase in tertiary education (diploma and degree level) to produce the trained manpower needed for the Second Industrial Revolution. In 1980, following Sir Frederick Dainton's Report on University Education in Singapore (1979), the government merged Nanyang University and the University of Singapore to form the single, and stronger, National University of Singapore (NUS) at Kent Ridge.

In his review of higher education (1989), Dainton argued that, with rapid economic growth and growing demand for graduate manpower, Singapore should build two strong, comprehensive universities. Consequently, Nanyang Technological Institute (NTI, established in 1981) was renamed Nanyang Technological University (NTU) in 1991. The National Institute of Education was also established as part of NTU. In 2000, the government set up a third university, the Singapore Management University (SMU), offering courses in management. The government is now looking into establishing a fourth university in Singapore.

It is interesting to note that about 65 per cent of the education establishments commenced operations in 1990 and later. Table 1 lists the number of establishments by commencement year as at 2001. Foreign-owned organisations represented 5.9 per cent of the education industry, with an employment share of 3.5 per cent. Some of the

Table 1. Number of education establishments by commencement year, 2001

Commencement year	Locally owned		Foreign owned	
	(No.)	(%)	(No.)	(%)
Total	2,765	100.0	143	100.0
Before 1950	73	2.6	1	0.7
1950–1959	52	1.9	1	0.7
1960–1969	56	2.0	2	1.4
1970–1979	162	5.9	5	3.5
1980–1989	662	24.0	17	11.9
1990–1999	1,422	51.4	88	61.5
2000 and after	338	12.2	29	20.3

Sources: Commercial Establishment Information System and Census of Education Services.

more well-known foreign-owned education organisations in Singapore include the British Council English Language Teaching Centre (UK), the University of Chicago Graduate School of Business (US) and INSEAD (France).

2.2 Singapore Education System — Policies and Practices

The Ministry's 1997 mission statement, 'Thinking Schools, Learning Nation' (TSLN), has directed the transformation in the education system in recent years. Since 2003, the Ministry has focused on nurturing a spirit of innovation and enterprise (I&E). Prime Minister Lee Hsien Loong's call on teachers to 'teach less, so that our students could learn more' forms the basis for the TSLN (as shown in Fig. 1). The Ministry of Education (MOE) also introduced an instructional approach, Strategies for Active and Independent Learning (SAIL), to enhance teaching and learning, to engage students in active and reflective learning, and to nurture independent learning habits.

The structure of education in Singapore is diagrammatically shown in Fig. 2. This shows that education at all levels (primary, secondary and tertiary) is flexible and broad-based to ensure all-round or holistic development. In addition, individuals enter the

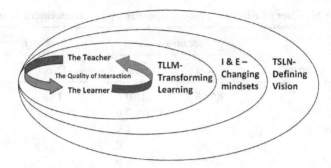

Figure 1.   Teach less, learn more — transforming learning form quantity to quality

Source: Ministry of Education (2005). Singapore Education Milestones 2004–2005: Teach less, learn more. http://www.moe.gov.sg/about/yearbooks/2005/teach.html.

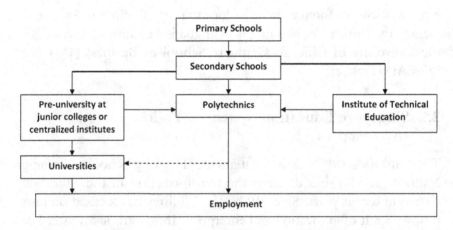

Figure 2.   Structure of education in Singapore

employment market from different educational levels (Institute of Technical Education (ITE), polytechnic and university).

Singapore's local tertiary education institutions are unable to meet existing demand, resulting in a considerable need for international education. There are two types of transnational education in Singapore: 'external' distance education programs and foreign university branch campuses. External programs are offered by a local institution in conjunction with a foreign awarding university, and since the mid-1990s the government has encouraged a select group of elite foreign universities to offer programs and establish centres.

Singapore has attracted 10 world-class universities, including INSEAD, Massachusetts Institute of Technology (MIT), Stanford University, Chicago Graduate School of Business and Technische Universiteit Eindhoven.

The education market is segmented, with demand perceived to come from both consumers (students) and corporations (Singapore is a major base for the regional headquarters of multinational corporations). Four broad supplier categories are delineated, with the acknowledgement that the supporting services sub-sector (e.g., testing and assessment services) could also be attracted to locate in Singapore. Figure 3, from the Economic Review Committee (2002b) report, conveys this segmented conceptualisation.

Singapore's education industry has progressed from supplying basic academic education to catering to varied needs ranging from personal enrichment, skills building, and professional training. The industry structure has also transformed with the entry of more foreign-owned establishments (see Table 2).

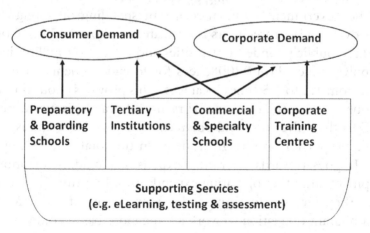

Figure 3.   The market segments for educational services in Singapore

Source: Singapore Economic Review Committee (2002b), p. 4.

"One of the major challenges for a foreign organization to establish itself in Singapore lies in establishing a brand unless there is a global brand.

Brand is equated with quality; priority is given to the rankings and not to the wholesome development. For example here in Singapore, our institution has primarily students from Indian origin and lacks diversity.

One of the reasons is that the students graduating from the local institutions (local students) are given preference by many employers. The Government should also look into this dimension for not only helping foreign institutions to set up their infrastructure here but providing them equal opportunity in the job market as well."

— Dr Vijay Sethi, Dean, Global Masters in Business Administration (GMBA), S P Jain Center of Management.

By 2012, the Singapore government hopes to attract more than 100,000 full fee-paying international students and an equal number of corporate executives ('Going global', 2004).

The government's annual recurrent spending on foreign students over the last three years is estimated at about $154 million in the three publicly funded universities and about $69 million in the five polytechnics. From 2008, fees for foreign students have been raised from 1.1 to 1.5 times local fees. This provides about one-fifth and one-tenth of the total annual recurrent grants disbursed by the MOE to the universities and polytechnics respectively, and is based on the proportion of foreign students in the total student population. It goes towards operating expenses, including manpower, equipment and other operating expenditures. In return for the subsidies they receive, foreign students are bound by the MOE's Tuition Grant obligation to work at Singapore-based companies for three years after graduation. Those who do not wish to meet this obligation pay full fees with no public subsidy (MOE, 2008).

Table 2. Number of education establishments by type of education services and commencement year, 2001

Type of education services	Total	Before 1950	1950–1959	1960–1969	1970–1979	1980–1989	1990–1999	2000 onwards
Total	**2,908**	74	53	58	167	679	1,510	367
Locally Owned	**2,765**	73	52	56	162	662	1,422	338
Music, dance & language	275	1	3	3	9	40	184	35
Academic subjects & tuition	1,278	70	39	37	35	462	506	129
Commercial, information technology & technical	495	2	1	6	13	72	329	73
Higher learning	16	0	2	2	1	3	4	4
Others	701	0	7	8	104	86	399	97
Foreign Owned	**143**	1	1	2	5	17	88	29
Music, dance & language	52	1	0	0	1	5	32	13
Academic subjects & tuition	31	0	1	2	3	7	13	5
Commercial, information technology & technical	19	0	0	0	1	4	12	2
Higher learning & others	41	0	0	0	0	1	31	9

Sources: Commercial Establishment Information System and Census of Education Services.

2.3 In-Employment Education System in Singapore

During 2000–2001, two separate studies were carried out by the Ministry of Manpower (MOM) and the National University of Singapore (NUS). The MOM study focused on adult training and employer-supported training while the NUS study focused on the training needed to address skills shortages and human resource development strategies of the multinational companies based in Singapore. The studies found that:

- The public sector and multinational companies spent the most on corporate training/in-employment education for their employees, especially those with a sizable labour force.
- Smaller firms were more likely to have their training provided by external agencies while larger firms tended to have a mix of both in-house and external training agencies.
- Participation in training was strongly skewed towards those with higher educational achievement. Such participants are more likely to be employed in skilled jobs and more active in the learning process.
- The largest amount of training was expended in the banking and finance sector for managers, professionals, technicians and clerks.
- Employees engaged in public administration, defence, education and financial services sectors were more likely to attend some form of structured training.
- Employees in the hotel, restaurant and wholesale and retail trade sectors had the lowest rate of training. This may be explained by low training participation, the large presence of temporary workers and the use of unstructured on-the-job training.

In September 2002, the education working group of the Economic Review Committee (also known as the Services Sub-Committee) found that, *inter alia*:

- The education industry was estimated to contribute USD1.72 billion to the Singapore economy or about 1.9 per cent of GDP (Singapore Department of Statistics, 2000). By capturing a large share of the global education market, the industry's contribution to GDP could be increased by 3 to 5 per cent of GDP in 10 years.

- Education is a significant service export for countries such as Australia, the United Kingdom and the United States. Education also tends to be a counter-cyclical industry, even during a recession.

- Singapore has several competitive advantages that could allow it to position itself as an education hub, including its strategic geographic location, reputation for educational excellence, its vibrant business hub, and a safe and cosmopolitan environment.

- There are approximately 6000 multinational corporations in Singapore, half of which have regional manpower training responsibilities. As such, one of the Economic Review Committee's recommendations is to encourage such multinational corporations to establish their regional training centres in Singapore.

- Corporate training, in-employment education and executive education have been identified by the sub-committee as offering good growth potential. It further recommended that efforts should be made to attract foreign executives for such training, given that it would be a force multiplier for the economy. Table 3 shows the number of foreign-owned education establishments by country of ownership as of 2001.

One of the suggestions of the sub-committee includes localising the product and addressing the needs of the end-user, *vis-à-vis* mere

Table 3. Number of foreign-owned education establishments by country of ownership, 2001

Country of ownership	Number	Per cent
Total	143	100.0
United Kingdom	48	33.5
Japan	30	21.0
Australia	15	10.5
United States	7	4.9
Malaysia	5	3.5
Switzerland	4	2.8
Others	34	23.8

Source: Census of Education Services.

promotion of ready-made products/services. For example, one local training provider, which offers MBA and bachelor's degree programs through an Australian university, is now translating some of its course material into Mandarin.

Collaboration between corporate training centres and local universities is also encouraged, especially in pursuit of applied research and joint training programs.

3 CHALLENGES AND ISSUES

While identifying the factors that contributed to the successful transformation of Singapore from a low productivity trade centre to a high value-added international business centre, the role of the government has been acknowledged as a major determinant (World Bank, 1993). The policy instruments used in Singapore to supplement market forces in directing scarce resources, particularly labour, to high-growth economic activities may be classified into four major policies: education, fiscal, industry and wage. The first policy aimed at regulating the supply of labour while the other three sought to restructure the demand for labour (Kalirajan, 1992).

The analyses by Krugman (1994) and Young (1994) concluded that input (physical and human capital) growth contributed to output growth and that the contribution of technological progress to output growth was negligible between 1960 and 1986. These studies concluded that Singapore has to devote more resources to research and development as well as to innovation in order to maintain positive growth rates in technological progress for future sustained growth. However, the amount of research and development undertaken by an economy is dependent on the quality of its labour force and the availability of physical capital.

In the present context, Singapore's economy faces several key challenges including, vitally, the growth of India and China and their capacity to attract foreign investment. Also important are the ageing workforce and changing demographics, rising cost of operations/living, and the shift towards a knowledge economy requiring global talent. All of these affect the in-employment education market.

Based on the latest estimates, Singapore's total population, including over 1 million non-residents, was 4,588,600 as of the end of June 2007. The proportion of elderly persons aged 65 years and over had reached 8.5 per cent in 2007, up from 7.4 per cent in 2003 (Singapore Department of Statistics, 2008).

About 66 per cent of the aged population has no formal educational attainment while only 4.3 per cent has completed primary education. The current education level expected in the technological labour market is at least secondary level (which stands at 3.5 per cent) (Fig. 4). Obviously, the lack of qualifications and commensurate training may actually discourage aged workers from seeking employment beyond retirement, as there could be less demand for their skills.

Realising this, the government has taken a series of initiatives to provide financial incentives to employers, such as the Lifelong Learning Endowment Fund and the Skills Development Fund (described later in this chapter), to promote in-employment education and training and to ensure that the present and future workforce is more adaptable.

In 2007, inflation was about 2 per cent and could rise to 5 per cent or more in 2008 (The Economic Times, 2008). This rising cost has

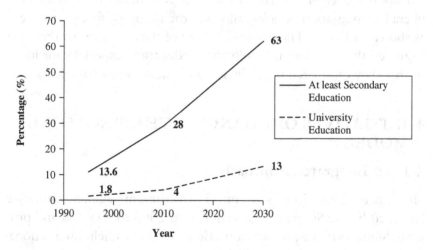

Figure 4. **Education profile of resident population aged 65–74 years, 2000–2030 (% of resident population aged 65–74 years)**

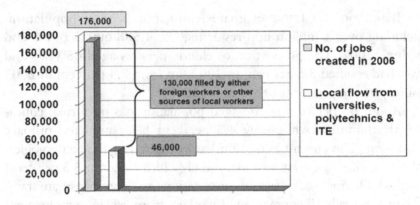

Figure 5.   Number of jobs created and filled — Singapore Scenario

Source: General Household Survey, 2005 and Labour Force Survey, 2006.

prompted many companies (including in-employment education providers) to revisit their expansion plans in Singapore.

Singapore is gradually moving towards a knowledge-based economy (KBE). To hasten this transition, from 1 January 2005, withholding tax on royalty payments was lowered from 15 per cent to 10 per cent, which was especially helpful to smaller businesses. The Singapore government has created a large number of jobs and has liberalised migration policies, allowing the inflow of foreign workers, as shown in Fig. 5. The growing inflow of these foreign workers has triggered the need for in-employment education, especially for locals so that they can match the skills sets and equal the global talents.

4 INITIATIVES OF CHANGE — THE SINGAPORE MODEL

4.1 An Integrated Approach

Singapore Education is a multi-government agency initiative launched by the Singapore government in 2003 to establish and promote Singapore as a premier education hub and to help international students make an informed decision on studying in Singapore.

This initiative is led by the Singapore Economic Development Board (EDB) and supported by the Singapore Tourism Board (STB), Standards, Productivity and Innovation Board, Singapore (SPRING), International Enterprise Singapore (IE) (all under the Ministry of Trade and Industry (MTI)) and the Ministry of Education. The key roles of each agency are:

- STB (Education Services Division): to promote and market Singapore Education overseas;
- EDB: to attract internationally renowned educational institutions to set up campuses;
- IE: to help quality schools develop their businesses and set up campuses overseas;
- SPRING: to administer quality accreditation for private educational organisations; and
- MOE: to oversee the public school system in Singapore.

The Ministry of Trade and Industry is the most important formal institutional mechanism for governance, with the Ministry of Education and the Ministry of Manpower following its lead, although in an integrated fashion.

The government has devoted $6 to $7 billion annually over the past years to education — the bulk going to student subsidies (Budget Highlights — Financial Year 2007). Government expenditure on education (primary, secondary and post-secondary) has remained relatively stable at about 10 to 11 per cent of total expenditure. However, expenditure on tertiary education has increased from an average of about 7 per cent before 2001 to about 9 per cent since 2001. This is largely attributed to higher operating grants and subsidies to Institutes of Higher Learning as well as the establishment of Republic Polytechnic and Singapore Management University to cater to the growing demand for tertiary education.

Between 2006 and 2010, the government plans to invest an additional $5 billion to build up Singapore's R&D capabilities through the National Research Foundation. An additional $0.5 billion is scheduled to be invested in education to nurture the diverse talents of the children and to equip every child with the skills to succeed in a fast-changing world.

4.2 Continuing Education and Training (CET)

The government continues to invest in the quality of the workforce, with programs to enhance the competitiveness of services and promote workplace safety and work–life harmony. As the Singapore government propounds, education will not just be about pre-work education, but also in-employment and post-work education as well as continuing education and training (CET) for workers at all levels. These will become a key focus of national efforts to safeguard the employability of workers. The Singapore government has also liberalised the law to promote international cooperation in education and lifelong learning.

'Our objective is to make Singapore a "Global Schoolhouse" providing educational programmes of all types and at all levels from pre-school to post-graduate institutions, and that attracts an interesting mix of students from all over the world', stressed Foreign Affairs Minister George Yeo (EDB, 2003). He explained that a three-pronged initiative has been set in place to realise Singapore's vision: 'First, we need to attract good foreign institutions into Singapore. Second, we need to develop our own local institutions and enterprises. And, third, we need to bring in large numbers of international students' (EDB, 2003).

The Ministry of Manpower launched the Manpower 21 Report in 2000. This blueprint to develop Singapore's manpower base includes the following initiatives:

- The National Skills Recognition System, launched in September 2000, is a national framework for establishing job skills, alternative skills acquisition routes and certification of workforce skills.
- The Strategic Manpower Conversion Programme (SMCP) aims to train and re-skill Singaporean workers in relevant fields to meet the manpower needs of key sunshine industries.

The government made further headway in its drive to foster a vibrant intellectual climate when Universitas 21 Global — a consortium of 21 well-known universities and Thomson Learning — established its global headquarters in Singapore in 2001. Not only is the online university the first of its kind in Asia, it adds another dimension to Singapore's global schoolhouse vision — e-learning.

The Singapore Workforce Development Agency (WDA) was established in September 2003 to enhance the employability and competitiveness of the labour force. The WDA has two main arms: the Industry Network and the Learning Network. The Industry Network works closely with industries to identify the skill needs of the workforce and to develop industry-focused continuing education and training (CET) programs for both employed workers and jobseekers. The Learning Network builds new CET capabilities, including skills and curriculum development, and research in adult learning and teaching methods. Currently, about 80 training institutions have partnered the WDA in delivering the Singapore Workforce Skills Qualifications (WSQ) system and the Singapore Employability Skills System (ESS) training programs. Many have also incorporated career guidance as part of their services.

The ESS prepares people for careers by offering training in essential workplace skills that are portable, essential and relevant in any industry and that will help workers to remain employable in the ever-changing economy. The ESS was developed by the WDA with inputs from employers and industry associations. These 10 basic skills are critical in improving the efficiency and effectiveness of workers at the workplace: workplace literacy and numeracy; information and communication technologies (ICT); problem-solving and decision-making; initiative and enterprise; communications and relationship management; lifelong learning; global mindset; self-management; work-related life skills; health and workplace safety.

4.3 Re-Skilling for Employment

Re-skilling for Employment is another program initiated by the WDA that aims to select displaced workers from other industries and equip them with relevant trade skills to enhance their employability for trade jobs in the marine industry. The program adopts a place-and-train approach where jobseekers are first employed by companies before being sent for training. For example, Marine Re-skilling for Employment (MariNE), a collaborative effort between the WDA and the Association of Singapore Marine Industries (ASMI), was launched in May 2004. Training under MariNE is skills orientated and includes 352 hours of practical training over eight weeks. On completion of this training, the trainees sit for the relevant skills test in the specific trade. Successful trainees are awarded an industry-recognised Skills Evaluation Test (SET) Level 1 and commence work with the respective companies.

The WDA now also collaborates with industry to offer composite skills assessment under the WSQ system to help experienced and competent workers gain recognised national accreditation of their current skills set. This is an extension of the WSQ Assessment-Only Pathway (AOP) route, which takes workers' prior work experience into account in certifying their skill levels. In addition, WSQ certification is recognised by the MOM in assessing work-pass eligibility. For instance, foreign workers who obtain a manufacturing composite assessment certificate may upgrade their work permit status from unskilled to skilled. The composite skills assessments will be administered by WDA-appointed assessment centres for each sector.

4.4 Role of the Corporate Sector

The modalities of corporate education have matured over time — while most companies conduct their own employee training as a cost centre, some have set up autonomous training centres and some have established for-profit entities. Other companies have outsourced their training to specialised training providers such as the Forum Corporation (part of the Pearson Group).

Many in-employment education/training centres in Singapore are fairly lean, i.e., they have a small full-time administrative team, leverage internal trainers or freelance professional trainers and use hotel facilities to conduct training. Companies are not keen to invest in permanent training facilities, either because of cost considerations or lack of economies of scale.

4.5 Role of Unions

The National Trades Union Congress (NTUC) is a national federation of trade unions of workers in the industrial, service and public sectors. In October 2006, it comprised 63 trade unions and 6 associations. The NTUC includes 9 cooperatives and 6 affiliated organisations — the Singapore Labour Foundation, NTUC Club, NTUC Link, the Ong Teng Cheong Institute of Labour Studies, NTUC LearningHub, and the Consumers' Association of Singapore. Nearly 99 per cent of unionised workers are affiliated with the NTUC, which promotes non-confrontational, amicable dispute resolution and participates in the formulation of policies affecting workers.

The government took steps to control the labour movement through the NTUC by opening the Employment and Employability Institute, or e2i, in September 2007. The e2i will be a key CET provider that all workers will be able to access for training, job search or career guidance.

The government, the NTUC and employers have established a tripartite relationship, an interesting concept in Singapore. A key role of the NTUC has been to enhance workers' employability for life, encouraging them to take full advantage of the opportunities for in-employment education and training. With its strong outreach capabilities and direct links with employers resulting from the tripartite arrangement, the NTUC can mobilise large numbers of workers to undertake training and can match trainees to jobs when they graduate.

Union leaders and employers serve on key institutions such as the National Wages Council, the Economic Development Board, the Central Provident Fund and the Singapore Productivity and Standards Board. Government and employer representatives also give the benefit of their experience to the labour movement by serving on the boards of cooperatives, business ventures and other organisations within the NTUC.

4.6 Role of Professional Bodies

Professional bodies, such as the Singapore Human Resources Institute (SHRI), the Marketing Institute of Singapore and the Singapore Institute of Architects, exist for the benefit of their members. They play a key role in developing occupational qualifications and providing quality assurance in these professional programs. An example is the SHRI–HR Accreditation Framework. To maintain professional standards, SHRI developed a Singapore model for accrediting human resources practitioners, based on the KSC: the HR Competency Framework.

4.7 Financial Incentives

Companies and training providers can capitalise on funding opportunities provided by different government agencies to help develop workforce training programs in specific sectors. The Ministry of Manpower provides the largest number of financial incentives to industries for in-employment education and corporate training programs. The Lifelong Learning Endowment Fund (LLF) is an example. This scheme provides employer-based training as well as individual and community-based training. Its aim is to improve employment prospects and opportunities by promoting and facilitating the acquisition of skills.

Through financial incentives, the Skills Development Fund (SDF) encourages employers to upgrade their workers' skills to enable Singapore to sustain its competitiveness and economic growth. Its key schemes include the Training Assistance Scheme (TAS), which encourages employers to initiate structured training and development programs for employees; the Training Plan Scheme (TPS), which subsidises training costs and helps employers to adopt a systematic training approach; and the Consultancy Assistance Scheme, which encourages companies to undertake projects to improve productivity through raising the skill levels of workers.

The industry-wide initiatives of the Manpower Development Assistance Scheme (MDAS) aim at improving the employability of the older and less-educated, and training workers needed for strategic industries. It complements the employer-based incentives provided under the SDF and LLF. It is currently promoting the Workforce Development Program, which retrains workers at risk of structural unemployment. Another initiative is the Critical Training Program Development, which funds training organisations, associations or leading companies to develop new training programs for Singapore's strategic industries. This specific fund is available only to the top industry bodies, such as industry associations, groups of companies and economic agencies.

The Learning Infrastructure Development Scheme shares the development costs of industry training centres for critical industries to encourage industry associations and leading Singapore-registered companies or societies to play a stronger role in training. The scheme also encourages companies to share their expertise with other players in the same industry or in the same value chain through expanding their corporate training outfit.

5 QUALITY ASSURANCE

The growing number of local and foreign suppliers of content, technologies and services makes it increasingly difficult for companies to choose high-quality training service providers. Thus, the government has established a quality assurance system to help providers upgrade their standards and to introduce transparency in the marketplace.

The presence of world-renowned universities providing executive education and in-employment programs in the market is forcing most training providers to improve the quality of their services and to use their branding to differentiate themselves.

Corporate customers of training products and services also increasingly prefer to connect to a single company capable of promoting a full range of products and services. This relates to the need to have a company that can offer training in both technical and non-technical areas and deliver it across various platforms, be it classroom, online or both.

Singapore has an Education Excellence Framework (Fig. 6) designed in 2004 to protect learner interests and to build high-quality

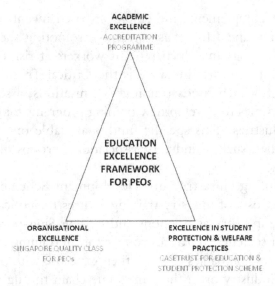

Figure 6.   Education excellence framework for Professional Employment Organisations (PEOs)

education providers, and which is aimed primarily at Private Education Organizations (PEOs). The framework focuses on three key components: academic excellence, organisational excellence, and strong student protection and welfare practices.

The MTI has established an Education Services Accreditation Council to accredit institutions for their capabilities to deliver quality programs. The second component of the framework focuses on enhancing the organisational excellence of PEOs by encouraging them to upgrade through the SQC (Singapore Quality Class) for PEOs Scheme, which provides a benchmark for PEOs in business and management excellence. The third component focuses on PEOs adopting good practices in student protection and welfare through the CaseTrust for Education scheme, which includes the Student Protection Scheme.

CaseTrust is a collaborative accreditation scheme between CASE, the Building and Construction Authority (BCA), EDB, National

Association of Travel Agents of Singapore (NATAS), Singapore Retailers Association (SRA), SPRING Singapore, STB and the Infocomm Development Authority of Singapore (IDA), supported by the Ministry of Manpower, for the accreditation of employment agencies and private education organizations, respectively. It also identifies businesses that have good business practice and a reputation for fair trading.

6 CONCLUSION

Singapore's economy is growing rapidly. Employment is expanding strongly, creating a dearth of skilled manpower to fill the gaps and sustain the growth. It is a balancing act between optimising local manpower resources and the inflow of foreign workers. The government is attempting to maintain a balance and hence there is a consolidated effort from many departments and agencies to promote lifelong learning. The phenomenon of in-employment education is therefore a priority.

ACKNOWLEDGEMENTS

The authors are grateful to PECC, Professor Tan Teck Meng, Dr David Wan and Dr Vijay Sethi for their guidance, support and valuable inputs.

REFERENCES

All-Party Committee on Chinese Education (1956). *Report of the All-Party Committee of the Singapore Legislative Assembly on Chinese Education.* Government Printer, Singapore.

Altbach P and Kelly G (eds.) (1984). *Education and the Colonial Experience.* Transaction Books, London.

Altbach PG (2000). Asia's academic aspirations: Some problems. *International Higher Education*, 19, 7–8. http://www.bc.edu/bc_org/avp/soe/cihe/newsletter/News19/text4.html (accessed 12 May 2008).

APEC (2001). *Measures Affecting Trade and Investment in Education Services in the Asia–Pacific Region.* Report to the APEC Group on Services.

Arrow K (1962). The economic implications of learning by doing. *Rev Econ Stud*, 29, 155–173.

Association of Singapore Marine Industries. Marine Reskilling for Employment Programme (MariNE). http://www.asmi.com/index.cfm?GPID=129 (accessed 7 July 2008).

Branson L (2001). Singapore tops in globalisation. *Straits Times*, 10 January, p. 1.

Brown D (1998). Globalization, ethnicity and the nation-state: The case of Singapore. *Aus J Int Aff*, 52(1), 35–46.

Carnoy M (1974). *Education as Cultural Imperialism*. David McKay, New York.

Coleman J (ed.) (1965). *Education and Political Development*. Princeton University Press, New York.

Cunningham JB and Gerrard P (2000). Characteristics of well-performing organisations in Singapore. *Singapore Management Review*, 22(1), 35–64.

Dainton FS (1979). *Report on University Education in Singapore*. Prime Minister's Office, Singapore.

Dainton FS (1989). *Higher Education in Singapore*. Ministry of Education, Singapore.

Economic Times (2008). Singapore PM sees inflation at 5%: Newspaper. *Economic Times*, 4 February. http://economictimes.indiatimes.com/News/International_Business/Singapore_PM_sees_inflation_at_5_Newspaper/rssarticleshow/2754350.cms (accessed 7 July 2008).

Education (2000). Profile of an educationist: Dr Thomas Khoo. *Education: Singapore's Knowledge Industry Journal*, June/July, 21.

Gopinathan S (1974). *Towards a National System of Education in Singapore 1945–1973*. Oxford University Press, Singapore.

Gwee YH (1969). Education and the multi-racial society. In *Modern Singapore*, JB Ooi and HD Chiang (eds.), pp. 208–215. University of Singapore Press, Singapore.

Hofstede G (1997). *Cultures and Organizations*. McGraw-Hill, New York.

Kalirajan KP (1992). Modelling earnings distorting government intervention: The case of Singapore's managerial earnings. *J Comp Econ*, 16, 105–117.

Kalirajan KP and Shantakumar G (1998). Ageing labour force in a labour shortage economy: The case of Singapore. *Int J Soc Econ*, 25(2–4), 486–503.

Krugman P (1994). The myth of Asia's miracle. *Foreign Aff*, 73, 62–79.

Lee KY (2000). *From Third World to First: The Singapore Story: 1965–2000*. Times Editions, Singapore.

McNutty S (2000). Singapore aims to be centre of advanced academic excellence. *Financial Times*, 23 August, p. 4.

Ministry of Education (1961). *Report of the Commission of Inquiry into Vocational and Technical Education in Singapore*. Ministry of Education, Singapore.

Ministry of Education (1970). *Education in Singapore*. Ministry of Education, Singapore.

Ministry of Education (1998). *Education in Singapore: An Overview*. Ministry of Education, Singapore.

Ministry of Education (1998). *Learning to Think, Thinking to Learn: Towards Thinking Schools, Learning Nation*. Ministry of Education, Singapore.

Ministry of Education (2000a). *Education Statistics Digest*. Management Information Branch, Planning Division, Singapore.

Ministry of Education (2000b). *Information Notes: Registration of Distance Learning Programmes*. Private Schools Section, Ministry of Education, Singapore.

Ministry of Education (2001). *Private Schools in Singapore*. Ministry of Education, Singapore. http://www1.moe.edu.sg/privatesch/privates.htm (accessed 27 May 2001).

Ministry of Education (2005). *Singapore Education Milestones 2004–2005: Teach Less, Learn More*. http://www.moe.gov.sg/about/yearbooks/2005/teach.html (accessed 16 June 2008).

Ministry of Education (2008). *Parliamentary Replies*, 21 January. http://www.moe.gov.sg/media/parliamentary-replies/2008/01/foreign-students.php (accessed 14 May 2008).

Ministry of Finance (2007). Budget highlights — Financial Year 2007. http://mof.gov.sg/budget_speech/downloads/FY2007_Budget_Highlights.pdf (accessed 12 May 2008).

Ministry of Manpower (2008). Expressway for skilled workers to obtain national qualifications. http://www.mom.gov.sg/publish/momportal/en/press_room/press_releases/2008/20080129-WSQ.html (accessed 7 July 2008).

Patton MA (1999). Changes in the Singapore university student demand since the currency crash. *Higher Education in Europe*, 24(2), 203–206.

Riley N (2000). Chicago Graduate School of Business. *Education: Singapore's Knowledge Industry Journal*, 34–36.

Romer P (1986). Increasing returns and long-run growth. *J Polit Econ*, 94(5), 1002–1037.

Schultz T (1971). *Investment in Human Capital: The Role of Education and Research*. The Free Press, New York.

Singapore Department of Statistics (2000). Educational upgrading through external degree programmes, 1998. *Statistics Singapore Newsletter*, January, 17–18.

Singapore Department of Statistics (2001). Educational upgrading through external degree programmes, 1999. *Statistics Singapore Newsletter*, January, 13–14.

Singapore Economic Development Board (2004). 'Going global' with Singapore-based education. http://www.sedb.com.cn/edb/sg/en_uk/index/news_room/publications/singapore_investment04/singapore_investment11_12/0.html (accessed 12 May 2008).

Singapore Economic Review Committee (2002). *Developing Singapore's Education Industry: ERC Report*. Government of Singapore, p. 4.

Singapore Management University (2000). *Background Information*. Singapore Management University, Singapore.

Song OS (1984). *One Hundred Years' History of the Chinese in Singapore*. Oxford University Press, Singapore.

Tan S (1994). *First and Foremost: Training Technologists for the Nation: Forty Years of the Singapore Polytechnic*. Singapore Polytechnic, Singapore.

Teo CH (2000). 'Education Towards the 21st Century' — Singapore's Universities of Tomorrow. http://www.moe.gov.sg/media/speeches/2000/sp10012000.htm (accessed 7 July 2008).

US & Foreign Commercial Service and US Department of State (2004). Corporate Training, Singapore, available at Industry Canada. http://strategis.ic.gc.ca/epic/site/imr-ri.nsf/en/gr109643e.html (accessed 7 July 2008).

Wong FHK and Ee TH (1971). *Education in Malaysia*. Heinemann, Singapore.

Wurtzburg C (1990). *Raffles of the Eastern Isles*. Oxford University Press, Singapore.

Yeo G (2003). Singapore: The Global Schoolhouse. Speech by Minister for Trade and Industry, 16 August. http://www.sedb.com/edbcorp/sg/en_uk/index/in_the_news/2003/20030/singapore_-_the_global.html (accessed 20 February 2004).

Young A (1994). The Tyranny of Numbers: Confronting the Statistical Realities of the East Asian Growth Experience. NBER Working Paper No. 4680.

Japanese Higher Education: Seeking Adaptive Efficiency in a Mature Sector

Christopher Pokarier

1 INTRODUCTION

In 2005, Japan had 726 universities and 488 junior colleges, with many of the latter affiliated with the former. Japan has more than enough domestic higher education places to accommodate anyone who has completed an approved high school program, is 18 years old or over, and has the desire and financial resources to enrol. Many institutions fail to fill their enrolment quotas, while select institutions are oversubscribed by a dozen times or more. Since the initial development of higher education institutions in the mid-Meiji era — the period of rapid modernisation in the last two decades of the nineteenth century — Japan has been characterised by a plurality of institutional types, funding sources and educational entrepreneurship. Although Japan's pre-war higher education institutions represented the pinnacle of elite education reached by relatively few, by 1930 it already had achieved a higher education participation rate comparable to Canada's and well above that of France, Sweden and Finland (Mosk and Nakata, 1987, p. 379). Japan's post-war policy settings showed considerable 'adaptive efficiency' (North, 2005) in supporting mass expansion of the higher education system in response to rapidly growing demand. Although the absolute number of Japanese undertaking higher education studies abroad since has been relatively large, these flows have generally reflected pull factors (e.g., the foreign destination's cultural attractiveness or specialist expertise) rather than the push factor of insufficient domestic higher education capacity to meet demand. Japan is currently unusual in having both its total outbound and inbound student flows roughly in balance (IIE, 2006). Yet international students represent only 3.06 per cent of all students in Japanese universities and junior colleges (MEXT, 2006). This is in contrast to some 13.4 per cent for the UK, 17 per cent for Australia and possibly as high as 28 per cent for New Zealand, but is in line with the share of international students in total enrolments in countries such as Norway (OECD, 2006, p. 293). Inbound international students therefore have had little general transforming effect on Japanese higher education. Rather, the historical drivers of higher education expansion in Japan have been domestic.

Japan's liberal approach to chartering new institutions from the mid-1950s, coupled with fiscal caution and considerable institutional entrepreneurship, quickly brought about a higher education system with high participation rates and a striking reliance on private institutions to meet the bulk of growing demand. Undergraduate education was seen primarily as a private good; the costs were not to be heavily socialised.[1] Consequently, in contemporary Japan 73.7 per cent of

---

[1] James (1986) provides a sophisticated political economy account of differing rates of private and public sector provision of education across prefectures, consistent with the electoral constituencies of the long-ruling Liberal Democratic Party, in addition to the varying presence of NPO providers of education services. See Pempel (1973, 1978) specifically on the earlier politics of higher education expansion and Schoppa (1991) on a later period.

higher education students are in private institutions (77 per cent of undergraduates but only 24 per cent of doctoral candidates), public outlays on the sector are about half the OECD average at 0.7 per cent of GDP, and private outlays are double the OECD average (MEXT, 2006; OECD, 2007, p. 230). In addition, Japan is distinguished by a large private 'shadow education' sector geared to the market for university places (Stevenson and Baker, 1992). State policy objectives, such as those in relation to science and engineering education and research, as well as equity-of-access objectives, were pursued principally through the simultaneous support of nearly a hundred national universities and institutes.

Yet the rapid expansion of Japan's higher education sector brought both immediate problems of quality and profound longer-term problems of structural adjustment. With declining domestic demand and a limited capacity to attract and accommodate international students, Japan finds itself with too many small, unfocused institutions and formidable challenges in realising rationalisation of a fragmented college and university system. Moreover, as leading pre-war institutions provided a model for the creation of numerous new colleges and universities, certain norms, organisational forms and governance practices that could hinder quality teaching and research were inadvertently propagated throughout the system (Nagai, 1971). New institutions recruited academic staff from amongst those trained at the older institutions and often also replicated their curriculums, albeit at a lower level.

Facing this legacy and the high fixed costs of aging tenured staff, many universities struggle to differentiate themselves through a strategic focus on boutique areas of expertise. Moreover, all institutions generate their own interests and legitimating ideas, which may become barriers to adaptation to changed circumstances. This is particularly true in universities that have venerable antecedents and a distinctive social mission. In the Japanese case, a dark historical experience of state intervention in academic affairs at the time of the Pacific War hardened subsequent attitudes amongst many academics towards both state control and executive managerialism (Marshall, 1992; 1994). Although the national bureaucracy retains the capacity to micromanage some aspects of both national and private university operations, its capacity to change established governance practices and professional norms is inevitably constrained.

Intense competition amongst institutions for a shrinking domestic undergraduate market provides some impetus for change. Yet exclusive institutions generally owe their appeal more to their historical exclusiveness than the quality of the educational experience they offer and the established hierarchy of universities has remained strikingly stable. The university and faculty that one enrolled in is a powerful signal to potential employers, which in turn may be life-determining in a labour market characterised by leading firms offering permanent employment and near exclusive recruitment of executives from within. Distinctive features of the market for new graduates therefore deeply affect student aspirations and expectations *vis-à-vis* universities. Similarly, the character of the market for university admission has profound impacts on the entire schooling system and perpetuates an enormous private shadow education industry that, in turn, becomes an influential constituency for the status quo.

2 HISTORICAL DEVELOPMENT OF JAPANESE HIGHER EDUCATION

Japan has experienced several striking periods of higher education entrepreneurship. The active role of the modernising Meiji state in late nineteenth-century Japan in promoting learning from abroad is well known. In addition to compelling local mobilisation of resources for general schooling, creating a lasting positive legacy, the Meiji leadership accepted higher education initiatives by missionaries and domestic educational visionaries, and initiated the establishment of elite imperial universities. The pre-eminence of the first two, the universities of Tokyo and Kyoto, continues as both have the most highly contested undergraduate programs and centres of research endeavour. In the pre-war period, other imperial universities — such as Nagoya, Tohoku, Kyushu and Hokkaido — were founded as well as a number of boutique institutions. The state has therefore been heavily involved for over a century as a direct provider of higher education, with extensive micromanagement of the national institutions being the established norm. Yet such microcontrols were constrained, and sometimes co-opted by, a university governance model that was essentially an extreme form of continental European-style professorial chair systems — an 'academic baronial model' (Clark, 1979).

During the occupation period, student numbers recovered and grew impressively, despite it being a period of economic hardship and reconstruction resulting from the devastation of war. Yet this demand was principally met through the expansion of existing institutions, even as they often struggled with the costs of physically reconstructing damaged campus facilities and then supplementing their pre-war capacity. This was a policy objective of the education ministry (the then Monbusho, now Monkasho or 'MEXT') that favoured a policy of strict criteria for chartering new higher education institutions. While the preservation of quality was an explicit rationale, perceptions of national resource constraints, and the interests of stakeholders in existing institutions, also played a part. In addition to the formal and rather strict chartering process coordinated by the education ministry, an American-influenced voluntary accreditation system for private institutions came into being with the creation of the Japan University Accreditation Association (JUAA) in 1947 (Yonezawa, 2002, pp. 129, 136).

Yet the mid-1950s marked a profound shift towards a liberal chartering regime as the ministry came under pressure from members of the ruling Liberal Democratic Party to take a less restrictive approach to accrediting new junior colleges and universities. This pressure arose in response to constituencies interested in creating entirely new institutions, as well as existing private schools wishing to expand into college and university education. Although the voluntary accreditation system was not embraced by many of the newly emerging institutions, it helped to legitimate the shift to a far more liberal chartering regime.[2] However, new institutions felt no market or

---

[2] Between 1947 and 1956 the JUAA standards effectively set the chartering criteria that the ministry imposed but the ministry then moved to issuing its own standards. In a dual-standard environment most universities did not concern themselves with JUAA accreditation (Yonezawa, 2002, p. 130).

regulatory pressure to seek JUAA accreditation at a time of rapidly growing demand for university places. As a consequence, Japan's standards enforcement regime for higher education became almost entirely centred on the initial foundation period of an institution (or new faculty or program with them). While an institution's poor standing might impact on the granting of ministerial approval for future expansion plans, mature private institutions could effectively escape direct scrutiny of their standards.

Observers in the late 1970s noted that this profound expansion in the number of tertiary institutions had occurred with very little change in the established status hierarchy of institutions (Amano, 1979, p. 11; cited also in McVeigh, 2002, p. 67). Moreover, the curriculum, structures and practices of prestigious institutions were often mimicked by newer institutions. This was compounded by the flow of research degree graduates and, later, retiring academics from the established universities into the staff of new colleges and universities.

2.1 Returns to Higher Education and Equity

A number of scholars have explored the 'internal rate of return' to individuals undertaking higher education in Japan in various periods; Oshio and Seno (2007) provide a good overview of this literature. The weight of research suggests a significant but declining rate of return to university graduates as a whole as the overall participation rate grew substantially. Nakata and Mosk (1987) found evidence that demand for higher education has shown some sensitivity to price, opportunity costs and perceived quality. Studies have confirmed the popular perception in Japan that graduation from a prestigious institution significantly increases the probability of gaining employment in major firms and institutions, as well as bestowing considerable social prestige (Dore, 1976; Pempel, 1973, p. 83). Ishida, Spilerman and Su (1997, p. 880) found evidence that this 'credentialism' effect may be much stronger in Japan than in the United States. There is mixed evidence for subsequent effects on internal promotion although there is considerable evidence that elite graduates are more likely to succeed in the 'delayed competitions' for the scarce senior management ranks (Oshio and Seno, 2007, pp. 54–55). Kawaguchi and Ma (2004) have found evidence that there are returns to the Tokyo University credential independent of the talents of its graduates.[3] Systematic patterns of higher returns to more prestigious university and faculty programs are frequently revealed in research that finds its way into the popular media, which in turn influences preferences for institutions. Some analysis does show that difficulty of entry — as measured by *hensachi* scores — does not always directly correlate, leading *President* magazine (14 October 2007) to create tables of 'cost performance' with competitiveness-of-entry measured against expected income.

Japan's reliance primarily on private institutions and direct contributions by students' families in growing its higher education system in the 1950s and 1960s inevitably involved inequalities of access (Cummings, 1979). Yet arguably the rapid growth of private institutions took some demand pressures off the national institutions in the context of a dynamic 'shadow education' industry in Japan for those who could afford to pay for such entrance exam preparation. Many studies and official policy documents recognise a widening and hardening of class divides in Japan over the last two decades, and an apparent diminishment of social mobility through higher education (Ishida, 1993; Kondo, 2000; Dore, 2007, p. 398).

In 2005, about 8 per cent of the 576,724 domestic students at state-run universities (some 21 per cent of all students) were granted fee exemptions based on financial needs while a ¥2 billion subsidy was provided to private universities for similar purposes (*Daily Yomiuri*, 1 November 2006). MEXT seeks additional government revenues to

---

[3] This clever piece of social science research takes advantage of a historical anomaly to disentangle the market return to a university credential from the talent of the students who were able to enter and graduate from a prestigious university. Owing to student political unrest, the University of Tokyo did not admit a class in 1969, compelling talented students to go to other prestigious universities. In time, the alumni of those universities from this year should have outperformed career-wise, as some of their number would have been Todai graduates in other years. They did not.

substantially increase such fee relief, while the standard national university fee has been raised by 26.5 per cent over the last decade to ¥535,800 per annum in 2006. This still compares favourably with private university fees, which typically range between ¥750,000 and ¥1,300,000 for general humanities and social sciences courses. Yet prospective students are still only permitted to apply to one national university (similar restrictions apply to public high schools), which means that poorer, more risk-averse, students are less likely to gamble on applying to a prestigious national institution. They aim instead for a lesser national option for fear of failing and having to go to a more expensive private institution or being a *ronin*, cramming to try again the following year. In May 2007, Prime Minister Abe's Education Rebuilding Council proposed that students be allowed to apply to two, rather than one, national institutions (*Yomiuri Shimbun*, 27 May 2007).

3 THE MARKET FOR UNIVERSITY ENTRY

The university entrance point became the key signal to employers of individual aptitude largely because there is no standardised school exit qualification in Japan. In contrast to, for instance, the baccalaureate in France, the English A-levels and the HSC or OP scores of particular Australian states, there are no ready means to compare the attainment of graduating students across schools. Hence, the particular university and faculty one is accepted into becomes a crucial proxy measure of relative academic aptitude, with profound consequences for both students and academic providers at all levels (Cummings, 1979; Amano, 1990). Unsurprisingly, the academic standing of high schools is primarily determined by which tertiary institutions their graduates end up in, and likewise all the way back to elementary and even pre-school institutions.

Japan's market for undergraduate entry is notable for, and deeply patterned by, the absence of a centralised 'clearinghouse' for matching students to places. Students apply directly to a limited number of individual faculties within institutions at considerable expense (typically ¥30,000–40,000). Applications are limited not only by the immediate financial costs involved, but also by the particularities of each faculty's application process. The entrance examinations take up the best part of a day, sometimes more, and the concentrated period in which these are held (February to early March) means that the scope for students to apply to multiple institutions is physically limited. The creation, conduct and timely grading of these examinations entails significant burdens on academic and administrative staff in institutions, offset, however, by the significant revenues that entrance examinations have typically brought the more popular institutions.

Even the most prestigious institutions systematically strategise the timing of their entrance examinations to maximise revenues. Typical practices include setting a deadline for payment of non-refundable place acceptance fees for less popular faculties prior to the announcement of passing candidates for more prestigious faculties, effectively compelling the payment of placement fees as a form of insurance against failing to secure a place in the preferred faculty. Within universities, entrance examination processes are the most closely scrutinised of all activities and are widely considered to be where both institutional and individual staff reputations are most on the line. The establishment of the National Center Test for University Admissions had the potential to attenuate some of the inefficiencies of the faculty-based examinations but many universities still require additional examinations or take more students through a solely faculty-based entrance exam.[4] While the ostensible rationale for this is the particular programmatic attributes of the faculty in question, it has the effect of blunting comparisons between faculties and institutions that would make apparent their relative standing in the market.

Perhaps the greatest cost of the established entrance exam system, but one that is impossible to put a figure on, is in the impact on learning styles and skills outcomes arising from essentially pragmatic decisions on the scope and form of entrance exams. Many faculties only set examinations in limited curriculum areas (e.g., such as Japanese language, English, mathematics and one of either Japanese

---

[4] The 'center' exam is administered in late January each year across a wider range of subject areas and students can take the test on even just one subject.

or world history — with mathematics often as an elective). Moreover, the requirement to grade exams and release results within a week or so has meant widespread use of multiple choice questions and scanned mark sheets, with many institutions now doing away with the writing component in exams. This guards against criticism from cram schools and other constituencies about discretionary grading but may weaken the development of students' analytical and communication skills. Such fact-based examinations also favour cram schools and other private providers of exam preparation services.

The centrality of university entrance as a signal has resulted in very high levels of private expenditure on pre-tertiary education, much of it delivered alongside the school system by private for-profit providers. Cram schools (*juku*) supplement regular classes and students may attend these from the early elementary school years.[5] The so-called *yobiko* offer preparatory courses to those who fail to gain a desired university place and so choose to study privately until the following year's entrance exams. Given the large personal returns to gaining acceptance into a prestigious faculty, it is not surprising that a vibrant private market has evolved for the analysis of the relative competition for entry. Central to this are the standardised mock examinations developed and administered by large private cram schools. Students' relative performance in these, coupled with data on university offers, provide measures of the relative standing of each faculty. These unofficial rankings (via the *hensachi*, a standard deviation measure) determine the relative stature of faculties and provide some basis for students to strategise their university applications and exam preparation.

Another striking feature of the Japanese system is the mismatch between the broad compulsory high school curriculum, determined

---

[5] Historically, the key points of competition were for entrance into the final three-year high school, and then into university, and private expenditures on *juku* and other educational services (home tutors, supplementary study materials, etc.) typically rise significantly in the two years preceding these points. In the Tokyo area, competition for prestigious private schools has centred increasingly on the middle school entrance point, and this is one of the few areas of market growth for the *juku* industry.

by the national government, and the far narrower subject range required for entrance to most universities (Tokyo University is noted for its broad requirements). The latter have the effect of weakening student, and even school, commitment to the national school curriculum (and, perhaps, inculcating a tactical, calculating mindset). Indeed, in 2006 a major national scandal broke as it was revealed that over 540 schools were certifying students as having completed certain course requirements for graduation when in fact the students had been permitted to take additional entrance examination cram classes in core disciplinary areas instead (*Yomiuri Shimbun*, 27 October 2006; 3 November 2006). Yet this blatant 'gaming of the system' by many schools was nonetheless somewhat understandable from a social justice perspective: the schools concerned were predominantly in regional areas not well served by specialist private cram schools and/or students did not have the means to pay for such services.[6]

The standing of schools is profoundly influenced by the performance of their former students in getting into prestigious universities. Schools therefore are tempted into tactical conduct to enhance their perceived relative performance. In one prominent recent instance, Osaka Gakugei High School sought to substantially enhance its record of acceptances into prestigious institutions by having one outstanding student apply — successfully in every instance — to 73 different faculties, for which the school paid ¥1.3 million in application fees. The faculties would all accept students on the basis of the National Center Test for University Admissions. The school rewarded the student with ¥50,000 and a watch (*Yomiuri Shimbun*, 21 July 2007). The school had also been paying the university examination fees of other good students over a five-year period.

At the same time, universities have been making significant pragmatic changes to their admissions processes. This is most notable with

---

[6] A policy decision was taken not to revisit the situation of many certified past graduates but 2006–07 (i.e., late March 2007) graduates were required to take make-up classes to meet a contact hour requirement in order to be certified as high school graduates, a precondition for being accepted into a university under national rules.

the so-called AO (from the English 'admissions office') mechanism, which 45 national and public universities and 380 private institutions utilised in 2006 (*Daily Yomiuri*, 18 January 2007; 12 June 2007). This creates an alternative application path, separate from the general entrance examination, which involves a comprehensive review of the students' school records, personal accomplishments, application statement and, not infrequently, performance in a distinctive examination and in an interview. Some lesser institutions are even making AO offers to third-year high school students prior to their August summer break in the hope of securing more students that way (*Daily Yomiuri*, 12 June 2007). The AO process is designed ostensibly to apply a broader range of criteria in the selection process, partly in response to the growing diversity of student backgrounds. Issuing AO offers is attractive to institutions in an era of declining domestic demand because they can fill their enrolment quotas without impinging heavily on their *hensachi* rankings of relative demand owing to the opaqueness of the AO system. Partly for this reason, the Education Ministry is proposing to introduce a new standardised test for the AO process (something akin to the SAT). This would be attractive to the *juku*, which have been much less successful in developing preparatory services for the AO process than for regular entrance examinations. With even the Japan Association of National Universities permitting institutions to increase the proportion of AO admissions from 30 per cent to 50 per cent, beginning with the 2008 Spring intake, these moves by both the education bureaucrats and cram schools are unsurprising (*Daily Yomiuri*, 18 January 2007).

The potential impact on institutions of the shrinking domestic university-age cohort is profound. A survey and analysis by the Promotion and Mutual Aid Corporation for Private Schools of Japan found that in the Spring of 2005, 29.5 per cent of private universities (160) did not meet their intake quota; 17 institutions filled less than 50 per cent of places; and one institution attracted only 14 per cent (*Yomiuri Shimbun*, 27 July 2005; 21 August 2005). A year later, 40 per cent of private universities did not meet their intake quotas (*Daily Yomiuri*, 22 November 2006). Underlying this is the simple maths of supply and demand. Enrolee numbers peaked at 810,000 in

1993 and fell to 690,000 in 2006. Despite this evident trend, the number of private universities actually rose substantially during the same period (*Daily Yomiuri*, 22 November 2006). The forced closure of a recently established institution, Hagi International University in Yamaguchi Prefecture, in 2005 finally made the very real threat of financial disaster in colleges and universities cognitively salient for many.

4 CORPORATISATION OF NATIONAL UNIVERSITIES AND SECTORAL RATIONALISATION

In 2001, the Koizumi government initiated a significant reform and structuring process for the national university system that is still unfolding and contested (Murasawa, 2002; Goldfinch, 2006). Rationalisation of the 99 institutions was an explicit policy objective and by 2007 mergers had reduced the number to 87. Boutique public institutions have been merged with larger general public counterparts, such as the integration of Yamanashi Medical College and Yamanashi University. The Koizumi reforms also altered the legal foundations of national universities, turning them into (more) independent incorporated bodies.

National universities historically had been administered as an extension of the national educational bureaucracy, with administrative staff rotated through various institutional and other postings. While offering certain benefits in terms of accountability, bureaucratic inflexibility was problematic, and the professional gulf between academic and administrative staff was profound. The Koizumi reforms of national universities were predicated on the view that significant changes in the internal governance of institutions would be required to enable mergers, and the removal of direct bureaucratic controls, to result in favourable institutional evolution. As a consequence, the authority of the president, the central administration and deans has been substantially increased *vis-à-vis* professorial faculty meetings, which historically could be a powerful force for resisting change (Goldfinch, 2006, p. 598). Yet, post-reform, there is much anecdotal evidence that institutional autonomy has brought new managerial rigidities and heavy compliance and accountability burdens that have frustrated many academics. An October 2007 survey by the Opposition Democratic Party of Japan (DPJ) found that 65 former education ministry bureaucrats held executive positions across 60 state-run institutions, including two who were serving as university presidents (Kyodo, in *Daily Yomiuri*, 9 October 2007). The DPJ criticised this as an instance of the recently maligned but previously common pattern of *amakudari* ('descent from heaven'), where retired officials take positions in organisations that they previously oversaw.

Data on both student and staff numbers in national universities following the 2001 reforms are revealing: there has been no growth for five years as institutions are compelled to generate an efficiency dividend to cope with certain rising costs (such as age-indexed salaries) in the context of declining public funding.[7] In fiscal 2007, the national government provided some ¥1.2 trillion in subsidies to these institutions. Tuition fees accounted for ¥360 billion of revenue and external funding of various kinds amounted to another ¥210 billion. In addition, public university hospitals generated revenues of ¥620 billion but also entailed heavy operating costs.

Debate is currently raging over the funding model to be put in place from the 2010 academic year. A proposal was submitted to the Abe government in late February 2007 by four members of the Council on Economic and Fiscal Policy, including Nippon Keidanren Chairman Fujio Mitarai, for a radical shift to competitive funding that would hasten institutional rationalisation and specialisation. While resisted by MEXT, the Japan Association of National Universities and the National Institute of Natural Sciences, the reform proposal won support from Finance Minister Koji Omi and prominent figures from private university and Tokyo University. Central to the ongoing

---

[7] With the transformation of national universities into independent legal entities has come a certain discretion over fees. The former imperial institutions reportedly could put fees up by some 10 per cent over the previously standard tuition level without impacting on demand from 'quality' students while regional institutions find that their markets are more price sensitive (*Mainichi Shimbun*, 24 December 2004).

disagreement is the likely redistributive impact away from regional institutions to the leading research universities, the economic impact on regional economies, and specific issues of what performance metrics would be applied. Ministry modelling of the proposal suggested that as many as 47 national universities would become financially unviable under the current proposal (Murai and Hashimoto, 2007). A Japan Center for Economic Research study estimated Hirosaki University's regional economic contribution to be in the order of ¥40.6 billion and Yamaguchi University's at ¥66.7 billion (*Yomiuri Shimbun*, 28 May 2007).

The precipitous decline in domestic student numbers has sparked a range of collaborative endeavours among other types of institutions. At the regional and municipal level, this has ranged from outright mergers between public institutions, such as those involving municipal and prefectural institutions in Tokyo and Hyogo, respectively. No merger between private universities had occurred for over 50 years, a situation that has now dramatically ended with several prominent merger developments. The prestigious Keio University, with its leading medical and nursing faculties, will merge with Kyoritsu University, which is well known for its pharmacy program (*Daily Yomiuri*, 22 November 2006). Kwansei Gakuin University and Seiwa College plan to merge in April 2009. More modestly, but still of historical significance, is the formalisation of reciprocal admissions and credit transfer systems, such as that seen between Osaka Prefecture University and Osaka City University (*Yomiuri Shimbun*, 13 January 2007). Among universities of particular standing, there have been fresh initiatives to promote student mobility as well as research collaboration. For instance, Tokyo, Kyoto, Keio and Waseda Universities have formalised a graduate student mobility mechanism that would allow students to spend up to a year at one of the other institutions (*Daily Yomiuri*, 27 December 2007).

5 SECTORAL ADJUSTMENT AND REGULATION

Debate continues on how liberal policy should be in relation to both the founding and ongoing conduct of private universities. Given declining domestic demand, pressures arise for restricting any further expansion of capacity and for enforcing the enrolment quotas of institutions. Yet in an era when anybody can go to university, arguably students place greater value on institutions differentiated by established prestige or, alternatively, distinctive expertise in a particular field. Reflecting the former, Waseda University, amongst others, has been warned against enrolling over its quota (it was between 1.2 to 1.4 times over quota recently) in a 2007 independent review by the Japan University Accreditation Association (*Daily Yomiuri*, 18 April 2007).

One subset of new university ventures, corporate for-profit institutions, is of particular interest owing to the peculiar regulatory basis for the experiment, for ongoing controversy, and for sharply varied outcomes. Although a general ban on corporate universities remains in place, five institutions nonetheless were formed officially from 2003 through being located in specially designated structural reform zones. One such institution, LEC Tokyo Legal Mind University, based in Tokyo's central Chiyoda Ward, was the first corporate university established but was later subject to a stringent MEXT improvement advisory order (*Yomiuri Shimbun*, 27 January 2007). LEC is a long-established private preparatory school specialising in national examinations for professionals such as lawyers and accountants. Its university program was found to be largely a façade, with most of the courses being the existing offerings in its cram school business.[8] Notably more successful is Digital Hollywood University, based in Tokyo's Akihabara, which offers undergraduate and graduate programs in creative digital arts. Growing out of a specialist vocational school of the same name, its founders have had strong industry support in both curriculum delivery and student placements. Digital Hollywood was commissioned to draft major digital content policy papers for METI, and former Foreign Minister Taro Aso made a substantial policy statement at the institution (Sugiyama, 2006; www.dhw.ac.jp). Digital Hollywood easily fills its assigned undergraduate enrolment quota, in

---

[8] Paradoxically, many of its students in the non-degree classes are 'double schooling' there while being enrolled at prestigious established universities.

contrast to many generic low-status universities. Yet considerable hostility to lifting the general ban on corporate universities remains in the education ministry and a proposal to do so in the 2006 academic year was shelved (*Yomiuri Shimbun*, 26 January 2007). Meanwhile, the existing corporate universities are subjected to close scrutiny of their operations by ministerial assessors, some drawn from established research universities, where practices are not always up to the standards they demand of new institutions.

5.1 Regulating for Quality?

In the absence of effective direct regulatory controls on education quality, the national bureaucracy has tended historically to microregulate inputs into higher education. There has been a gradual unwinding of some of these controls as universities have repeatedly drawn attention to their counter-productive impact on institutional innovation. Only in January 2007 did MEXT revise regulations that obliged private universities to have ownership of their land and buildings (*Daily Yomiuri*, 13 January 2007). The rules had severely constrained institutions' development of branch campuses. Reform came about in part as a result of pressure from local government authorities seeking to attract educational institutions. Yet the impact of the changes will be seen most clearly in existing universities' rationalisation of campus facilities, and their move back into central urban districts in particular. Prospective students do not want the inconvenience of outer-suburban campuses, however lush, that many formerly centrally situated institutions moved to in the 1960s and 1970s. In Tokyo, Hosei University has built a prominent tower in central Kudan and bought the facilities of a girls' middle and high school nearby (*Daily Yomiuri*, 21 August 2005). In nearby Ochanomizu, Meiji University has built the equally large 'Liberty Tower' and its students mingle with those from Nihon University across the street and several other closely situated institutions. Toyo University recently followed suit by moving first- and second-year classes from distant Saitama to new facilities in its central Bunkyo-bu campus.

Since 1991, universities have had greater latitude to design their own curricula. The post-war curriculum model of two years of general education followed by more specialist training is no longer enforced. Ironically, given its prior role in enforcing the general studies requirements, MEXT currently plans to introduce 'attainment targets' in specified disciplinary areas that universities should demonstrate their graduates can meet. The explicit rationale is that many universities' curricula are insufficiently structured, permitting students to take diverse courses on an *ad hoc* basis (*Daily Yomiuri*, 26 March 2008). Underlying ministry statements is the concern about declining academic standards in an era of too many universities for domestic demand.

With the 1991 liberalisation of curriculum controls came a new requirement that institutions undertake self-monitoring and self-evaluation. Proposals for compulsory external evaluation were successfully opposed on the grounds of academic freedom and on the grounds that increasing competition between institutions with a shrinking demographic would be a disciplining force (Yonezawa, 2002, p. 130; see Horio, 1988, on notions of academic freedom). By the early 2000s, neither argument carried much weight. Within policy-making circles there seems to be no faith that market pressures (from employers, mediated through students as well as other channels) will influence institutions to offer coherent academic programs and enforce minimum standards. On the contrary, the Central Council for Education subcommittee report, reflecting MEXT views, stated that: 'With universities giving priority to the immediate securement (sic) of students, the ability levels guaranteed by universities is not clear'. (*Daily Yomiuri*, 26 March 2008).

In 2002, the Central Council for Education 2002 determined that from the 2004 academic year all universities must be independently evaluated once every seven years, with institutional discretion over both the assessing body and how the institutions act upon evaluations. The National Institution for Academic Degrees and University Evaluation, the Japan Institution for Higher Education Evaluation, and the Japan University Accreditation Association are the three authorised lead evaluators, and institutions may choose to submit to scrutiny from more than one. Perhaps not insignificantly, the new evaluation regime created more demand within universities for staff with experience of working in the education ministry.

Private universities historically have shown some market sensitivity, creating and renaming faculties and programs in response to moves by rival institutions and trendsetters. Comparative cultures, cross-cultural communications, international studies, liberal studies and, most recently, international liberal studies, have been some of the buzzwords around which institutions have reorganised existing staff and courses.

Yet both institutional leaderships and government officials have faced considerable barriers to addressing fundamental issues of teaching and research quality, in no small part owing to established patterns of university governance and norms about the nature of academic work.

5.2 Governance and Managerial Change

The old professorial chair system (*kyoza*), where the full professor had exclusive responsibility for a disciplinary area and more junior staff, was often criticised for reinforcing patronage systems, poor governance, and resistance to innovation in both educational practice and research (Clark, 1979; see Hall, 1998, for a very critical perspective). Medical faculties are notorious for the residual hierarchical patronage practices of the old professorial chair system which have even been dramatised recently in a fictional television series.[9] Yet market pressures, following regulatory change, might also attenuate some of these problems — albeit at considerable social cost. University hospitals, especially in the regions, are at crisis point as residents shift en masse for their two-year final training period to general hospitals — where they get more experience, specialist training, and

---

[9] Such perceptions were reinforced in March 2008 with a controversy over the dean of Yokohama City University's Graduate School of Medicine having taken substantial cash gratuities from successful doctoral candidates (*Yomiuri Shimbun*, 13 March 2008).

more money (Sakagami and Tamura, 2006). The last regulatory and policy vestiges of the old chair system ended from April 2007. This was reflected, for instance, in a formal change of titles from 'assistant professors' (*jokyoju*) to 'associate professors' (*jun kyoju*) and the introduction of regulations granting them more independence and responsibility in teaching, research and administration. Many institutions had moved in that direction even before this change (*Yomiuri Shimbun*, 1 May 2006). This regulatory move on so-called vertical segmentation and hierarchy has also been reflected in graduate school policy priorities. In June 2007, the Abe government's so-called Education Rebuilding Council proposed limiting the number of students in graduate programs who had taken their undergraduate degree in the same institution to 30 per cent (*Daily Yomiuri*, 27 December 2007).

5.3 Graduate School and Other Reform Issues

Since 1991, and particularly in the last decade, public policy has placed greater emphasis on strengthening Japanese graduate education. For instance, the creation of professional graduate schools has been seen as an impetus to other reforms in the sectors they pertain to. The creation of professional law schools is a profoundly significant development. In 2007, the school-level education reform championed by the Abe Cabinet was linked to ministerial approval of proposals by 19 universities to establish graduate schools for teacher training (*Daily Yomiuri*, 28 November 2007). Regulatory reform has paved the way for universities to introduce some early graduation mechanisms that, in effect, belatedly recognise that many students were taking sufficient credits to graduate in less than the specified four years. More creative interfaces with graduate programs are permitted and indeed encouraged. Yet recent proposals, such as those drafted by Nobel Laureate Ryoji Noyori as head of the Education Rebuilding Council, would extend graduate school programs from two to three years (creating a 3 + 3 + 2 system — the latter for a doctorate). This would be a shift away from the direction of the EU Bologna process and further diminish the attractiveness of Japanese master's degree programs *vis-à-vis* foreign offerings (which have become as short as a year) (*Daily Yomiuri*, 13 April 2007). Yet the internationalisation of Japanese graduate schools is also an explicit objective of government policy. For instance, MEXT seeks more public funding to bring talented foreign graduate students from developing countries, but is also promoting a change of tax and other laws to facilitate corporate donations to graduate schools (*Daily Yomiuri*, 24 June 2008).

Graduate education reform is seen as inexorably tied to the broader promotion of Japan's research performance and the development of 'world class' institutions (Arimoto, 2007; Kobayashi, Yan and Shi, 2006). A National Institute of Science and Technology Policy study of scientific publishing suggested that Japanese researchers had had a significant impact in fields such as material science and physics, but less so in fields such as environmental science and engineering, in which Japanese researchers might be expected to be prominent (*Daily Yomiuri*, 6 April 2007). Japan came fourth, with 9 per cent of papers surveyed, following the US at 61 per cent then Germany (13 per cent) and Britain (12 per cent). A number of national universities, led by Tokyo University, figure prominently in international rankings but are still seen as needing to do more to attract promising foreign researchers (and to coax talented Japanese back home). Tokyo University has established an engineering 'Nobel Prize' program to attract resources and promising younger researchers (Hasebe, 2006). The Japanese Society for the Promotion of Science (JSPS) provides some 200 postdoctoral fellowships and 70-odd senior fellowships a year (www.jsps.go.jp), but few foreign researchers who come under such programs stay on beyond the fellowship period (Osborne, 2007).

6 OPENNESS, INTERNATIONAL MOBILITY AND COMPETITION

As noted earlier, Japan is unusual in having its numbers of inbound and outbound cross-border student flows roughly in balance (IIE, 2006). Strikingly, degree students are predominantly from Japan's Asian neighbours while visiting students are primarily from American and European institutions (although a substantial minority of the former, in particular, are of Asian background or are actually foreign students in the US). Notably, even in 1965 86 per cent of foreign students in Japan were privately funded, rising to 90 per cent in 2005 (MEXT, 2006). Outbound Japanese student flows are predominantly to Western countries.

For more than a decade, policy statements in relation to inbound international students have often implied that they might be an impetus for improved practice in Japanese universities. Yet there is also sufficient realism to recognise that they are unlikely to compensate numerically for the severe decline in domestic demand for undergraduate education. Over half of foreign graduate students in Japan are in national universities, reflecting their strengths as research institutions, and graduate students represent over a third of total international students (Huang, 2006, p. 527). Undergraduate degree students account for over 40 per cent and the remainder are students in shorter visiting programs of a year or a semester abroad.

Perceived competition from foreign universities, at both the undergraduate and graduate level, figures increasingly prominently in official policy statements and proposals. For instance, the Education Rebuilding Council suggested a significant (and rather problematic) reorientation of the academic calendar to a September start, on the grounds that elite North American and European institutions are on that calendar (*Daily Yomiuri*, 19 September 2007). Universities already can, and indeed some do, enrol students who are graduates of a regular Japanese high school in September. Japanese institutions are well aware of the barrier that the Japanese language presents to attracting international students, except those from neighbouring countries such as China and South Korea, where Japanese language ability confers considerable career opportunities. Some institutions are committed to offering full academic programs in English, such as the private Waseda University at both undergraduate and postgraduate level, and the boutique Asia Pacific University (APU) at Beppu, which is a spin-off from Ritsumeikan University. Yet such initiatives are the exception, apart from small-scale offerings to accommodate limited numbers of inbound exchange students. Japan is still far from establishing the wide range of English-based programs (more often graduate programs) that has been witnessed in Sweden, the Netherlands and even France. Militating against such initiatives are the rigid human resource practices that severely constrain the capacity of faculties to provide incentives to Japanese staff to teach in English. This is despite a significant increase in the number of Japanese faculty who have had foreign graduate training or who have spent at least a significant period abroad in a visiting research capacity.

An official policy statement released in late 2007 urged the doubling of foreign academic staff in Japanese higher education institutions and a significant expansion in international student numbers (*Daily Yomiuri*, 27 May 2007). This further elaborates a view from within MEXT that the 'internationalisation' of Japanese institutions may be an impetus to improved quality. The period from 1992 to 2002 marked a quite substantial rise in the total number of foreign faculty members across Japanese higher education, from 3955 to 9378 (Huang, 2006, p. 531). A total of 77 per cent of all foreigners employed in the Japanese tertiary sector were in private institutions. The hiring of foreign staff in some institutions remains contentious, with claims that special categories of staff appointment entail higher teaching loads and less job security. Yet there has been a notable increase in the preparedness of a number of Japanese institutions to both give tenure to foreign academic staff and post position notices in English as part of a general shift to more open recruitment practices. Nonetheless, in 2005 only 52 of Tokyo University's 2,800 full-time teaching staff were non-Japanese (*Yomiuri Shimbun*, 4 July 2005).

7 CONCLUSIONS

In a cross-country study, Jongbloed and Vossensteyn (2001, p. 141) noted that Japan had a largely output-oriented public research funding model, especially for the sciences, while its public funding of teaching was predominantly input-oriented (i.e., based on total enrolments). While the UK and the US also largely applied such a categorisation, Japan fared less well against Jongbloed and Vosensteyn's recommended criteria for efficient input-oriented funding of teaching. Enrolment caps, barriers to inter-institution student mobility and limited information on the relative quality of academic programs may all compound inefficiencies associated with public subsidies for teaching (Jongbloed and Vossensteyn, 2001, p. 142).

Japan's saving grace, in terms of their funding, should be the predominant role of private fees paid directly to institutions in driving student-centred quality. Yet, as seen above, distinctive features of Japan's labour market and employment systems have made Japanese higher education consumers less sensitive to educational quality while being acutely sensitive to institutional prestige as measured through competitiveness of entry. With the general exceptions of some science and engineering sub-fields, and professional training such as medicine, the value proposition a Japanese undergraduate education represents (relative to many other OECD members' systems) is a more positive signalling effect to the waiting labour market than saleable human capital formation. This is reflected in IMD's ranking of the effectiveness of university education as applied to future careers, which at 58th, had Japan ahead of only South Korea and Indonesia in a 60-nation sample. Japan came last in a small sample in 2000 and 2002 (*Yomiuri Shimbun*, 13 July 2005). Enders and Teichler (1997, pp. 367–368) found that Japanese academics generally rate their commitment to teaching, in contrast to research, significantly lower than do their counterparts in the Netherlands, Sweden, Germany, the US and the UK. Yet the Japanese academics' classes are generally larger, and they are also more likely to be teaching at another institution as well.

Enhanced international mobility — inbound and outbound — of students, academic and administrative staff can facilitate institutional innovation. Students with solid academic credentials and experience of studying abroad are in strong demand from leading Japanese employers given the scale of their international operations. Those institutions, such as Waseda University, that have made an extended study abroad component integral to some of their academic programs are then challenged to meet higher expectations about the quality of teaching, services and facilities from students upon their return.

Inbound international students, especially semester and year abroad undergraduate students from leading foreign institutions as well as postgraduates, create another constituency for better practice. Where such students are integrated with domestic students in common programs and social networks, their impact is all the greater. Yet in even the most internationalised of Japanese institutions, the impact of such visiting international students remains quarantined in specialist host faculties and boutique programs. As discussed above, foreign students in Japanese higher education institutions currently represent only some 3.06 per cent of total students so their impacts are likely to be patchy and incremental. Moreover, some Japanese institutions with low academic standards accept international students with limited Japanese language and academic attainment levels to stave off financial ruin, while some other Japanese institutions with strong brand cache in the domestic market still show little interest in recruiting talented international students.

Graduate training abroad, foreign sabbaticals and conference participation — the latter two being well supported by Japanese institutions — also have important roles to play in the dissemination of good practice. Yet a continuing weakness in the Japanese higher education sector is the tiny proportion of academics, Japanese and indeed foreign, who have held regular teaching posts in foreign universities. Consequently there is still little direct transmission of foreign experience of such practices as performance management, program innovation, assessment and reporting, accreditation applications and the like. Attracting Japanese academics back from foreign employment and addressing continuing barriers to full engagement of experienced foreign academic staff in both the teaching and management of Japanese institutions will assist in institutional innovation.

Policymakers recognise the ongoing weaknesses of Japan's higher education institutions and the potential economic and social implications. The Abe government's Innovation 25, strategic guidelines for a prosperous nation in 2025, explicitly identified university reform, doubling the number of foreign faculty, requiring teaching in English to be doubled, and breaking down programmatic divides between science and humanities majors. Even the conservative *Yomiuri Shimbun* embraced this vision (*Daily Yomiuri*, 27 May 2007). Yet little can be achieved through regulation alone, and the government does not have the fiscal capacity to create powerful incentives for reform where institution-level interests or inertia may currently inhibit innovation. As most of Japan's higher education capacity grew through private institutional entrepreneurship in a near laissez-faire regulatory environment during the nation's high growth period, so must much painful adjustment be market-driven now. Yet a plethora of interdependent microregulations and private institutional practices diminish the pace of sectoral adjustment and impact adversely on educational outcomes.

The tools of state might best be deployed in hastening the 'work-out' process in Japanese higher education while providing some structural adjustment assistance. At the same time, the basic architecture of the Japanese domestic higher education market could be overhauled so that prospective students could be more efficiently matched to academic institutions with regard to academic calibre and career aspirations. This would come at the expense of the large cram school, testing and exam prep publishing businesses but would have positive effects backwards into the school system and forwards into university practice. The historical evolution of Japan's higher education system provides deep insights into how promptly individuals and firms will respond entrepreneurially to institutional flaws, and how the resulting structures of incentives and of legitimating ideas in turn can make institutional reform in such a mature system profoundly difficult.

REFERENCES

Amano I (1979). Continuity and change in the structure of Japanese higher education. In *Changes in the Japanese University: A Comparative Perspective*, WK Cummings, I Amano and K Kitamura (eds.), pp. 10–39. Praeger, New York.

Amano I (1990). *Education and Examination in Modern Japan*. WK Cummings and F Cummings (trans.). University of Tokyo Press, Tokyo.

Arimoto A (2007). The competitive research environment in the Japanese context. Paper presented to the Regional Research Seminar for Asia and Pacific: Competition, Cooperation and Changes in the Academic Profession, 17–18 September, Zhejiang University, Hangzhou, China.

Clark BR (1979). The Japanese system of higher education in comparative perspective. In *Changes in the Japanese University: A Comparative Perspective*, WK Cummings, I Amano and K Kitamura (eds.), pp. 217–240. Praeger, New York. Previously published as Yale Higher Education Research Group Working Paper 33, Yale University Institute for Social and Policy Studies, New Haven, CN.

Cummings WK (1979). Expansion, examination fever, and equality. In *Changes in the Japanese University: A Comparative Perspective*, WK Cummings, I Amano and K Kitamura (eds.), pp. 83–106. Praeger, New York.

Dore R (1976). *The Diploma Disease: Education, Qualification and Development.* University of California Press, Berkeley.

Dore R (2007). Insider management and board reform: For whose benefit. In *Corporate Governance in Japan: Institutional Change and Organizational Diversity*, M Aoki, G Jackson and H Miyajima (eds.), pp. 370–395. Oxford University Press, Oxford.

Enders J and Teichler U (1997). A victim of their own success? Employment and working conditions of academic staff in comparative perspective. *High Educ,* 34, 347–372.

Goldfinch S (2006). Rituals of Reform, policy transfer and the national university corporation reforms of Japan. *Governance,* 19(4), 585–604.

Hall IP (1998). *Cartels of the Mind: Japan's Intellectual Closed Shop.* WW. Norton, New York.

Hasebe K (2006). Todai aiming for Nobel prizes. *Daily Yomiuri,* 16 November.

Horio T (1988). In *Educational Thought and Ideology in Modern Japan: State Authority and Intellectual Freedom,* S Platzer (ed. and trans.). Tokyo University Press, Tokyo.

Huang F (2006). Internationalization of curricula in higher education institutions in comparative perspectives: Case studies of China, Japan and the Netherlands. *High Educ,* 51, 521–539.

Institute for International Education (IIE) (2006). *Open Doors.* www.iienetwork.org (accessed 12 March 2008).

Ishida H (1993). *Social Mobility in Contemporary Japan: Educational Credentials, Class and the Labour Market in a Cross-National Perspective.* Macmillan, London.

Ishida H, Spilerman S and Su K-H (1997). Educational credentials and promotion chances in Japanese and American organizations. *Am Sociol Rev,* 62, 866–882.

James E (1986). The private nonprofit provision of education: A theoretical model and application to Japan. *J Comp Econ,* 10, 255–276.

Jongbloed B and Vossensteyn H (2001). Keeping up performances: An international survey of performance-based funding in higher education. *J High Educ Pol and Manag*, 23(2), 127–145.

Kawaguchi D and Ma W (2008). The causal effect of graduating from a top university on promotion: Evidence from the University of Tokyo's admission freeze in 1969. *Econ Educ Rev*, 27, 184–190.

Kobayashi M, Yan C and Shi P (2006). *Comparison of Global University Rankings*. Center for Research and Development in Higher Education, University of Tokyo, Tokyo.

Kondo H (ed.) (2000). *Nihon no Dansou Shisutemu 3: Sengo nihon no kyouiku shakai [Japan's Class System 3: Education Society in Postwar Japan]*. University of Tokyo Press, Tokyo.

McVeigh BJ (2002). *Japanese Higher Education as Myth*. ME Sharpe, Armonk, NY.

Marshall B (1992). *Academic Freedom and the Japanese Imperial University, 1868–1939*. University of California Press, Berkeley.

Marshall B (1994). *Learning to be Modern: Japanese Political Discourse on Education*. Westview Press, Boulder, CO.

Ministry of Education, Culture, Sports, Science and Technology (MEXT) (2006). Statistics. www.mext.go.jp (accessed 12 March 2008).

Nakata Y-F and Mosk C (1987). The demand for college education in postwar Japan. *J Hum Resour*, 22(3), 377–404.

Murai MI and Hashimoto J (2007). Government mulls university fund cuts. *Daily Yomiuri*, 6 May.

Murasawa M (2002). The future of higher education in Japan: Changing the legal status of national universities. *High Educ*, 43(1), 141–155.

Nagai M (1971). *Higher Education in Japan: Its Take-off and Crash*, J Dusenberry (trans.). University of Tokyo Press, Tokyo.

North DC (2005). *Understanding the Process of Economic Change*. Princeton University Press, Princeton and Oxford.

Organisation for Economic Cooperation and Development (OECD) (2006). *Education at a Glance*. OECD, Paris.

Organisation for Economic Cooperation and Development (OECD) (2007). *Education at a Glance*. OECD, Paris.

Osborne P (2007). Japanese system stifles foreign scientific talent. *Japan Times Online*, 5 June.

Oshio T and Seno W (2007). The economics of education in Japan: A survey of empirical studies and unresolved issues. *Jpn Econ*, 35(1), 46–81.

Pempel TJ (1973). The politics of enrolment expansion in Japanese universities. *J Asian Stud*, 33(1), 67–86.

Pempel TJ (1978). *Patterns of Japanese Policymaking: Experiences from Higher Education*. Westview Press, Boulder, CO.

Sakagami H and Tamura Y (2006). University hospitals haemorrhaging staff. *Daily Yomiuri*, 17 April.

Schoppa LJ (1991). *Education Reform in Japan: A Case of Immobilist Politics.* Routledge, London.

Stevenson DL and Baker DP (1992). Shadow education and allocation in formal schooling: Transition to university in Japan. *Am J Sociol*, 97(6), 1639–1657.

Sugiyama T (2006). *Kuuru Japan: Sekai ga kaitagaru nihon [Cool Japan: the Japan the World Wants to Buy]*. Shodensha, Tokyo.

Yonezawa A (2002). The quality assurance system and market forces in Japanese higher education. *High Educ*, 43, 127–139.

11

Transnational Higher Education in China

Rui Yang

1 INTRODUCTION

Transnational education refers to any education delivered by an institution based in one country to students located in another (McBurnie and Ziguras, 2007). While the international mobility of students is a well-established and growing feature of higher education, the transnational mobility of institutions and courses on a large scale is a recent phenomenon. During the past decade, the transnational provision of education has increased so dramatically that it is at the leading edge of the most fundamental change taking place in higher education, evincing the invisible hand of the market at work and allocating educational resources across borders efficiently. This is a new evolutionary phase within the global development of higher education in the context of emerging international trade agreements for services, the opening of education markets with insufficient capacity to meet the anticipated demands of citizens for advanced degrees, and the ever-present demand for colleges and universities to establish additional revenue streams.

China has been well documented as one of the world's largest education-importing countries, sending millions of students to study abroad. It has, most recently, attracted attention as a fast-growing receiver of students from overseas, but relatively few have noticed that transnational higher education is growing rapidly in China, that China is increasingly significant and, given its size, has the potential to dwarf all traditional offshore markets. The development of for-profit and non-profit transnational institutions operating in an international education market is more akin to international business than traditional academic expansion, a fact that has not always been understood within Chinese education circles. Realising that China is perhaps the world's most complex, over-hyped and under-analysed market for transnational higher education, this report delineates a general picture of transnational higher education provision in China, covering its policy context, major features and issues of concern.

2 THE SOCIAL AND POLICY CONTEXT

The development of transnational higher education is a result of China's overall policy arrangements during the recent decades of reform, and several contextual factors have directly impacted on it. The first, and most fundamental, is the educational reforms that are aligned with those in the economic sector. Since 1978, building close links between education and the market has been the most prominent orientation, together with decentralisation in finance and management in the reform of education. For the past 25 years great efforts have been made to introduce the function of the market in education. The role of the market has been particularly prominent in higher education, endorsed by the Decision on the Reform of the Educational Structure in 1985. As the market gained more significance in China, especially in the more developed coastal and urban areas, more substantial reform policies were introduced to make structural changes in education, including the Program for Education Reform and Development in China in 1993 and the Education Act of the People's Republic of China in 1995.

The second is the commercialisation of education, which is much related to and indeed an aspect of China's market-oriented reforms, reflecting radicalism in a pseudo-market. China's education policies are produced by economists to 'meet the needs of a socialist economy'. In 1992, the Decision on the Development of the Tertiary Industry stated clearly that education was a tertiary industry and those who invested in it would own and benefit from it. The government raised the idea of education as a stimulus for economic growth in the Decision on Further Educational Reform to Promote Quality Education in 1999. Private investment in education was strongly encouraged. The Decision on Reform and Development of Basic Education in 2001 and the Decision on Further Reform of Basic Education in Rural Areas in 2002 provided further bases for ownership transfer from the public to the private sector.

The third is China's bid to enhance its international competitiveness in a globalising world. To achieve this, the Chinese government has implemented major projects to enable a handful of its national flagship higher education institutions to achieve world class standards. Realising the intensified global competition among leading universities and feeling the pressure for better rankings in the global university league, China plans to develop its own knowledge production capacity by strategically identifying key research bases and establishing major national laboratories on the one hand, and by importing good practices from foreign universities on the other. China thus allows overseas universities, in collaboration with local institutions, to jointly develop academic programs in China to help Chinese institutions develop their own capacity, status and innovation quickly (Garrett, 2004).

For the Chinese government, transnational education is seen as a means of rapidly boosting the capacity of Chinese universities by accessing the world's most advanced education systems, thereby accelerating the process of human capital building and ultimately economic development. For individual Chinese institutions, the appeal is in being able to offer a program in partnership that they could not provide alone because of their lack of resources, expertise and insufficient prestige to attract students on their own account. By partnering, they can capitalise on the demand for foreign qualifications and/or the shortage of places available at universities. They also hope that in the longer term such collaboration can help build their capacity to deliver their own programs without foreign partners.

Despite the massive expansion of higher education, local institutions alone cannot meet the demand for higher education. The Chinese government has gradually taken a favourable view of in-country activity by foreign institutions, especially after China's accession to the World Trade Organisation on 11 December 2001 and its agreement signed with the GATS. Specific legislation has governed transnational education in China since the 1990s, including the Interim Provisions for Chinese–Foreign Cooperation in Running Schools (1995) and the Regulations of the People's Republic of China on Chinese–Foreign Cooperation in Running Schools (2003). These regulations stipulate that foreign institutions must partner with Chinese institutions, that partnerships must not seek profit as their objective, that no less than half the members of the governing body of the institution must be Chinese citizens and the president or the equivalent must be a Chinese citizen residing in China, that the basic language of instruction should be Chinese, and that tuition fees may not be raised without approval (Garrett, 2004). They also restrict levels and forms of the joint academic programs, excluding China's compulsory education and the education and training conducted under special provisions by the state.

Compared with the provisions in 1995, the 2003 regulations have some important features, including extending government encouragement from vocational to higher education; strongly promoting Chinese universities to cooperate with prominent overseas higher education institutions in launching new academic programs to improve the quality of teaching and learning and to import excellent overseas educational resources to local institutions; and relaxing the restrictions on profit making.

3 MAJOR FEATURES OF TRANSNATIONAL HIGHER EDUCATION IN CHINA

Hard statistical data on transnational education are lacking internationally. China publishes its regulations and some (not always timely) information including a list of 'approved higher education joint programs in China leading to the award of overseas degrees or degrees of the Hong Kong Special Administrative Region' on China–Foreign Cooperation in Education, a website specifically on Chinese–overseas joint programs. According to the information provided by the website and recent studies by Chinese scholars, it is clear that the scale of foreign higher education activity in China has developed rapidly in recent years, the extent of foreign commitment is growing, and the types of providers involved are becoming increasingly diverse.

3.1 Scale of Foreign Activity

Since the promulgation of the 1995 regulations, there is evidence of increasing ambition and greater commitment on the part of joint ventures. Both the University of Nottingham in the United Kingdom and Oklahoma City University in the United States were expressly invited by the national authorities to set up operations in China, marking the first official push in this direction. In 1995, there were only two programs that could offer an overseas degree. By June 2004, the number of joint programs between overseas and Chinese institutions had increased to 745, with 169 programs qualified to award overseas (including Hong Kong) degrees (Ministry of Education, 2004).

According to the official website information (updated on 23 March 2006), by 30 June 2004, there were 668 approved partnerships,[1] with a total student enrolment of 51,893. New partnerships have formed annually following the 1995 provision, as shown by Table 1.

---

[1] Partnership in this study refers to the formal collaboration between different institutions to offer education programs in a chosen field. Once established, it is still considered as one partnership even after it has continuously recruited different batches of students.

Table 1.   New partnerships established 1995–June 2004

Year	1995	1996	1997	1998	1999	2000	2001	2002	2003	2004
Number of partnerships	2	3	4	7	9	11	22	37	45	24

Source: Based on information in Ministry of Education (2004). List of joint programs leading to degrees of foreign universities and universities in Hong Kong. http://www.cfce.cn/web/List/Info/200603/20.html (accessed 18 February 2008).

While government control has always been strong in Chinese education at all levels, transnational higher education is seriously challenging China's administration (Mok, 2007). Because of China's size, devolved systems of authority and its relatively undeveloped legal system, there are both officially approved and non-approved foreign provision, as well as various types of approval. Whether the status is approved or non-approved is not clear as approval is given at various 'official' levels. The range of known partnerships suggests that the relationship between government regulation and local practice is flexible (Garrett, 2004). Many non-approved joint programs in China lead to the award of an overseas qualification.

In May 2003, for example, the Australian Vice-Chancellor's Committee (AVCC) (2003) listed 200 current offshore programs in China undertaken by Australian universities, 157 (79%) of which were Australian bachelor's or master's programs, indicating that the real extent of foreign degree activity is in excess of that reported on the official ministry list. Given the number of non-approved programs, the number of certifying bodies outside the ministry (e.g., municipal, provincial and local governments) and the likelihood that some of the programs have no government approval at all, the total number of ventures involving degree programs from overseas institutions is certain to exceed the number reported on the official ministry list (Garrett, 2004).

3.2 Details of Partnerships

3.2.1 *Countries of origin of overseas partnership institutions*

The degree programs approved by the Chinese government are in collaboration with 164 overseas universities or colleges. These overseas partners are predominantly from countries or regions with developed economies and advanced technology. With the biggest shares of educational service export in the world, the dominant providers of these overseas partnerships with Chinese institutions are from Australia and the United States. Some other institutions, including universities from Hong Kong and Europe, have also been approved to grant degrees to students enrolled in the joint programs.

As Fig. 1 demonstrates, Australia is the source of the highest number of partnerships (29.27%), followed by the United States (26.83%), Hong Kong (13.41%), Canada (8.54%), France (6.71%) and the United Kingdom (5.49%). This is in line with the finding of the AVCC 2003 report that 27 Australian universities (representing

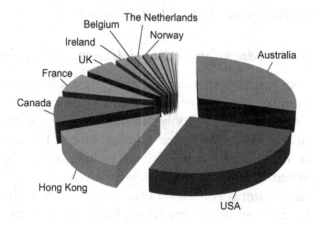

Figure 1. Countries of origin of partnership institutions

Source: Based on information in Ministry of Education (2004). List of joint programs leading to degrees of foreign universities and universities in Hong Kong. http://www.cfce.cn/web/List/Info/200603/20.html (accessed 18 February 2008).

71% of its 38 members) had offshore programs in mainland China in 2003, suggesting that China is a major site of offshore activity for a large majority of Australia's universities. Offshore programs in China represent 13 per cent of all reported current offshore activity by AVCC members. More than half (53%) of Australian joint programs in China are offered by three universities — Charles Sturt, Southern Queensland and Victoria, none of which are considered to be major institutions within the Australian system.

While Australian universities are known for their aggressive marketing globally, especially within the Asia–Pacific region, it is interesting to note that Hong Kong, a city with only eight university-level institutions, has been actively participating in the China market. Similar to the Australian picture, a closer inspection reveals that only four Hong Kong institutions were listed: the University of Hong Kong, the Chinese University of Hong Kong, Hong Kong University of Science and Technology and Hong Kong Polytechnic University. Of the total shared by Hong Kong institutions, their percentages are respectively 13.64 per cent, 9.09 per cent, 9.09 per cent and 68.18 per cent, showing great institutional differentiation, with Hong Kong Polytechnic University dominating.

3.2.2 Levels of education and disciplinary distribution

As noted above, strictly speaking, a joint program with China needs approval from the Ministry of Education. While it is almost certain that many joint programs are only authorised to offer certificates and diplomas, it is hard to obtain their actual numbers. The analysis here is based on the official list, which only includes the programs formally approved to grant overseas degrees. As shown in Fig. 2, an overwhelming majority (68.26%) of the programs are at the master's level, 27.54 per cent at the bachelor's level, and 2.4 per cent and 1.78 per cent, respectively, at the postgraduate diploma and doctoral level.

Since the Ministry of Education has the power to approve joint programs, it has a direct impact on the disciplinary distribution of the programs and tends to favour certain subject areas depending on the needs it perceives in the country at that time. In general, English

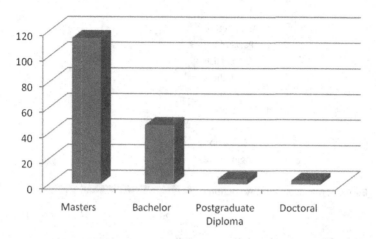

Figure 2. Levels of joint education programs

Source: Based on information from the Ministry of Education (2004). List of joint programs leading to degrees of foreign universities and universities in Hong Kong. http://www.cfce.cn/web/List/Info/200603/20.html (accessed 18 February 2008).

language programs were popular in the 1970s, science and technology were in high demand in the 1980s and 1990s, and management has become the most desirable in the last 10 years. As illustrated by Fig. 3, 61.02 per cent of provision is in the broad area of business and management, followed by IT (13.56%), engineering (7.91%), education (7.34%), law (2.26%), sports management (1.69%), real estate (1.69%), English language (1.13%) and 0.56 per cent each for psychology, architecture and a few others.

3.2.3 *Geographical distribution*

Most of the Chinese–overseas joint education programs are run by institutions concentrated in the eastern coastal areas, the most prosperous region in China. As demonstrated by Fig. 4, the regional distribution is Beijing (28.92%), Shanghai (19.28%), Tianjin (7.83%), Zhejiang (7.23%), Jiangsu (6.02%), Jiangxi (4.82%), Liaoning (4.22%), Guangdong (4.22%), Heilongjiang (3.01%), Hubei (2.41%), Yunnan (2.41%), Shaanxi (1.81%), Jilin (1.81%), Sichuan (1.81%), Hebei (1.2%), Fujian (1.2%), Henan (0.6%), Shanxi (0.6%) and

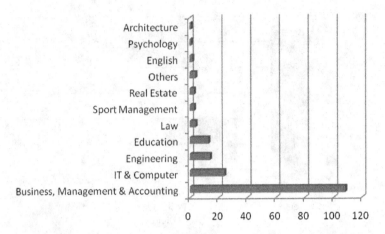

Figure 3.   Disciplinary distribution of joint programs

Source: Based on information from the Ministry of Education (2004). List of joint programs leading to degrees of foreign universities and universities in Hong Kong. http://www.cfce.cn/web/List/Info/200603/20.html (accessed 18 February 2008).

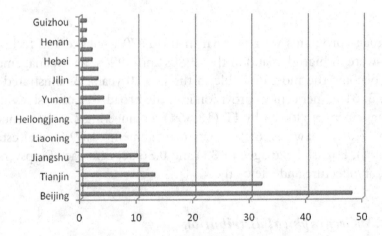

Figure 4.   Geographical distribution of joint programs

Source: Based on information from the Ministry of Education (2004). List of joint programs leading to degrees of foreign universities and universities in Hong Kong. http://www.cfce.cn/web/List/Info/200603/20.html (accessed 18 February 2008).

Guizhou (0.6%). By 2004, there had been no officially listed joint programs in provinces such as Anhui, Gansu, Guangxi, Hainan, Inner Mongolia, Ningxia, Qinghai, Tibet and Xinjiang, all of which are relatively underdeveloped.

3.2.4 *Teaching, teachers and assessment*

Chinese students enrolled in the joint programs are normally satisfied with the teaching approaches employed by their teachers from overseas, despite the fact that they often find it difficult to communicate effectively with the teachers because of their lack of English proficiency. They also generally perceive their teachers to be competent. The Chinese regulations require that foreign teachers and administrators of the joint programs have at least a bachelor's degree and certification, respectively. Teachers are also required to have at least two years' teaching experience before joining the programs. Such criteria are fairly low and are usually met easily by overseas institutions. Thus, Chinese students are generally happy with the quality of teaching staff in their programs, especially when measured by qualifications. Another major dimension of student satisfaction with their education programs relates to the teaching facilities offered by the joint programs. In this aspect, most Chinese students are equally satisfied.

An important and closely related aspect of the teaching activities is that assessment of student performance is not only to verify the knowledge and technical ability that students have acquired but also to assure academic quality. Although the methods of assessment in the joint programs differ greatly from the Chinese methods that students are familiar with and like, it has been reported that they have a highly positive attitude towards the methods used by the joint programs. They have, however, clearly expressed their concern that any assessment could be out of the control of the Chinese side. In this, some differentiation between undergraduate and postgraduate students can be identified.

3.2.5 *Tuition and fees*

Tuition is one of the most important deciding factors for students in selecting programs offered by different institutions. Chinese regulations provide guidelines for tuition fees. The partner institutions decide how much to charge based on a related price policy issued by the government, and cannot add further items or elevate criteria without government permission. Although the cost of enrolling in Chinese–overseas joint programs is substantially lower than that of studying abroad, most of the students enrolled in these programs think their tuition fees are quite high. Most domestic students in China are unable to pay for these relatively expensive programs. Since the joint programs are a service offered by the overseas institutions as trade, it is inevitable that these institutions aim to make a profit. It is therefore a significant issue for overseas partner institutions to consider affordability when setting their fee level. The difficult part is deciding on a reasonable level of tuition fees, which will depend on a variety of factors, from the subject area of the joint program to the local living standards. For reference, most students enrolled in joint programs in Zhejiang province, one of China's most developed regions, consider that a reasonable tuition level should currently lie between 25,000 and 30,000 RMB.

4 ISSUES OF CONCERN

4.1 Quality Assurance

Transnational higher education is especially vulnerable to the perils that consumerism creates in higher education. It is sometimes suggested that increases in the number of fee-paying students may lead to pressure on institutions and academics to engage in 'soft marking' or grade inflation in order to satisfy their increasingly influential customers (Tierney, 2001). With the recent global rise of transnational education programs, quality assurance has become a major issue for those program-offering institutions. Australian universities, for instance, have started to re-examine their quality assurance systems in order to maintain similar academic standards between the home and overseas academic programs.

The quality assurance issue has been raised for transnational higher education in China as well. According to Chinese regulations, the government takes legal responsibility for approving or chartering the establishment of transnational education programs in line with the existing legal frameworks and guidelines. The problem, however, lies in the lack of intervention after the approval. The responsibility for quality assurance in effect falls almost entirely into the hands of the individual teaching staff and their program coordinators. Thus, it is not surprising that Chinese students are concerned about the quality of their programs, especially when individual teachers and their departments are the sole arbiters of quality assurance. The Chinese government should consider exploring the possibility of developing new regulatory frameworks to govern the operation of transnational higher education programs.

4.2 Legal Status

Chinese regulations stipulate clearly that transnational higher education is only a supplementary part of China's higher education sector, and foreign higher education activity has not been regarded as an integrated part of the system. In this legal sense, it is fundamentally different from the services provided solely by Chinese national, provincial and even private higher education institutions. Because all the joint programs are run by overseas universities in collaboration with Chinese public (national and provincial) universities, there is a misconception that the programs are publicly owned. In contrast, the operation of these joint programs is strikingly different from that of the education programs at Chinese public universities, especially from a legal perspective. While these joint programs are set up by public universities as encouraged by the Ministry of Education, they are run privately. How transnational higher education programs are defined legally remains a challenge to Chinese policymakers.

The Chinese government has not permitted overseas institutions to set up their branch campuses on the mainland to recruit local students and offer teaching programs. Here, an oft-cited example is the University of Nottingham, Ningbo, China. Even after years of effort, the University of Nottingham has not been able to establish a branch campus in China and has only been allowed to found a university in collaboration with Zhejiang Wanli University. Although the majority of programs taught at this university have been imported from the University of Nottingham, it is strongly emphasised that it is not a branch campus of the University of Nottingham but a completely independent university owned by Zhejiang Wanli University.

One explanation of China's ambiguity regarding the legal status of transnational higher education is the fact that such joint education is relatively new to China. There is, however, another more fundamental reason: China's concern about its possible loss of educational sovereignty, something that has never stopped perplexing Chinese policymakers, theorists and partner institutions. Such a concern, however, is not China-specific. A report commissioned by European university heads warned that, as a result of the development of transnational education, 'national autonomy and sovereignty in the domain of higher education (and tertiary education) have never before been challenged on such a scale' (Adam, 2001, pp. 6–7).

4.3 Cultural Appropriateness

There has been an increasing awareness of the appropriate level of adaptation of content and pedagogy of foreign programs and the impact of foreign providers on the culture of students and the nation. According to GATE (1999), materials and learning resources should normally be adjusted to be culturally appropriate to the range of students to whom the courses are being offered.

In reality, this is not always the case. Some providers even advocate the 'global template', a generic product that has no trace of the local character of knowledge, in current transnational higher education courses (Luke, 2005). On the one hand, this is a continuity of the longstanding 'sanctioned ignorance' that enables an individual discipline or nation to proceed without reference to any others and without fully acknowledging the legacies of colonialism and imperialism. On the other hand, there is a miscalculation of the global dominance, failing to acknowledge that the global–local nexus is a twofold process of give and take, an exchange by which global trends are reshaped to local ends, and a dynamic interaction between global trends and local responses.

This has great implications for the transnational provision of higher education in China. Considering that students who are enrolled in joint programs come to buy Western education and degrees and are usually keen to learn Western experiences, most consider their course arrangements reasonably appropriate. At the same time, to ensure that they can benefit from their Western knowledge and degrees, they demand a well-balanced combination of both Western and Chinese experiences. Indeed, they are required to have knowledge of both the global and the local. Unique perspectives and values based on rich local experience and awareness of the society and culture would allow them to seize the initiative in identifying the real needs of their local societies and in setting up their own agendas and targets.

However, it is the local perspective that is overshadowed by the dominant, hegemonic global. This is being realised as transnational higher education provision in China booms. Cultural appropriateness of the curriculum has begun to catch greater attention. Individuals are becoming more critical of the proportional arrangement between foreign (often Western) and Chinese course content. While most of the students still accept current arrangements, those holding negative views are increasing. Studies of the joint programs have shown that Chinese students regard curriculum adaptability to their local context as a key aspect, and the power relationship between Western and indigenous knowledge remains unequal (Yang and Yao, 2007).

While the export of the foreign into China has been viewed positively within the corporatisation of higher education, there are a number of problematic issues, including the commodification of knowledge and the hegemony of Western knowledge and pedagogies. There are a number of pedagogical concerns in achieving high-quality transnational higher education courses in China. The danger of the 'global template' is that it dissociates education from China's social, cultural and political origins. Such decontextualised 'globalised' curricula reflect a particular view of what is claimed to be 'universal', which is informed by the geographical and social location of the curriculum developer, typically the Western (English-speaking) world. The implicit social values of these exporting countries inform curriculum, and the Chinese social and cultural context in which students live is largely ignored by such courses, raising the longstanding question of what counts as 'scholarship'.

4.4 Public Good or Private Commodity

To many critics, the rapid growth of income-generating transnational programs looks like an unseemly gold rush threatening to undermine the public service orientation that should be paramount to higher education institutions. The approach of Western universities is often described as aggressive or even predatory in developing countries, leading South Africa's Kader Asmal (1999) to ask: 'Are we entering a Darwinian nightmare, when higher education is red in tooth and claw and only the fittest survive?' Exporting universities often see the establishment of overseas operations as a profitable means of responding to unmet student demand in other countries, arguing that transnational education is a vital means of expanding educational opportunity and student choice in places with excess demand. While transnational education serves to build educational capacity selectively in areas in which local providers are constrained or unwilling to respond to commercial demand, it is seen to pose potential threats to traditional conceptions of education as a public good because of its marketised and foreign nature.

The clearest motivation for institutions on both sides of the partnership is the promise of expanding enrolment and revenue by attracting students who are unlikely to enrol in a distance education program or to undertake an entire course overseas. The danger that excessive focus on the financial bottom line can compromise commitment to the community service responsibility of the publicly funded body is real. In this sense, the approach suggested by McBurnie and Pollock (2000) is useful for decision-makers to evaluate transnational opportunities: strategic (does this advance our goals for the institution in the medium to long term?); academic (how does this fit with our educational expertise and interests); and business (will this yield a profit or at least cover costs?). A judicious combination of the rationales allows a university to evaluate revenue-raising opportunities critically while giving appropriate priority to the overriding academic values that guide the future of the institution.

5 CONCLUDING COMMENTS

As a response to supply shortages that have arisen because of the local system's inability to meet the rapidly growing demand, and as an approach to development assistance that focuses on improving the capacity of the local education system to provide for itself, the Chinese government expects transnational joint programs to help improve the quality of China's human resources, upgrade China's educational system, meet the national educational demand, prevent brain drain, and attract foreign capital into education. For Chinese universities, the stated expectations are to learn practical and effective ways to improve their academic quality, upgrade standards, and build new programs that are badly needed for China's development yet cannot be offered by the universities themselves.

While such expectations have not materialised fully, transnational higher education certainly has much room for further development in China, as indicated by the fact that no more than 100 of the 1671 higher education institutions had joint programs with overseas partners in 2004 at undergraduate level and below, and that only about 10,000 students (0.5%) of the annual recruitment (4,473,400) were enrolled in the joint programs offered by Chinese and overseas partners.

However, the road to future development will most likely be bumpy. Transnational higher education has risen in China against a backdrop of a significantly transformed Chinese higher education sector, with an increasing number of providers, diversified financial resources, and a growing yet pseudo market. The intensified diversification and marketisation of higher education has challenged China's conventional higher education governance. Rather than building new regulatory frameworks to govern the increasingly complex and diversified higher education sector/market, the Chinese government unwisely still places hope on its state-oriented regime.

REFERENCES

Adam S (2001). *Transnational Education Project Report and Recommendations.* Confederation of European Union Rectors' Conference, Brussels.

Asmal K (1999). Speech at the *Mail and Guardian* Graduate Career Fair, 26 August. http://www.info.gov.za/speeches/1999/990914425p1008.htm (accessed 19 February 2008).

AVCC (2003). *Offshore Programs of Australian Universities.* Australian Vice-Chancellors' Committee, Canberra.

Garrett R (2004). Foreign higher education activity in China. *Int High Educ,* 34, 21–23. Available online at http://www.bc.edu/bc_org/avp/soe/cihe/newsletter/News34/text012.htm.

GATE (1999). *Trade in Transnational Education Services.* The Global Alliance for Transnational Education (GATE), Washington, DC.

Luke C (2005). Capital and knowledge flows: Global higher education markets. *Asia Pac J Educ,* 25(2), 159–174.

McBurnie G and Pollock A (2000). Decision making for offshore activities: A case study of Monash University. In *Transnational Education Providers, Partners and Policy: Challenges for Australian Institutions Offshore,* D Davis, A Olsen and A Bohm (eds.), pp. 53–66. IDP Education Australia, Canberra.

McBurnie G and Ziguras C (2007). *Transnational Education: Issues and Trends in Offshore Higher Education.* Routledge, New York.

Ministry of Education (2004). List of joint programs leading to degrees of foreign universities and universities of Hong Kong. http://www.cfce.cn/web/List/Info/200603/20.html (accessed 18 February 2008).

Mok KH (2007). One country, diverse systems: Politics of educational decentralization and challenges for the regulatory state in post-Mao China. *China Rev,* forthcoming.

Tierney WG (2001). Academic freedom and organizational identity. *Aust Univ Rev,* 44(1/2), 7–14.

Yang R and Yao WH (2007). Whose knowledge counts? A case study of a joint MBA Program between Australia and China. In *The World Yearbook of Education 2007: Educating the Global Workforce: Knowledge, Knowledge Work and Knowledge Workers,* L Farrell and T Fenwick (eds.), pp. 41–53. Kogan Page, London.

Index